Soviet Strategic Forces
Requirements and Responses

ROBERT P. BERMAN AND JOHN C. BAKER

As the United States undertakes to reshape its strategic forces and alter its approach to arms negotiations, Americans need to have a clear idea of the threat facing the country and its allies. This study examines the strategic posture of the Soviet Union for signs of strengths and weaknesses in Soviet nuclear forces and indications of how Soviet leaders set defense priorities.

Robert Berman and John Baker believe that strategic planning and missile development are closely related. As a guide to the evolution of Soviet strategic posture in the nuclear age, they trace the development of Soviet ballistic missiles since World War II. Their accounts of the design and development of Soviet weapon systems reveal how Soviet technical capacity has changed and what effect important political and military events have had on missile development.

The authors warn that before 1985 Soviet leaders will have to make critical decisions that will govern weapon development until the turn of the century. The trends within the design bureaus and the disruptions in individual weapon programs that the authors have detected suggest what the USSR can reasonably be expected to do. The confines within which Soviet strategic planners must work are apparent in the appendixes to this study, which describe the process of missile design and development, the design and operating characteristics of missiles, regional and intercontinental targeting assignments, the use of military reconnaissance satellites, and the strategic defense forces of the Soviet Union.

At the time this study was prepared, Robert P. Berman and John C. Baker were members of the staff of the Brookings Foreign Policy Studies program. In 1981 Baker joined the staff of Pacific Sierra Corporation.

STUDIES IN DEFENSE POLICY

SOVIET STRATEGIC FORCES: REQUIREMENTS AND RESPONSES

Robert P. Berman and John C. Baker

THE BROOKINGS INSTITUTION
Washington, D.C.

Copyright © 1982 by

THE BROOKINGS INSTITUTION

1775 Massachusetts Avenue, N.W., Washington, D.C. 20036

Library of Congress Cataloging in Publication data:

Berman, Robert P., 1950–
  Soviet strategic forces.

  (Studies in defense policy)
  Includes bibliographical references and index.
  1. Strategic forces—Soviet Union. 2. Soviet
Union—Military policy. 3. United States—Military
policy. I. Baker, John C., 1949– . II. Title.
III. Series.
UA770.B45 1982   358′.17′0947   82-70889
ISBN 0-8157-0926-9
ISBN 0-8157-0925-0 (pbk.)

9 8 7 6 5 4 3 2 1

THE BROOKINGS INSTITUTION is an independent organization devoted to nonpartisan research, education, and publication in economics, government, foreign policy, and the social sciences generally. Its principal purposes are to aid in the development of sound public policies and to promote public understanding of issues of national importance.

The Institution was founded on December 8, 1927, to merge the activities of the Institute for Government Research, founded in 1916, the Institute of Economics, founded in 1922, and the Robert Brookings Graduate School of Economics and Government, founded in 1924.

The Board of Trustees is responsible for the general administration of the Institution, while the immediate direction of the policies, program, and staff is vested in the President, assisted by an advisory committee of the officers and staff. The by-laws of the Institution state: "It is the function of the Trustees to make possible the conduct of scientific research, and publication, under the most favorable conditions, and to safeguard the independence of the research staff in the pursuit of their studies and in the publication of the results of such studies. It is not a part of their function to determine, control, or influence the conduct of particular investigations or the conclusions reached."

The President bears final responsibility for the decision to publish a manuscript as a Brookings book. In reaching his judgment on the competence, accuracy, and objectivity of each study, the President is advised by the director of the appropriate research program and weighs the views of a panel of expert outside readers who report to him in confidence on the quality of the work. Publication of a work signifies that it is deemed a competent treatment worthy of public consideration but does not imply endorsement of conclusions or recommendations.

The Institution maintains its position of neutrality on issues of public policy in order to safeguard the intellectual freedom of the staff. Hence interpretations or conclusions in Brookings publications should be understood to be solely those of the authors and should not be attributed to the Institution, to its trustees, officers, or other staff members, or to the organizations that support its research.

FOREWORD

Since the late 1940s the growth of Soviet strategic power has been a continuing concern of the West. Relying heavily on long-range nuclear missiles, the USSR has sought to acquire modern strategic forces capable of supporting historical Soviet interests as a continental power, and of expanding its reach beyond its borders. In this study Robert P. Berman and John C. Baker analyze the Soviet Union's strategic forces and examine how they have been shaped by the changing political and military conditions of the post-World War II period.

The Soviet strategic force posture is unique in its combination of regional and intercontinental offensive nuclear forces, a combination that arises from the USSR's varied security requirements. The Soviet Union attempts to meet its security needs by military domination of the surrounding regions and by acquiring forces adequate to offset any strategic threat posed by the United States.

The authors focus on the USSR's strategic missiles because of the importance accorded them in the Soviet strategic force structure. The methodical process of Soviet missile development and deployment since the 1950s serves as a useful indicator of critical decisions and shifts of emphasis. The authors portray Soviet strategic force development as a persistent effort frequently marked by technical setbacks and programmatic redirections. They conclude that in certain critical periods, such as the early 1960s, decisions were made that determined the development of Soviet strategic forces for years to come. They argue that the USSR entered another such period in the early 1980s.

This is the twenty-eighth publication in the Brookings Studies in Defense Policy series. As in all such studies, the authors have used only publicly available material. Their purpose is to contribute to public discussion and professional judgment on a subject that has often been an issue of national debate.

Robert P. Berman and John C. Baker were research associates in the Brookings Foreign Policy Studies program when the manuscript of this study was written. Both authors contributed to several other studies on defense policy while at Brookings. Robert P. Berman is the author of *Soviet Air Power in Transition,* published by Brookings in 1978.

The authors received assistance from many persons during the course of their work. They are particularly grateful for the comments of Edward L. Warner III, Benjamin S. Lambeth, and Ronald H. Stivers, who reviewed their manuscript for Brookings. Among their Brookings colleagues the authors are indebted to Raymond L. Garthoff, Michael MccGwire, Helmut Sonnenfeldt, and John D. Steinbruner, who were instrumental in helping them define their approach to the subject, and to Desmond Ball, Richard K. Betts, Bruce Blair, James D. Farrell, William P. Mako, and Barry Posen for their comments and encouragement. Gregory C. Baird, Duncan L. Clarke, Bradford Dismukes, Mark Flanigan, Dennis M. Gormley, Sidney N. Graybeal, Robert W. Herrick, Louis Holliday, David Holloway, Ned I. Len, Margrethe Lundsager, James M. McConnell, K. J. Moore, Mary A. Munday, James Peak, Dennis Ross, and Robert G. Weinland also earned the authors' gratitude for advice and help of various kinds.

This study was initiated by Henry Owen, former director of the Brookings Foreign Policy Studies program, and Barry M. Blechman, former director of the Brookings Defense Analysis staff. John D. Steinbruner, the present director of the Brookings Foreign Policy Studies program, guided the study to completion; Alice M. Carroll edited the manuscript; Virginia Black, Ruth Conrad, Ann Ziegler, and Delores Burton typed it; and Clifford E. Wright verified its factual content. M. Cristina Gobin and Jacqueline A. Martin directed the secretarial support for the project. The authors are grateful to them all.

The Brookings Institution gratefully acknowledges the financial assistance of the Ford Foundation, whose grant helped to support this study and other work on national security. The views expressed are those of the authors and should not be ascribed to the persons who provided information or commented on the manuscript, to the Ford Foundation, or to the trustees, officers, or other staff members of the Brookings Institution.

BRUCE K. MACLAURY
President

October 1982
Washington, D.C.

CONTENTS

Text Figures

Appendix Figures

CHAPTER ONE

THE EVOLUTION
OF SOVIET STRATEGIC FORCES

As THE United States faces a series of choices concerning the future of its strategic forces and its approach to limiting strategic arms, its assessment of the role and character of Soviet strategic forces is extremely important. Too often in shaping and directing plans for its strategic nuclear force, the United States has tended to see Soviet military forces and strategy as a reflection of its own stance or simply to accept the worst plausible projection of Soviet intentions and capabilities. The result has been that U.S. strategic programs and approaches to arms control have not always been responsive to the real threat posed by the Soviet Union's strategic forces.

The United States needs to develop an understanding of the underlying priorities, purposes, and nature of the USSR's strategic forces. Such an understanding would not only help to make U.S. forces a more effective instrument of Western security but also would alleviate unnecessary anxiety about Soviet intentions. This study seeks to contribute to Western knowledge by examining the development and organization of the USSR's strategic missile forces, the heart of the Soviet strategic forces.

The Soviet Record

The Soviet strategic forces are as much a product of military traditions as of changing circumstances. Certain patterns and practices in Soviet force development can be discerned from the historical record. It is possible to relate the changes that have occurred in the composition of forces to changes in Soviet strategy or military requirements. By examining Soviet strategic forces as a whole it is possible to recognize

1

trade-offs and interactions between different components of the armed forces and to relate Soviet weapon developments and operations to Soviet military doctrine and strategy.

Both regional and intercontinental strategic objectives have been important in the development of Soviet strategic forces. The Soviet Union seeks politically and militarily to dominate the regions surrounding it and to forestall the use of U.S. political and military power against the Soviet homeland. The development of the ballistic missile, which has the central role in Soviet strategic posture, reflects the interaction and choices that Soviet leaders have made in pursuit of these objectives.

The Soviet strategic forces are composed of substantial regional forces directed against adjoining areas such as Western Europe and China as well as intercontinental-range nuclear forces capable of striking targets in the U.S. mainland. Historically, the most vital interests of and greatest threats to the USSR have been in neighboring areas. Hence the Soviet tendency—not fully appreciated in the United States—to attribute a strategic importance to its regional nuclear forces. The Soviet need for intercontinental strategic forces became critical by the early 1960s when the United States began to deploy large numbers of intercontinental ballistic missiles (ICBMs) and other intercontinental weapons that could not be effectively offset by Soviet defenses or regional forces. In response, the USSR undertook a series of expedient measures and long-term programs that determined the shape of its missile programs into the 1980s.

The critical determinants of Soviet weapon programs and deployments are the requirements that Soviet military forces must meet in order to support the various security interests of the Soviet Union and offset the military forces of its potential adversaries. This study analyzes the Soviet strategic forces posture by relating weapon programs, command structures, and operating patterns to underlying Soviet political and military requirements. As with any nation, the country's geographical position, its particular military heritage and doctrinal values, the strengths and weaknesses of its technical production base, and institutional and political interests within the country also are important in shaping the character of weapon programs.

The long lead-times necessary for development of modern strategic weapons complicate the process of acquisition. Typically, it takes seven to ten years from the time when initial design requirements for a weapon system are set until the first models are tested, and several more years may pass before the system is fully operational. These long lead-times, combined with the USSR's tendency to use established technologies to develop follow-on systems, create a basic stability in the process. The long lead-times, however, also make the process susceptible to being upset. When a strategic program meets with a major technical failure, or significant changes occur suddenly in military requirements, the USSR is forced to redirect programs, with the result that strategic weapons may have to serve in roles they were never envisaged to fill. Recognizing the "quick fixes," or interim measures, resorted to during critical periods is essential to understanding the development of Soviet strategic forces.

The military requirements that determine how Soviet strategic force programs develop can only be surmised. But the evolution of strategic requirements is so intimately associated with the development of critical weapon systems that recasting the histories of Soviet ballistic missiles offers a reasonable means of judging how each has affected the other. For most weapons the approximate date when design requirements were established and a development program begun can be extrapolated from the dates of flight-testing and deployment. The military requirements that existed or were anticipated at the time that a specific system was initiated suggest what mission the weapon was originally intended to perform. Once the design characteristics of the weapon are determined, the influence of changing requirements, technical problems, and organizational changes on the development, deployment, and modifications of the system can be analyzed.

At each stage in the life cycle of a weapon program—research and development, deployment, and operation—different participants are likely to be predominant. In the first stage, when the initial design requirements are set and the weapon is being developed, the weapon design bureaus probably have greatest impact (see appendix A); in the second stage, when the deployment decision is made and the USSR must make choices with regard to basic allocation of resources, the top political and military leaders are critical; and in the third stage, when the new system begins to operate in peacetime deployments or annual exercises, the operational patterns and preferences of the individual services or commands the weapons are assigned to become of the greatest importance. All of these groups have distinct interests that can affect the character and operation of weapon programs.

The case histories of the major strategic weapon programs exhibit the dynamic nature of Soviet strategic force development and the changes in threats and in technology they have been forced to respond to (see appendixes B and C). The most instructive era is the 1960s, when both the threat facing the Soviet regional and intercontinental strategic forces and the technology available for responding to new requirements were changing rapidly.

Evidence of these changes can be found in information relating to the hardware, operation, doctrine, and bureaucratic organization of the Soviet strategic forces. Most important for this analysis is information concerning the performance characteristics of strategic weapon systems. While estimates of the operational accuracy or actual yield of Soviet missiles must be used with caution, trends in overall numbers and deployment rates of new systems and modifications of the original models can be discerned from generally more reliable information. Any fact indicating when a particular system was initiated, entered into testing, or began being deployed is critical for determining the weapon case histories. Data on the operational patterns of the Soviet strategic forces are scarce, but the occasional revelations of such details as the operating tempos or readiness levels of particular strategic systems as well as their general deployment location contribute significantly to the construction of historical profiles.

By comparison, Soviet military writings on doctrine and strategy are generally useful as indicators of Soviet force priorities and employment considerations. Statements by high-ranking military and naval leaders can reinforce hypotheses suggested by hardware and operations data. Because these writings usually reflect official policy, a sudden proliferation of statements on a new subject may be a signal of internal debate or the adoption of a new policy. Information on the organization and composition of the Soviet strategic forces is also instructive. The dedication of an independent service, the Strategic Rocket Forces, to command both regional and intercontinental missiles highlights the priority attributed to this service and its integral role at various levels of conflict.

This chapter describes how the Soviet strategic forces are organized, while chapter 2 speculates on how they might be employed in the event of war. From information on the nature and output of the Soviet missile design bureaus, chapter 3 and the appendixes to this study reconstruct the lineage of Soviet land- and sea-based missile systems and thus the choices that have been available to the USSR for meeting its changing requirements.[1]

Soviet Command Structure

In the event of war the Soviet military command structure would undergo an important transformation. The daily activities of military districts and groups, such as training, would decrease and emphasis would shift to military activities in each affected theater of war (*teatr voyny,* or TV) and theater of military operations (*teatr voyennykh deystviy,* or TVD). Control of the Soviet political apparatus as well as combat forces would be turned over to the State Defense Committee. Commanders-in-chief of the military services would become part of the Supreme High Command (Verkhovnoye Glavnoye Komandovaniye, or VGK), directly responsible to the State Defense Committee, while top-level commanders responsible for operations would become part of the VGK's General Staff Operations Directorate and of the high commands in the TVDs (see figure 1-1).

The Supreme High Command in Wartime

The peacetime Defense Council is likely to become the State Defense Committee in wartime. The council, the highest forum of defense decisionmaking in the USSR, is headed by General Secretary and President Leonid I. Brezhnev and is probably composed of selected members of the Politburo of the Communist party and senior representatives from the Soviet military high command as well as party and state

1. Estimates of the current structure and an appreciation of the development of Soviet strategic posture are important in understanding the threat that the Soviet Union poses to the United States and other foes. This study is based on information drawn from the public record in the United States and other Western countries, scholarly analyses of military affairs, journalists' reports, and translations of Soviet military works. Among the most important sources are the declassified statements of the secretary of defense on the defense budget for fiscal years 1962 to 1974, issued by the Department of Defense; the U.S. Foreign Broadcast Information Service's translations from *Voyennaya mysl'* (*Military Thought*), issued by the Library of Congress; and Nikita Khrushchev's *Khrushchev Remembers: The Last Testament,* ed. and trans. Strobe Talbott (Little, Brown, 1974).

Figure 1-1. The Probable Soviet Wartime Command Structure

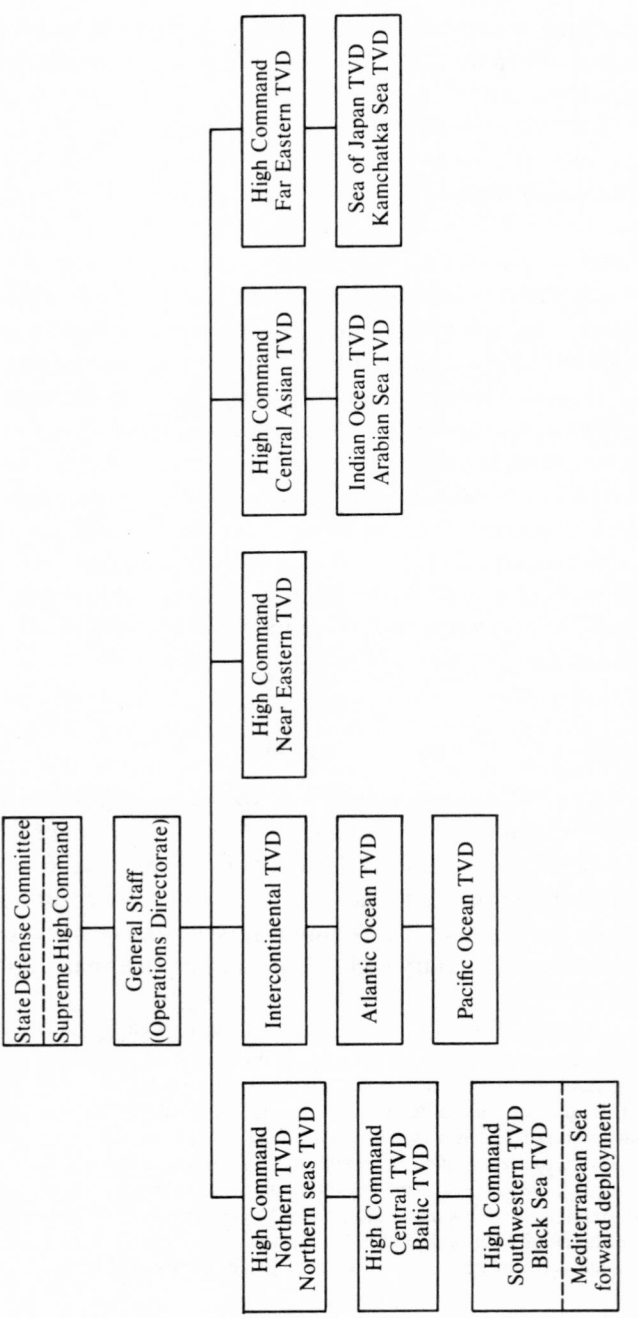

Sources: Derived from Gregory C. Baird, *Soviet Intermediary Strategic C² Entities: The Historical Experience* (McLean, Virginia: BDM Corp.), p. 91; James T. Westwood, "Soviet Naval Theater Forces: Their Strategy and Employment" (October 1978), p. 8.

TVD Theater of military operations.

organizations concerned with defense.[2] The most fundamental issues of Soviet defense policy are believed to be considered and decided on by the Defense Council. In wartime its function would be similar to that of the State Committee of Defense (Gosudarstvennyy Komitet Oborony, or GKO) that existed during World War II. A major task of the VGK, once the political decision has been made, would be to authorize the release of nuclear weapons; and, like the earlier GKO, it would coordinate and mobilize the overall war effort.

In peacetime the Soviet armed forces are administered by the Ministry of Defense under the leadership of the minister of defense, currently Marshal Dmitri F. Ustinov. The ministry is composed primarily of uniformed officers and is responsible for day-to-day management of the military establishment (figure 1-2). The General Staff of the ministry— thought of as the essence of Soviet military professionalism, and often characterized as the "brain of the army"[3]—is deeply involved in running the Soviet armed forces. It has a critical role in formulating military plans and shaping force requirements and has direct links to the main staffs of the services and other commands.[4] The chief of the General Staff, currently Marshal Nikolai V. Ogarkov, is also a first deputy minister in the Ministry of Defense. Broader consideration of military policy and the peacetime direction of the Soviet armed forces[5] fall to the Main Military Council, a collegial body within the Ministry of Defense made up of the minister, the chief of the General Staff, and other top military officers of the ministry. Leonid Brezhnev, as chairman of the Defense Council and supreme commander, also may be a member of this body.[6] It is the Main Military Council that is likely to assume the most important role in the wartime command structure by transforming

2. Thomas W. Wolfe, "The Military Dimension in the Making of Soviet Foreign and Defense Policy," in *The Soviet Union: Internal Dynamics of Foreign Policy, Present and Future,* Hearings before the Subcommittee on Europe and the Middle East of the House International Relations Committee, 95 Cong. 1 sess. (U.S. Government Printing Office, 1978), p. 99.

3. Edward L. Warner III, *The Military in Contemporary Soviet Politics: An Institutional Analysis* (Praeger, 1977), pp. 24–25; Thomas W. Wolfe, "The Soviet General Staff," *Problems of Communism,* vol. 28 (January–February 1979), pp. 51–54. Also see Army Gen. V. G. Kulikov, "The Brain of the Army," in *Selected Soviet Military Writings, 1970–1975: A Soviet View,* U.S. Air Force translation series (GPO, 1977), pp. 185–89.

4. Kulikov, "Brain of the Army," pp. 185–89; Arthur J. Alexander, *Decision-Making in Soviet Weapons Procurement,* Adelphi Papers 47 and 48 (London: International Institute for Strategic Studies [IISS], 1978), pp. 17–18; Wolfe, "Military Dimension," p. 105.

5. Alexander, *Decision-Making,* pp. 15–16; Wolfe, "Military Dimension," p. 105.

6. Wolfe, "Military Dimension," p. 105.

Figure 1-2. The Soviet Peacetime Command Defense Structure

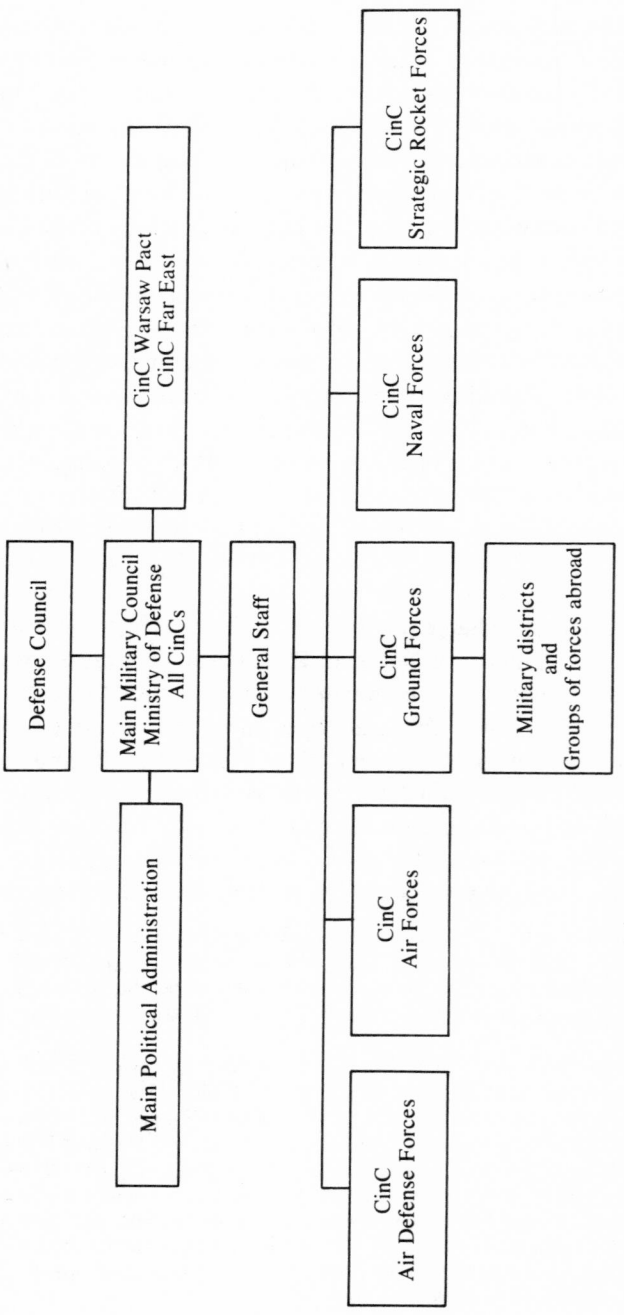

Source: Adapted from U.S. Central Intelligence Agency, "USSR Organization of the Ministry of Defense," chart CR-761407a (July 1976).

into the Headquarters of the Supreme High Command and operating along the lines of its World War II predecessor, generally known as the Stavka. Exercising command and control of the armed forces through a highly centralized system, this body would be critical in defining, planning, and directing the military tasks to be accomplished in the various theaters of military operations. The General Staff within the Ministry of Defense would become the working agent of the Supreme High Command, thus increasing in importance once war begins.

In peacetime, political and military organs are integrated in the Main Political Administration and in councils at the headquarters of the major territorial commands.[7] Such councils do not exist though for the Strategic Rocket Forces (SRF), which are controlled from Moscow.[8] In wartime, separate military councils (that in peacetime function only with groups of forces abroad and in key border areas) probably would become activated as part of the commands in the TVDs.

Operational Commands

The most extensive changes in the transition of the Soviet military to a wartime footing will occur at the level of the operating commands. The command structure, which for the purposes of administration and training in peacetime is organized functionally by services and geographically by military districts (or groups of Soviet forces outside of the USSR), would change fundamentally. The military services would no longer exist as separate operational entities but would be relegated by components to the commands in the various theaters of military operations (TVDs). (In peacetime the TVD serves as a management tool, allowing Soviet planners to establish targets, force levels, deployments, and logistic structures and to evaluate their suitability for land, intercontinental, maritime, or oceanic warfare.)[9]

In wartime the TVDs become the structure through which the VGK, the General Staff, and the local high commands compose, plan, and carry out operations. To satisfy the varied requirements that the Soviet

7. Timothy J. Colton, *Commissars, Commanders and Civilian Authority: The Structure of Soviet Military Politics* (Harvard University Press, 1979), pp. 11, 14.

8. Ibid.

9. Gregory C. Baird, *Soviet Intermediary Strategic C^2 Entities: The Historical Experience* (McLean, Va.: BDM Corp., 1979), p. 24. The concept of maritime and oceanic TVDs is treated in detail in James T. Westwood, "Soviet Naval Theater Forces: Their Strategy and Employment" (October 1978), pp. 1–9.

armed forces are responsible for meeting, the theaters of military operations probably are grouped into three theaters of war (see table 1-1). Soviet military forces, including strategic weapon units, are stationed throughout the USSR so that they can be deployed to engage in action in a single theater or to support broader military objectives as part of a general war.

Only when war is imminent would the administrative features of the Soviet military establishment fully convert to the lines of command in a TVD. The USSR relies on military reconnaissance satellites and other means of intelligence collection to monitor its adversaries' activities for important signs of change (see appendix E). Military operations under the control of the VGK would be directed by the General Staff's Operations Directorate, probably located around Moscow, which would issue orders to the major functioning operational directorates in the TVDs.[10] In theaters of war as politically and militarily important as the Western and Far Eastern theaters, high commands would be responsible for allocating resources to various fronts preparing for or engaged in combat. For TVDs not important enough to require the establishment of a high command, the VGK could designate high-ranking general officers as its representatives to the commands in the field.[11]

Theaters of Military Operations

The purpose of the TVD framework is to achieve particular military and political objectives relating to the defense of Soviet territory, the destruction of strategic groupings of the enemy, and the withdrawal from the conflict of specific hostile governments. In many theaters of military operations, such as the land TVDs, all arms would be integrated in pursuit of these objectives; thus tactical nonnuclear forces would be combined with regional nuclear forces that are armed with medium-range bombers and ballistic missiles. Other theaters, such as the intercontinental theater of military operations, would probably rely solely on long-range nuclear arms. In addition, certain military units would prob-

10. Baird, *Soviet Intermediary Strategic C² Entities*, p. 91.

11. This practice was clearly established during World War II. See Marshal of the Soviet Union I. Bagramyan and Col. I. Vyrodov, "The Role of Representatives of Headquarters, Supreme High Command (Stavka VGK) During the War Years: Organization and Method of Their Work," *Voyenno-istoricheskiy zhurnal*, no. 8 (August 1980), reprinted in Joint Publications Research Service, *USSR Report: Military Affairs*, JPRS 76953, December 8, 1980, pp. 27–36.

Table 1-1. Soviet Theaters of Military Operations, Grouped by Theaters of War

Theater of war (TV)	Theater of military operations (TVD)			
	Land	Maritime	Intercontinental	Ocean
Western	Northern Europe	Northern seas	. . .	. . .
	Central Europe	Baltic Sea	. . .	. . .
	Southern Europe	Black Sea[a]	. . .	. . .
	Near East	. . .	. . .	. . .
Far Eastern	Central Asia	. . .	. . .	Indian[b]
	Far East	Sea of Japan	. . .	Pacific
		Kamchatka Sea	. . .	. . .
Intercontinental	. . .	. . .	Northern hemisphere	Atlantic
			Southern hemisphere	Pacific

Source: Rear Adm. V. Andreyev, "The Subdivision and Classification of Theaters of Military Operations," U.S. Foreign Broadcast Information Service, *Soviet Military Theoretical Journal: Voyennaya mysl' (Military Thought)*, November 1964, pp. 15, 18–20; Gregory C. Baird, *Soviet Intermediary Strategic C² Entities: The Historical Experience* (McLean, Va.: BDM Corp., 1979), p. 91; James T. Westwood, "Soviet Naval Theater Forces: Their Strategy and Employment" (October 1978), p. 8.

a. Includes Mediterranean Sea forward deployment.

b. Includes Arabian Sea forward deployment.

ably be held in reserve, directly under the command of the VGK. For example, Delta-class submarines, which carry long-range ballistic missiles and are administered by the Navy in peacetime, are likely to be controlled by the intercontinental TVD directorate in the General Staff in wartime as part of a strategic reserve force for the TVD. Certain naval deployments under operational control of the Soviet fleet commanders in peacetime may be located in maritime and oceanic TVDs that in wartime will be subordinated to the commands of land TVDs. For instance, the naval squadron deployed in the Baltic Sea probably would be reassigned to the direct control of the High Command in the Central European TVD, a practice consistent with theater warfare requirements. Similarly, the Soviet Navy's squadron deployed in the Mediterranean Sea would support the operations of land TVDs through various anticarrier, antisubmarine, and amphibious assault operations. This command arrangement, in turn, would permit the use of strategic missile and bomber forces to support the naval squadron in combat if the situation warranted it.

There is evidence that certain commands of the Soviet military establishment operate in peacetime on a basis approaching that required in wartime. Most obvious are components of the Strategic Rocket Forces and the Air Defense Forces—the two services that stress maintaining "constant combat readiness."[12] A significant portion of the Strategic

12. Maj. Gen. M. I. Cherednichenko, "On Features in the Development of Military Art in the Postwar Period," in *Selected Soviet Military Writings*, pp. 121–22.

Rocket Forces reportedly is maintained on combat duty at high alert levels in peacetime.[13] Other components of the land- and sea-based strategic missile forces may operate at lower levels of readiness, although they may be capable of bringing forces on line more rapidly than the rest of the Soviet forces can. Air Defense combat commands (see appendix D) exist in peacetime at a high level of readiness as protection against any foreign intrusion that occurs with minimal warning.[14] These exceptions to the general operating patterns of the Soviet armed forces are prompted by Soviet leaders' fear that in certain situations strategic warning time required to convert the Soviet military to a wartime footing would not be available.

Another special arrangement that appears to foreshadow the wartime command structure is found in the Soviet Far East command. Historically, the Far East has been an important area of military concern for the USSR, although typically second in priority to Europe as a theater of war. In part, this concern arises from the Soviet Union's traditional fear of becoming involved in a two-front war split between its eastern and western borders. From the end of World War II until the 1970s (except between 1947 and 1953, when hostilities were occurring near the Soviet border) the eastern USSR was organized along the same military district command structure as the rest of the country.[15] In the 1960s, as Sino-Soviet relations deteriorated, the USSR began to expand the military forces deployed along its eastern borders and, by the late 1960s, it had re-created a Central Asian Military District from a part of the Turkestan Military District. No evidence exists, however, to suggest that the basic Soviet perception of the nature of a world war or of Soviet wartime operational strategy had changed. Instead, the possibility of armed conflict with China appears merely to have added requirements to the existing Soviet force plans.

By contrast, during the next decade a number of changes appear to have been made in Soviet planning regarding war with China. In particular, the early 1970s witnessed the increasing orientation of first-line Soviet strategic forces toward covering China. New SS-11 variable-range ballistic missiles supplanted the less survivable medium-range missiles at sites along the Sino-Soviet border.[16] Yankee-class ballistic-

13. *Department of Defense Annual Report Fiscal Year 1981*, p. 81.

14. Harriet Fast Scott and William F. Scott, *The Armed Forces of the USSR* (Westview, 1979), p. 148.

15. Ibid., pp. 192–94.

16. William Beecher, *New York Times*, March 3, 1972.

missile submarines were deployed in the Sea of Japan and in 1975 were used in firing exercises in conjunction with SS-11 missiles.[17] Subsequent modifications to the Soviet command structure for the Far East indicate that the USSR was creating a special operational arrangement for its force there. During 1978 General Secretary Brezhnev and Defense Minister Ustinov took a noteworthy tour through the Far East which included stops at a Strategic Rocket Forces base, the Far Eastern Military District headquarters, and the *Admiral Senyavin,* a command-and-control ship of the Soviet Pacific Fleet.[18] Quite possibly, these trips served to inaugurate the command autonomy of the Soviet forces in the Far East. By early 1979 it was reported that a major command reorganization had occurred in the Far East with the appointment of a senior Soviet military commander.[19]

The new command appears to form the basis of a Far East TVD high command charged with bringing the military districts along the Sino-Soviet border together as a special, more autonomous force that can respond quickly not only in wartime but also in peacetime. Perhaps the first active indication of this command change was the March 1979 Soviet military exercises, the largest ever held in the Far East, which took place coincidentally with the final stages of the Sino-Vietnamese border conflict.[20]

Reestablishment of the special Far East command in peacetime may indicate a growing Soviet interest in improving the operational responsiveness of its military forces through the use of the TVD high command framework. Despite Soviet interest in a highly centralized system to plan and to direct strategic operations, both the enormity and the diversity of Soviet regional and intercontinental operations in wartime necessitate that a more flexible command structure be utilized to fully exploit the military effectiveness of the Soviet military forces.

The Strategic Force Posture

The Soviet Union's regional forces are one of the principal elements of its military power. They are strategically important in part because

17. Fred S. Hoffman, *Washington Star,* August 18, 1975.
18. U.S. Foreign Broadcast Information Service, *Daily Report: Soviet Union,* March 31, 1978, pp. R2–R3; April 5, 1978, p. R1; April 7, 1978, pp. R1–R2.
19. The commander was Army Gen. Ivan Petrov. William Beecher, *Boston Globe,* March 29, 1979.
20. Ibid.

most of the world's vital political and economic centers lie in areas adjacent to the Soviet Union's borders but also because many of the nuclear delivery systems that are capable of attacking the Soviet homeland or its forces in wartime are located there. The rapid growth of the nuclear threat in adjoining regions in the 1950s was an important factor in leading the Soviet Union to develop a regional strategic posture that eventually manifested itself in the establishment of the Strategic Rocket Forces. Despite the subsequent growth of the Soviet intercontinental strategic forces, regional forces continue to have a prime role in providing for the political and military security of the USSR.

The Soviet Union's intercontinental forces seek to directly offset the strategic forces of the United States as a means of defending the Soviet homeland, supporting its global interests, and underpinning its aspirations for achieving regional predominance, both politically and militarily. Changes in the international political and military balance compelled the USSR to expand its security conception beyond its continental perspective. But in its traditional military fashion, the USSR sought to build a comprehensive strike capability against the U.S. strategic threat as a complement to its existing regional strategic strength.

Although long-range bombers and a few intercontinental ballistic missiles (ICBMs) began operation in the mid to late 1950s, it was not until the early 1960s that the intercontinental force structure began to take shape. Following a period of dramatic changes in the political and military balance between the United States and the USSR beginning in 1961, the USSR made a series of decisions—some expedient, others longer term—that determined the nature of Soviet intercontinental strategic forces well into the 1980s.

Deployment Patterns and Operating Levels of Forces

The land-based strategic forces of the Soviet Union are deployed across the entire country (figure 1-3). The Strategic Rocket Forces (SRF) comprise six armies which are subdivided into divisions, regiments, and batteries. The organization of the SRF by divisions and batteries is an indication of the substantial influence of the Ground Forces, and its artillery branch, on the SRF's operational philosophy. The divisions of the rocket armies may be apportioned among the various land, maritime, and intercontinental theaters of military operations (see table 1-2). The Soviet ICBM bases are mainly located along the Trans-Siberian Railway,

Table 1-2. Hypothetical Assignments of Soviet Regional and Intercontinental Strategic Rocket Forces, 1980

SRF army, by location in the USSR	Assignment of army	
	Missile employed	*Theater of military operations*
Northern	SS-4	Northern Europe
	SS-5	Northern Europe
	SS-20	Northern or Central Europe
Southern	SS-4	Near East
	SS-5	Near East
	SS-20	Central or Southern Europe or Near East
Moscow	SS-11	Central Europe and intercontinental
	SS-13	Intercontinental
	SS-17	Intercontinental
	SS-19	Central Europe or intercontinental
	SS-20	Northern, Central, or Southern Europe
Central	SS-11	Intercontinental
	SS-18	Intercontinental
	SS-20	Central or Southern Europe
Eastern	SS-18	Intercontinental
	SS-20	Central Europe, Near East, Central Asia, and Far East
Far Eastern	SS-11	Far East or intercontinental
	SS-20	Far East

while the medium- and intermediate-range ballistic missile (MRBM and IRBM) complexes and strategic bomber bases are more varied in their locations.

The SRF is currently capable of maintaining high alert levels. In the past the intercontinental force could be brought to full alert relatively quickly but could not be held there for long because of the limited operational lifetime of its missile guidance systems.[21] The regional force had problems with its SS-4 and SS-5 missiles, which took eight hours to be readied for firing and could only be held at that state for five hours and required another six hours to reload and refire.[22] The increasing reliance on variable-range ICBMs and the introduction of the SS-20 have eased these problems. The issue of who precisely physically controls

21. Based on information in *Air Force Magazine,* March 1978, p. 51; U.S. Department of Defense, *Soviet Military Power* (GPO, 1981), pp. 6–7, 55.

22. U.S. Central Intelligence Agency, "Major Consequences of Certain US Courses of Action in Cuba," SNIE 11-19-62, declassified (October 20, 1962), p. 2.

Figure 1-3. Deployment of Soviet Regional and Intercontinental Missile Forces, 1980

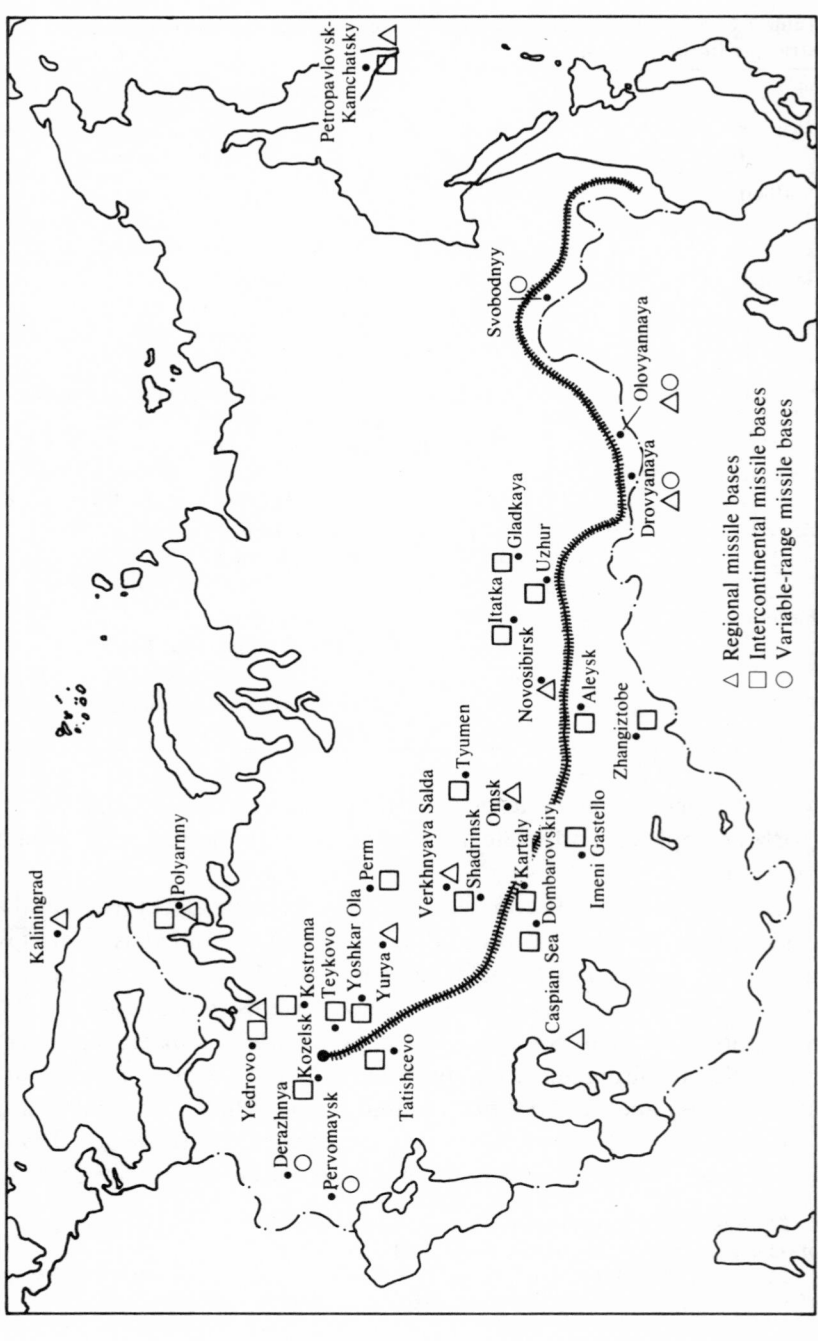

△ Regional missile bases		□ Intercontinental missile bases		○ Variable-range missile bases	
Yedrovo	SS-4, SS-5, SS-20	Yedrovo	SS-17	Derazhnya	SS-11, SS-19
Caspian Sea area	SS-4, SS-5, SS-20	Kozelsk	SS-19	Pervomaysk	SS-11, SS-19
Yurya	SS-20	Tatishcevo	SS-19	Drovyanaya	SS-11
Verkhnyaya Salda	SS-20	Kostroma	SS-17	Olovyannaya	SS-11
		Teykovo	SS-11	Svobodnyy	SS-11
Omsk	SS-20	Yoshkar Ola	SS-13		
Novosibirsk	SS-20	Perm	SS-11		
Drovyanaya	SS-20	Shadrinsk	SS-11		
Olovyannaya	SS-20	Tyumen	SS-11		
Polyarnny	SS-N-6, SS-N-8, SS-N-18	Kartaly	SS-15		
Petropavlovsk-Kamchatsky	SS-N-6, SS-N-8, SS-N-18	Dombarovskiy	SS-18		
		Imeni Gastello	SS-18		
Kaliningrad	SS-N-5	Itatka	SS-11		
		Gladkaya	SS-11		
		Uzhur	SS-18		
		Aleysk	SS-18		
		Zhangiztobe	SS-18		
		Polyarnny	SS-N-6, SS-N-8, SS-N-18		
		Petropavlovsk-Kamchatsky	SS-N-6, SS-N-8, SS-N-18		

Sources: *Hearings on Military Posture and H.R. 1872 [H.R. 4040] Department of Defense Authorization for Appropriations for Fiscal Year 1980,* Hearings before the House Armed Services Committee, 96 Cong. 1 sess. (U.S. Government Printing Office, 1975), bk. 1, pt. 3, p. 124; Clarence A. Robinson, Jr., "Soviet SALT Violation Feared," *Aviation Week and Space Technology,* September 22, 1980, p. 15; *Department of Defense Annual Report, Fiscal Year 1981,* p. 93.

the missile force also probably has been resolved with the installation of electronic safeguards on third- and fourth-generation missiles as well as in the new launch-control centers. In the past, nuclear warheads for the SS-7, for example, were located some distance from the missile itself and were probably controlled by special units of the KGB (Komitet Gosudanstvennoi Bezopastnosti, the Committee of State Security).[23]

An even more recent addition to the Soviet Union's strategic force is its nuclear-powered ballistic-missile submarines. They are deployed with three of the four main fleets of the Soviet Navy—about 70 percent of them with the Northern Fleet and about 25 percent with the Pacific Fleet.[24] It was not until late 1969 that the first of the ballistic-missile submarines, the Yankee class, initiated continuous patrols along the Atlantic coast of the United States.[25] By 1974 the Soviet Union began regular patrols with its new Delta-class nuclear-powered ballistic-missile submarines (SSBNs) that carry the extremely long-range ballistic missiles which permit them to cover U.S. targets from the Barents, Norwegian, and Greenland seas, as well as the northern Pacific, near their home bases. Currently the USSR maintains several Delta-class SSBNs regularly on station, mostly in these waters near the USSR, as well as a couple of Yankee-class SSBNs forward deployed off Bermuda and Nova Scotia in the Atlantic, and probably one near Hawaii in the Pacific.[26] The older Golf- and Hotel-class missile submarines primarily operate in areas such as the Baltic Sea and the Sea of Japan.

Rocket Force Targets and Mission Assignments

Soviet missiles have been developed to fulfill a wide range of targeting requirements. The combinations of ranges, yields, and reentry vehicles in the Soviet missile inventory allow military planners to chart single, group, or massed strikes aimed at meeting strategic objectives in a

23. John Barron, *KGB: The Secret Work of Soviet Secret Agents* (Reader's Digest Press, 1974), p. 15.

24. *Fiscal Year 1979 Arms Control Impact Statements,* Joint Committee Print, prepared for the House International Relations Committee and the Senate Foreign Relations Committee, 95 Cong. 2 sess. (GPO, 1978), p. 167; "Soviets' Nuclear Arsenal Continues to Proliferate," *Aviation Week and Space Technology,* June 16, 1980, p. 75.

25. *United States Military Posture for FY 1979* (Office of the Joint Chiefs of Staff, 1978), p. 30; William Beecher, *New York Times,* April 24, 1970.

26. George C. Wilson, *Washington Post,* April 28, 1975; Charles C. Petersen, "Trends in Soviet Naval Operations," in Bradford Dismukes and James M. McConnell, eds., *Soviet Naval Diplomacy* (Pergamon, 1979), pp. 77–84.

nuclear conflict. Each objective requires the neutralization or annihilation of certain targets in various theaters of military operation. Targets are ranked as either primary or secondary, depending on their urgency and military value.[27] The broad list of requirements compiled by Soviet planners is likely to be composed of strategic nuclear targets, including missiles, submarines, strategic aircraft bases, naval bases, nuclear storehouses, and command-and-control centers; operational and tactical nuclear targets, including aircraft carriers, aircraft, cruise missiles and tactical missile deployments, tactical airfields, nuclear storage sites, and command posts; conventional targets, including large ground-troop formations and reserves, logistical and fuel centers, naval bases, and air defense bases and facilities; and administrative and economic targets, including critical industrial facilities, national administrative and political centers, transportation centers and ports, and centers of state administration.

The assignments of Soviet rocket armies are a key to understanding the SRF's strengths and limitations.[28] The majority of the divisions of some rocket armies apparently are assigned for theater strike missions against NATO (the North Atlantic Treaty Organization) or China while the remaining divisions may be mainly oriented toward covering intercontinental military and industrial targets (although they are also available as theater reserves). Importantly, the deployment of variable-range ballistic missiles makes it possible for each rocket army to cover both regional and intercontinental targets. One army, in the Moscow area, seems capable of both high-intensity theater strikes and strikes against U.S. strategic targets. The major strength of this kind of organization is the flexibility and redundancy it offers the SRF in meeting the diverse targeting requirements outlined for it by the General Staff. Conversely, a certain tension must arise from the need to cover a variety of regional and intercontinental targets and yet withhold a portion of the land-based strike forces as a strategic reserve.

The basing locations and ranges of weapons assigned to the rocket armies suggest what the targeting responsibilities of units in various theaters of military operations are (see table 1-2). The northern-area rocket army effectively covers targets throughout Scandinavia and into Iceland with its SS-4s and can extend its reach to Greenland with SS-5s.

27. Joseph D. Douglass, Jr., *Soviet Strategy in Europe* (Pergamon, 1980), p. 74.
28. The targeting assignments are our estimates based on deployment locations and the presumed Soviet TVD planning framework.

Its SS-20s improve this coverage and make possible coverage of the Central TVD. The southern rocket army's SS-4s can reach Turkey, Israel, and Iran; its SS-5s add coverage of Greece, North Africa, and Saudi Arabia; and its SS-20s extend its coverage to Central and Southern Europe TVD targets.

Both the central and the eastern rocket armies seem to place a premium on intercontinental targets, especially since the missiles of these two armies can reach as far south as Missouri and cover the heart of the U.S. ICBM force. Interestingly, the longer range of the SS-18 is not necessary for coverage of the United States but to improve the chances of survival of the SS-18 complexes. Because of their southern locations, certain Soviet missile bases are out of the normal range of many Minuteman ICBMs, although the SS-18s can still reach all of the U.S. silos. Some SS-18s—in particular the third modification—offer the intercontinental TVD a distant reach, especially against targets in countries that could prove politically hostile in a long war. The 8,000-nautical-mile range of modification 3 permits coverage of areas as distant as South Africa and Brazil. Both the central and the eastern armies have SS-20 regiments that act as strategic theater reserves for various land TVDs. From these locations the SS-20s can cover targets in the Central Europe, Southern Europe, Near Eastern, and Central Asian theaters and even reach China in the Far East TVD.

The Moscow area rocket army has nearby as well as intercontinental targeting responsibilities. Its well-protected SS-19 force at Derazhnya and Pervomaysk can cover all of western and southern Europe as well as naval force deployments in the Mediterranean Sea. Regiments in the Moscow region, composed of SS-11s , SS-13s, SS-17s, and SS-19s, can cover most of the United States and all of Canada. Because of their centralized location, however, they may have diverse assignments. Some of the SS-13s could act as a booster for emergency transmitters to relay communications while the majority of the SS-13 regiments attacked early warning systems in Canada and Greenland. The SS-17s have sufficient range and warheads of high enough yields to strike Titan II ICBM bases as well as Strategic Air Command (SAC) bases and support facilities throughout the United States. The SS-19s can effectively attack various targets in the United States and Canada, including army, naval, and air bases. The SS-11s would be able to cover all the important administrative and economic targets in Canada and the eastern and central portion of the United States, and some of them have the range and characteristics necessary to bombard naval forces deployed at sea.

Some SS-20s may also be assigned to the Moscow army area. The SS-20's great advantage—besides its accuracy and its multiple warheads—is its ability to cover the same targets as the SS-4 and SS-5 but from the interior of the USSR. It can thus be used as a theater reserve weapon, a luxury not enjoyed by SS-4s or SS-5s in close proximity to many adversary states.

The Far Eastern rocket army, with a smaller list of targets than the other armies, can strike military and industrial targets in China in addition to the U.S. SAC base in Guam; nuclear ammunition sites and air force and naval bases in Guam, the Philippines, and Hawaii; and military, administrative, and economic targets in Australia. The SS-20 force is both a survivable and an accurate weapon system that enhances Soviet coverage of China.

Both the regional and the intercontinental theaters of operation have the additional support of ballistic-missile submarines located in maritime and oceanic theaters. The SS-N-5 and SS-N-6 missiles at sea with the various Soviet fleets are suitable for covering regional theater targets. Additionally, forward-deployed SS-N-6s can strike the home bases of U.S. command-post aircraft, as well as important American naval targets and command-and-control centers. And SS-N-8s and SS-N-18s, with their intercontinental ranges, offer a strategic reserve capability for use against remaining U.S. military targets and administrative and economic centers in the United States, if necessary. The sea-based missile forces round out the comprehensive targeting strategy of the Soviet forces which reflects the specific requirements of individual theaters of military operations as well as the overall need for flexibility of the strategic force itself.

CHAPTER TWO

SOVIET NUCLEAR STRATEGY

WHILE THE advent of the long-range nuclear missile altered Soviet military doctrine and strategy, both military tradition—largely shaped by the Ground Forces—and geographic and political reality have continued to have a strong influence in determining Soviet wartime objectives and operational philosophy. Probably the most influential factor is Russia's position as a large continental nation separated from powerful neighbors by long and relatively accessible borders. The vulnerability of its western border has been impressed on modern Soviet thinking by the devastating German invasion of June 1941. And the presence of potential threats along both its eastern and western borders has fostered Soviet concern about the possibility of a two-front war. Thus the current Soviet concept of what is strategically important encompasses developments in adjoining areas as well as the actions of its principal adversary, the United States.[1] The Soviet Union's geographical and political situation has also compelled it to place a premium on the maintenance of large ground forces. Historically, the USSR had to rely on a large army, often of uneven quality, to defend its vast territory against invasion. Until the establishment of the Strategic Rocket Forces in 1959, the Ground Forces were the most important of the Soviet military forces.[2]

The traditions of the Ground Forces are still reflected in the modern Soviet approach to the use of long-range, nuclear weapon systems. Soviet strategic doctrine accords high priority to decisively defeating the complete range of the enemy's military forces and occupying

1. See Thomas W. Wolfe, *Soviet Power and Europe, 1945–1970* (Johns Hopkins Press, 1970), pp. 32–42, 195–99; Fritz W. Ermarth, "Contrasts in American and Soviet Thought," *International Security,* vol. 3 (Fall 1978), pp. 146–48; William T. Lee, "Soviet Targeting Strategy and SALT," *Air Force Magazine,* September 1978, p. 120.

2. Edward L. Warner III, *The Military in Contemporary Soviet Politics: An Institutional Analysis* (Praeger, 1977), p. 30.

important portions of enemy territory even in the event of nuclear warfare.[3] Substantial nonnuclear forces are needed to meet such objectives. Reinforcing the tendency to rely on direct land combat with the enemy is a conservatism that is endemic to continental powers that lack the margin of error that a natural or political barrier provides. Russia has always been interested in creating a buffer zone of acquired territories and allies along its borders to protect its heartland from intrusion. This and many other traditional political and military values continue to be embodied in the Soviet strategy concerning the use of nuclear forces.

A perhaps less direct influence on Soviet strategic policy and strategy is the USSR's technological and industrial capacity for production of strategic weapons. One critical link in the building of Soviet weapon systems is the design bureau that brings together weapon design and development.[4] The design process instills stability in weapons acquisition through its long-term focus on steady improvement of existing systems and constant planning for follow-on systems. Such a process probably gives the USSR the confidence to commit itself to achieving the long-term technical goals required by its strategic objectives.

One of the major shortcomings of the weapons acquisition process has been the Soviet Union's relative inability to exploit certain technologies that, in the West, are critical to producing advanced weapon systems. The Soviet Union's inability to take advantage of passive sonar systems or advanced detection and guidance systems restricts its capacity to solve military problems, particularly in terms of strategic defense. However, this limitation is offset to some degree by the Soviet Union's capacity to regularly produce and deploy large numbers of major systems even during peacetime. In many cases its technological limitation appears to arise not from lack of knowledge and skill but from an economic system that encourages fulfillment of production targets at the expense of quality control, technological innovation, and exploitation of new technologies.[5]

In Soviet military writing the terms *military doctrine* and *military strategy* are used more precisely than in the West. Military doctrine, the

3. Marshal of the Soviet Union V. D. Sokolovskiy, *Soviet Military Strategy*, 3d ed., ed. Harriet Fast Scott (Crane, Russak, 1975), pp. 13 and 284.

4. William J. Perry, "The FY 1980 Department of Defense Program for Research, Development and Acquisition" (U.S. Department of Defense, 1979), pp. II-4–II-6; Arthur J. Alexander, *Decision-Making in Soviet Weapons Procurement*, Adelphi Papers 47 and 48 (London: International Institute for Strategic Studies [IISS], 1978), pp. 21–24.

5. Perry, "FY 1980, Department of Defense Program," pp. II-4–II-7.

highest level of military thinking, is dictated by the Communist party leadership as a set of official views about the types of warfare for which the Soviet military establishment must be prepared. Subordinate to Soviet doctrine are various levels of military thought, including military strategy, which develops the detailed organization, methods, and preparations for waging war.[6]

Both doctrine and strategy, which are discussed in great detail in Soviet military writings, are used for much broader purposes than outlining operational principles for the development and employment of military forces.[7] Soviet military treatises play an important role, for instance, in shaping public beliefs to conform with official thinking. Doctrine and strategy are also used to influence the adversary's perceptions—as for example in the stress on American inability to wage limited war in Europe. Finally, doctrinal precepts are often used to rationalize away intractable problems and to promote various institutional interests.[8]

Official statements of Soviet military doctrine and strategy obviously cannot be viewed as a binding blueprint for Soviet action. But they do shed light on the likely nature of Soviet military operations and mission priorities. Moreover, changes in Soviet statements on military doctrine and strategy may reveal the ideological, institutional, and technological influences that have shaped the Soviet Union's strategic posture.

Modern Doctrine and Strategy

Until Stalin's death in 1953, Soviet military doctrine and strategy were based solely on the experience of the prenuclear age.[9] After Stalin's death, a reevaluation that went on for several years resulted in Soviet proclamation that a "revolution in military affairs" had occurred.[10] The

6. Marshal A. A. Grechko, *The Armed Forces of the Soviet State* (U.S. Government Printing Office, 1975), p. 84; Benjamin S. Lambeth, "The Sources of Soviet Military Doctrine," in Frank B. Horton III, Anthony C. Rogerson, and Edward L. Warner III, eds., *Comparative Defense Policy* (Johns Hopkins University Press, 1974), pp. 200–02.

7. Lambeth, "Sources of Soviet Military Doctrine," pp. 214–15.

8. Benjamin S. Lambeth, *How To Think About Soviet Military Doctrine*, P-5939 (Santa Monica, Calif.: Rand Corp., 1978), pp. 15–16.

9. Raymond L. Garthoff, *Soviet Strategy in the Nuclear Age* (Praeger, 1958), pp. 61–63.

10. Among the several sources, see Col. Gen. M. Povaliy, "Development of Soviet Military Strategy," in U.S. Foreign Broadcast Information Service, *Selected Translations: Voyennaya mysl' (Military Thought)* (February 1967), pp. 67–71 (hereafter, *Military Thought*); Sokolovskiy, *Soviet Military Strategy*, pp. xx, 191–94.

basis of this transformation was the advent of long-range ballistic missiles armed with nuclear warheads, which offered the unprecedented capability to destroy targets around the world within a short time. The USSR adopted a new doctrine based on the belief that war between socialism and capitalism was no longer inevitable, but that a war between the two opposing coalitions of states would inevitably become a nuclear-missile war and would result in the crushing defeat of the imperialists.[11]

One important implication of the change in the nature of war was the possibility that massed nuclear strikes could accomplish strategic objectives at the outset of a war by their timely destruction of enemy targets.[12] This contrasted with the attainment of strategic goals in a prenuclear war through a relatively slow, sequential process of defeating the enemy's armed forces step by step and then seizing important enemy regions and political centers.[13] Long-range nuclear weapons also helped to erase the distinction in earlier Soviet strategy between the priority of front-line operations, where the enemy's armed forces were directly engaged, and the belief that attacks on the rear area targets that supported the war effort would have a negligible impact on the course of the war.[14] With the advent of nuclear-armed missiles, Soviet military strategy shifted to emphasize the importance of simultaneously attacking the enemy's front line and his economic and national control systems.[15]

In Soviet military writings the long-range ballistic missile was portrayed as far superior to the bomber for fulfilling military requirements. The missile's high speed and ability to reach its target (there were no effective defenses) were compared to the strategic bomber's low speed and vulnerability to enemy air defenses.[16] The initial Soviet lead in the

11. Sokolovskiy, *Soviet Military Strategy*, pp. 170–71, 194–95. The Soviet view of the inevitability of escalation was firm through the early 1960s; see Wolfe, *Soviet Power and Europe*, pp. 209–12.

12. Col. Gen. Nikolai A. Lomov, "The Influence of Soviet Military Doctrine on the Development of Military Art," in William R. Kintner and Harriet Fast Scott, eds. and trans., *The Nuclear Revolution in Soviet Military Affairs* (University of Oklahoma Press, 1968), pp. 160–61.

13. Sokolovskiy, *Soviet Military Strategy*, p. 242; Gen. N. A. Sbitov, "The Revolution in Military Affairs and Its Results," in Kintner and Scott, *Nuclear Revolution*, pp. 28–29.

14. Sokolovskiy, *Soviet Military Strategy*, pp. 11, 193–94, 274; Col. M. Skovorodkin, "Some Questions on Coordination of Branches of Armed Forces in Major Operations." *Military Thought*, February 1967, pp. 36–38; Col. Gen. N. A. Lomov, ed., *Scientific-Technical Progress and the Revolution in Military Affairs* (GPO, 1974), pp. 137–38.

15. Povaliy, "Development of Soviet Military Strategy," p. 71; Marshal N. Krylov, "The Nuclear-Missile Shield of the Soviet State," *Military Thought*, November 1967, p. 17.

16. Sokolovskiy, *Soviet Military Strategy*, pp. 193, 252.

development of long-range ballistic missiles, as opposed to the prevailing American advantage in strategic air power, provided the USSR with political and military incentives to belittle the bomber's utility.

Nuclear missiles also may have been more compatible with Soviet military heritage and values than the concept of strategic bombardment. The ballistic missile could be conceived of as a modern extension of battlefield artillery, the "god of war" that historically has provided the Russians with their main firepower in battle.[17] In many ways the artilleryman's mind-set best characterizes the Soviet approach to nuclear warfare, since it reflects both general Soviet military values and the specific involvement of artillerymen in the development of the Soviet strategic missile forces.

Although official doctrine relegated the traditionally predominant Ground Forces to a secondary role of exploiting nuclear strikes of the Strategic Rocket Forces, Soviet military writings have continually emphasized that final victory can be achieved only by the combined efforts of all branches of the Soviet armed forces.[18] The Ground Forces' ability to seize and occupy enemy regions and to defend the USSR against invasion is often cited as an example of the continuing importance of the traditional services.[19] To some degree, this is a convenient intermingling of Soviet doctrinal assumptions and institutional interests. Relying on the Ground Forces to seize and hold territory allows the traditional military forces to retain a significant wartime role despite Soviet doctrinal adherence to a concept of all-out nuclear war. Consequently, the "revolution in military affairs" notwithstanding, Soviet military strategy envisages that regional military forces in a world war might simultaneously employ conventional, chemical, and nuclear weapons to achieve their objectives.[20] And the shift in Soviet military strategy in the mid-1960s toward greater recognition that regional warfare could begin with an extended phase of conventional warfare ensures the continuing relevance of nonnuclear forces.[21]

Another traditional military priority that continues to be honored is

17. Ibid., pp. 241–42.

18. Ibid., pp. 198–99, 247.

19. Ibid.; see Army Gen. I. Pavlovskiy, "The Ground Troops of the Soviet Armed Forces," *Military Thought*, November 1967, p. 35.

20. Sokolovskiy, *Soviet Military Strategy*, pp. 199, 243.

21. Joseph D. Douglass, Jr., *The Soviet Theater Nuclear Offensive*, Studies in Communist Affairs, vol. 1, prepared for the Office of Director of Defense Research and Engineering and Defense Nuclear Agency (GPO, 1976), pp. 116–18; editorial, *Military Thought*, February 1966, p. 13; Col. B. Samorukov, "Combat Operations Involving Conventional Means of Destruction," *Military Thought*, August 1967, pp. 29–30.

the importance attributed to strategic reserve forces. The USSR learned in World War II that its strategic reserves were essential as a hedge against uncertainty and to assure the Supreme High Command that certain designated forces would always be available to be brought into battle at decisive points. While the nature of Soviet military forces has changed since that time, the principles governing their utility in wartime have not.

The Soviet military posture therefore represents a compromise between the old and the new in terms of military strategy as well as force structure. The balance leans heavily toward the modern nuclear side of the equation, but traditional Soviet military forces retain an important role.

From a broader perspective, the shift in military posture can be interpreted as the difficult but essential step of a power with a continental perspective toward a strategy that takes into account a transoceanic adversary strong in long-range strategic air and sea power and possessing a secure military and industrial mobilization base. Equally as important as the distant threat in the 1950s was the sudden growth of a nuclear threat (mostly in the form of nuclear-armed aircraft) in the regions surrounding the Soviet Union. Neither the intercontinental nor the regional threat could be directly or effectively countered by the traditional guardian of Soviet military security, the Ground Forces. Thus, the "revolution in military affairs" offered to the USSR both a possible solution and further challenge to its defense plans. Long-range, nuclear-armed ballistic missiles could counter the growing regional nuclear threat to the Soviet homeland effectively and also strike targets deep in the enemy's homeland. While the new weapons increased the strategic threat to the USSR itself, they also restored its ability to directly and decisively respond to all major military threats.

Wartime Objectives

The main Soviet military objectives in a world war have probably always been defense of the homeland, defeat and neutralization of military adversaries, and seizure and occupation of vital contiguous areas.[22] The existence of modern strategic forces has altered both the

22. Sokolovskiy, *Soviet Military Strategy*, pp. 282, 285; Benjamin S. Lambeth, *Selective Nuclear Options in American and Soviet Strategic Policy*, R-2034-DDRE, prepared for the Director of Defense Research and Engineering (Santa Monica, Calif.: Rand Corp., 1976), pp. 34–37; Lee, "Soviet Targeting Strategy," pp. 121–25; Joseph D. Douglass, Jr., and Amoretta M. Hoeber, *Soviet Strategy for Nuclear War* (Hoover Institution Press, 1979), pp. 14–33.

Table 2-1. Postulated Soviet General War Objectives in Various Theaters of Military Operations

Theater of military operations	Objective		
	Political neutralization	*Military neutralization*	*Military occupation*
Northern, Central, and Southern Europe			
Central Europe	...	X	X
Northern Europe	...	X	X
Southern Europe	...	X	X
Britain	...	X	...
Iceland	...	X	X
Spain	X	X	...
Sweden	X	...	...
Far East			
China	...	X	...
South Korea	...	X	...
Japan	X	...	...
Philippines	...	X	...
Near East and Central Asia			
Mediterranean Sea area	X	X	...
Persian Gulf area	X	...	X
Intercontinental			
Northern hemisphere	...	X	...
Southern hemisphere	X	X	...

Sources: *Dictionary of Basic Military Terms: A Soviet View* (U.S. Government Printing Office, 1976), pp. 52, 59, 120, 192; *Air Force Magazine*, September 1978, p. 122; Marshal of the Soviet Union V. D. Sokolovskiy, *Soviet Military Strategy*, 3d ed., ed. Harriet Fast Scott (Crane, Russak, 1975), p. 13.

nature and the relative priority of these objectives. Contemporary Soviet military strategy appears to focus on occupying Western Europe while relying on strategic forces to either politically or militarily offset the United States and any regional threats to its security such as China.[23] In other words, Soviet strategy concerns two sets of different but complementary military requirements—regional and intercontinental (table 2-1).

Europe is undoubtedly the most important regional theater of military operations for the Soviet Union. Soviet military writings suggest war in Europe could begin solely with conventional forces or with a combination of conventional and nuclear forces[24] and occur either simultaneously

23. Army Gen. S. Ivanov, "Soviet Military Doctrine and Strategy," *Military Thought,* May 1969, p. 47.
24. Douglass, *Soviet Theater Nuclear Offensive,* pp. 4, 45–53, 99–121; also see A. A. Sidorenko, *The Offensive (A Soviet View)* (GPO, 1975), pp. 40–70; Krylov, "Nuclear-Missile Shield," pp. 17–18; Povaliy, "Development of Soviet Military Strategy," pp. 70–71.

with intercontinental nuclear strikes or proceed at first only regionally. In any set of circumstances, defeat of the enemy's military forces and occupation of important territories would remain the wartime objectives. Soviet military strategy therefore attempts to integrate nuclear and nonnuclear responses at the tactical, regional, and intercontinental levels of combat.

The Soviet interest in occupying certain portions of Europe probably results from a belief that conventional warfare would be important in ending regional conflicts in a prolonged worldwide nuclear war. The seizure of important territorial objectives would deny the enemy forward staging areas and bases for its tactical forces as well as potential war-making resources. Furthermore, the acquisition of European industrial facilities and resources could help in the Soviet economic recovery following a nuclear war. This aspect of strategy reflects the Soviet Union's World War II experience of relocating its industry to avoid advancing German troops and drawing on the defeated German economy to revitalize its own.

The USSR's plans for the wartime occupation of Europe suggest that its nuclear strikes would be discriminate in their targeting. This is consistent with the Soviet all-arms approach that integrates the operations of tactical nonnuclear forces with those of regional nuclear strike forces. In the event that nuclear weapons are employed, Soviet military writings prescribe the use of nuclear strikes to destroy the enemy's military forces and other important targets.[25] Armored, mechanized, and airborne troops would then attempt to exploit these attacks by striking into the enemy's rear areas to destroy remaining enemy units and seize important territory.[26]

Soviet acceptance in the mid-1960s of the possibility of an extended phase of nonnuclear warfare thus did not require extraordinary changes in the Soviet military posture. The expansion in Soviet nonnuclear capabilities following this doctrinal decision was aimed at giving the USSR flexibility to effectively engage in combat under any conditions. Whether employing nuclear or nonnuclear weapons, the Soviet forces' most important mission is to neutralize the enemy's nuclear-armed

25. Another reason for Soviet interest in avoiding the nuclear devastation of Western Europe is said to be the problem of prevailing westerly winds (Lee, "Soviet Targeting Strategy," p. 124). Some analysts argue that it is therefore wrong to assume that Soviet strike forces are armed only with high-yield nuclear warheads. See Joseph D. Douglass, Jr., "Soviet Nuclear Strategy in Europe: A Selective Targeting Doctrine?" *Strategic Review*, vol. 5 (Fall 1977), pp. 19–32.

26. Sokolovskiy, *Soviet Military Strategy*, pp. 292–94.

systems and other important military forces.[27] The commonality of goals, targeting priorities, and operational approaches reflects the integral role of tactical, nonnuclear forces in Soviet regional nuclear planning.

The diverse Soviet objectives in the various theaters of military operations (TVDs) necessitate a multifaceted approach to regional operations. Objectives of defeating the enemy's military forces and occupying important areas are much less applicable to China, the Persian Gulf, Britain, and Japan than to continental Europe. Given the questionable feasibility and desirability of occupying large areas of China, for instance, the Soviet Union would probably attempt to neutralize that country in the event of world war. Using nuclear strikes, the USSR might seek to destroy China's important military installations and major administrative and economic centers. Soviet forces deployed along the Chinese border would probably act simply as a nuclear defense force against Chinese military incursions.[28] Soviet wartime strategy toward the Persian Gulf countries and Japan, with their great economic value and limited defense capability, may be oriented toward removing these countries from a worldwide conflict and bringing them under Soviet influence by means of political intimidation rather than through full-scale invasion. The military strength of the United Kingdom, on the other hand, combined with its geographic insularity, would probably lead the USSR to use nuclear force against it to neutralize it as a potential political and military threat to Soviet regional operations.

The most important of the Soviet Union's intercontinental strategic objectives in wartime would be to deter the use of U.S. nuclear forces. Failing that, Soviet military writings suggest the American threat would be countered by deep nuclear strikes at military and nonmilitary targets that would so devastate the United States that it could no longer influence the course of the war. Success in this mission would greatly improve the Soviet Union's chances of achieving its regional objectives and assuring the survival of its homeland.

Soviet strategy would aim at destroying U.S. strategic nuclear assets, command-and-control centers, general military forces, and administrative and economic centers. Effective nuclear strikes on command-and-control centers—not only those supporting strategic nuclear and con-

27. Maj. Gen. Kh. Dzhelaukhov, "The Infliction of Deep Strikes," *Military Thought,* February 1966, pp. 47–49; Sidorenko, *The Offensive,* pp. 132–37.

28. S. T. Cohen and W. C. Lyons, "A Comparison of U.S.-Allied and Soviet Tactical Nuclear Force Capabilities and Policies," *Orbis,* vol. 19 (Spring 1975), pp. 78–79.

ventional forces but also the national political control system—offer a way to disable and degrade the whole spectrum of military and political assets.[29] This element of Soviet strategy reflects both the high priority the USSR puts on a centralized command system and the Soviet view of nuclear war as a conflict waged between opposing political systems.

The American economic base is much more of a threat to the USSR than are European administrative and economic centers which could be occupied and eventually used to reconstitute the Soviet economy. Destruction of the American defense industrial base would end support for tactical forces in regions surrounding the USSR as well as the threat of postwar military and economic recovery of the United States. A strategy designed to destroy industrial facilities resembles U.S. plans in the 1950s for targeting the Soviet economic and transportation network as a means of supporting Western theater forces.[30]

Destruction of the enemy's administrative and economic base was proclaimed to be a major new tenet of the Soviet Union's military doctrine following its acquisition of strategic missiles. For the first time, comparable priority was put on attacking administrative and economic centers and military forces. The list of military targets (including strategic nuclear forces) that Soviet doctrine designates is much broader than what is usually thought of as nuclear targets in the West. Nonnuclear targets range from U.S. army, tactical fighter, and airlift bases to naval ports and conventional munitions depots.

The most important American military target is, of course, the missiles, submarines, and heavy bombers of the intercontinental strategic forces. Here again, Soviet targeting doctrine extends to destroying the supporting systems that enable these forces to perform effectively in wartime.[31] These targets include the national command-and-control system and its links to each major component of the U.S. strategic forces, as well as early-warning radar sites and navigational aids. The only means available for neutralizing or degrading such weapons as U.S. strategic submarines on patrol may be attacking their less survivable communications and navigation systems.

29. Skovorodkin, "Some Questions on Coordination," pp. 36–37.

30. For instance, see Henry Rowen's account in "A Strategic Symposium: SALT and U.S. Defense Policy," *Washington Quarterly,* vol. 2 (Winter 1979), p. 52.

31. Along this line, see Floyd D. Kennedy, Jr., "Attacking The Weakest Link: The Anti-Support Role of Soviet Naval Forces," *Naval War College Review,* vol. 32 (September–October 1979), pp. 48–55.

Soviet conceptions of intercontinental theaters of military operations are not confined to land masses but also include oceanic TVDs—both targets at sea, and ports and naval bases in the enemy's coastal zones.[32] The Soviet Navy has an important role in these theaters, but the Strategic Rocket Forces and long-range bombers may also be used to attack naval targets in the event of war.[33] The most important of these targets are ballistic-missile submarines and aircraft carriers armed with nuclear-capable aircraft.[34] The enemy's lines of communication at sea also can be disrupted by nuclear strikes on coastal installations as well as forces at sea.

Present Basis of Strategic Doctrine

Like other aspects of the Soviet strategic posture, strategic doctrine has been shaped by traditional attitudes heavily influenced by pragmatic military considerations.[35] Therefore, despite Soviet interest in avoiding nuclear conflict and maintaining a credible deterrent in peacetime, if war should occur, the USSR would seek to militarily prevail over the enemy as the best means of assuring national survival. Some Soviet military writings refer to victory as the goal in wartime, but few define its meaning in the context of all-out nuclear war.[36] Nevertheless, Soviet nuclear strategy continues to adhere to the traditional objectives associated with military victory of physically defending the homeland against enemy attack, decisively defeating the enemy's military forces, and occupying

32. Sokolovskiy, *Soviet Military Strategy,* pp. 299–302; Rear Adm. V. Andreyev, "The Subdivision and Classification of Theaters of Military Operations," in U.S. Foreign Broadcast Information Service, *Soviet Military Theoretical Journal: Voyennaya mysl' (Military Thought),* November 1964, pp. 19–20.

33. Sokolovskiy, *Soviet Military Strategy,* p. 302.

34. S. G. Gorshkov, *The Navy,* JPRS 72286 (Arlington, Va.: Joint Publications Research Service, 1978), p. 36. Also see James M. McConnell, "Strategy and Missions of the Soviet Navy in the Year 2000," in James L. George, ed., *Problems of Sea Power as We Approach the Twenty-First Century* (Washington: American Enterprise Institute for Public Policy Research, 1978), pp. 47–50.

35. Benjamin S. Lambeth, *The Elements of Soviet Strategic Policy,* P-6389 (Santa Monica, Calif.: Rand Corp.,1979), pp. 5–6; John Erickson, "The Soviet Military System: Doctrine, Technology and 'Style,' " in John Erickson and E. J. Feuchtwanger, eds., *Soviet Military Power and Performance* (Archon Books, 1979), pp. 24–28; Dennis Ross, "Rethinking Soviet Strategic Policy: Inputs and Implications," *Journal of Strategic Studies,* vol. 1 (May 1978), pp. 3–30.

36. For instance, see the recent statement by Marshal of the Soviet Union N. V. Ogarkov, chief of the General Staff, reprinted in *Strategic Review,* vol. 8 (Summer 1980), pp. 93–95.

enemy territory. Such goals have the benefit of creating relatively clear-cut military requirements and suggesting the kind of force structure that is needed. They also make it logical to integrate strategic and tactical operations, and nuclear with nonnuclear forces.

The tradition of direct, decisive battle against its enemies,[37] naturally fostered by its continental position, is an important link between the USSR's historical military approach and its modern strategic doctrine. The purer military perspective embodied in Soviet strategic thinking not only reflects Russia's continental heritage, but also the prominent role of the military in the formulation of strategy. With the exception of Nikita Khrushchev's short-lived attempt to dominate Soviet strategy and force planning, the USSR apparently has lacked the substantial civilian input characteristic of Western strategic thought since World War II.[38]

Soviet doctrine has also been able to develop relatively free of concern for external alliances. The USSR's geographical proximity to and political dominance of the neighboring Warsaw Pact countries obviates the kind of nuclear commitment that the United States has been compelled to make to its overseas allies. For the United States, this relationship has been a critical influence in leading it to embrace such doctrinal concepts as limited nuclear war and selective strategic targeting.

The Soviet approach to strategic doctrine contrasts in many ways with that of the United States and other Western nuclear powers. Instead of seeking to physically rebuff the enemy, as in Soviet doctrine, Western concepts rely on persuading the enemy that the cost of his actions (in terms of prospective losses) would far outweigh his gains. Thus, posing the threat of unacceptable losses in economic capacity, military power, and political cohesion, the Western concept attempts to dissuade the enemy from initiating nuclear war. If war should break out, the Western powers would continue to seek survival by means of deterrence by attempting to end the war through threats to escalate the conflict to increasingly higher levels of destruction. The Soviet Union has attempted to obtain additional insurance by striving for the capability not only to devastate the enemy's homeland, but also to prevail militarily in the event of a world war.

37. Lambeth, *Elements,* p. 5; Erickson, "Soviet Military System," pp. 25, 28.
38. Stanley Sienkiewicz, "SALT and Soviet Nuclear Doctrine," *International Security,* vol. 2 (Spring 1978), p. 92; Ross, "Rethinking Soviet Strategic Policy," p. 14.

In the final analysis, any speculation about the Soviet Union's perceptions concerning deterrence and its likely actions in the event of world war can at best be inferred only in general terms from military writings and Soviet choices of force posture. The uncertainty that underlies any analysis of Soviet strategic doctrine is due in part to the fact that the visibility of Soviet military writings on questions of strategy is generally unmatched by insight into the thinking of the top political leadership on questions of war and peace. Additionally, since the late 1970s the Soviet leadership has become more sensitive to the external implications of its doctrinal statements and appears to be tailoring its statements more to support its political position.

The traditional military values and the continental heritage of Soviet nuclear strategy are most clearly manifested in the Soviet operational philosophy for employing strategic forces in the event of nuclear war. The USSR's operational philosophy reflects skepticism concerning the possibility (or desirability) of controlling escalation in a major conflict. Soviet military writings tend to emphasize the likelihood that any direct conflict between the United States and the USSR would escalate into full-scale nuclear war.[39] Not surprisingly, the idea of limiting conventional or nuclear warfare to the theaters surrounding (and possibly including) the USSR has little appeal since even limited conflicts could result in substantial destruction to the Soviet Union. There is little acceptance in Soviet works of the various thresholds to escalation based on limitations in weapon types, or where they are used, outlined in Western writings.[40]

Rather than emphasizing measures that might limit escalation, Soviet military writings tend to portray decisiveness as the highest operational value in wartime operations. This reflects a propensity to engage the complete range of military resources available—once the threshold into war has been crossed—as the surest means of defeating the enemy and ensuring national survival. Such a strategic approach is consistent with traditional military values in its unconstrained pursuit of military victory once war begins.

---

39. Maj. Gen. V. Zemskov, "Characteristic Features of Modern Wars and Possible Methods of Conducting Them," *Military Thought*, July 1969, p. 23; Warner, *Military in Contemporary Soviet Politics*, pp. 156–57.

40. Sokolovskiy, *Soviet Military Strategy*, p. 195. Also see Douglass, *Soviet Theater Nuclear Offensive*, pp. 101–13.

Soviet emphasis on the inevitability of escalation also serves to undermine U.S. confidence in the possibility of limited warfare as well as to erode the political confidence of the U.S. allies in American defense assurances. In spite of the growth of Soviet conventional war capabilities in the late 1960s and early 1970s, and increasing acceptance in Soviet military writings of the possibility that a major U.S.-USSR conflict might not immediately escalate into nuclear war, Soviet military strategy continues to emphasize the likelihood of large-scale nuclear exchanges. Soviet doctrine appears to see the paramount threshold as that between war and peace rather than emphasizing, as Western doctrine does, the possible firebreaks once war occurs.

Another emphasis in Soviet military writings has long been on the decisiveness of the initial phase of a world conflict, and until the late 1950s on the value of a preemptive attack.[41] This concern may be as much a legacy of the traumatic experience of Germany's surprise attack in June 1941 as it is a recognition of the character of nuclear warfare.[42] But so long as modern warfare fails to offer an effective defense against strategic weapons, the preemptive strike will be a natural military solution to the problem of neutralizing the enemy's strategic forces.

The threat of nuclear escalation in a major NATO-Warsaw Pact conflict could convince the Soviet Union that restraining the use of its nuclear force would not be worth the risk of being exposed to a first strike by the enemy. Such a reaction is certainly possible, given the U.S. commitment to use nuclear weapons first if necessary to defend Europe against a major attack by the Warsaw Pact countries.[43]

Because a preemptive strike would depend on timely internal decisions and favorable external conditions (that is, the enemy has neither

41. Sokolovskiy, *Soviet Military Strategy*, pp. 202–05; Col. D. Samorukov and Col. L. Semeyko, "The Increase of Efforts in Nuclear Warfare Operations," *Military Thought*, October 1968, p. 44.

42. Sokolovskiy, *Soviet Military Strategy*, pp. 226–68; Lambeth, *How To Think About Soviet Military Doctrine*, p. 10. Also note the continuing reflection of this Soviet concern in the reported pledge of General Secretary Leonid I. Brezhnev that Soviet leaders are " 'taking into consideration the lessons of the past and are doing everything so that nobody catches us by surprise.' " Quoted in Maj. Gen. N. Vasendin and Col. N. Kuznetsov, "Modern Warfare and Surprise Attack," *Military Thought*, June 1968, p. 48.

43. James R. Schlesinger, *The Theater Nuclear Force Posture in Europe: A Report to the United States Congress in Compliance with Public Law 93-365* (Department of Defense, 1975), p. 15; Herbert Y. Schandler, *U.S. Policy on the Use of Nuclear Weapons, 1945–1975*, UC 650A (Library of Congress, Congressional Research Service, 1975), pp. 30–35.

launched a first strike nor is prepared to launch under attack),[44] it is unlikely that Soviet military leaders count on preemption in their strategic planning, nor could they rely on it to solve all their strategic problems since large numbers of U.S. forces on alert could survive even a successful preemptive attack. More likely, the USSR sees preemption as an option of last resort, to be employed when the enemy's nuclear attack appears imminent.

Other operational possibilities available to the Soviet Union include the choice of launching under attack or of riding out an attack and then responding with a second-strike attack. Soviet operational philosophy appears more disposed toward preemption and launch under attack than to riding out an attack. In the late 1960s Soviet military writings occasionally showed an interest in the launch-under-attack option and the USSR began deploying many of the weapon systems that were necessary for such a capability. Yet Soviet operational approach has not neglected the importance of maintaining strategic forces that can ride out an enemy first strike. The wide range of measures aimed at increasing the survivability of Soviet strategic forces, such as very hard silos for its intercontinental ballistic missiles (ICBMs), probably reflects a Soviet desire to hedge against the possibility that the USSR may be the victim of a first strike in wartime.

Another important aspect of the Soviet operational philosophy is the alert level of Soviet strategic forces. Until recently, the USSR was known to keep only a small portion of its land-based missiles on full alert,[45] and its bomber forces apparently have never been maintained in a peacetime ground-alert posture.[46] Only a small fraction of the strategic

---

44. Raymond L. Garthoff discusses the Soviet concept of preemption in the 1950s in *The Soviet Image of Future War* (Washington: Public Affairs Press, 1959), pp. 64–76, and the launch-under-attack (or launch-on-warning) concept in "Deterrence, Parity and Strategic Arms Limitation in Soviet Policy," in D. Leebaert, ed., *Soviet Military Thinking* (Allen and Unwin, 1981), pp. 101–03; see also Krylov, "Nuclear-Missile Shield," p. 18; Vasendin and Kuznetsov, "Modern Warfare and Surprise Attack," pp. 46–47.

45. *Allocation of Resources in the Soviet Union and China—1978*, Hearings before the Subcommittee on Priorities and Economy in Government of the Joint Economic Committee, 95 Cong. 2 sess. (GPO, 1978), pt. 4, pp. 67–68, 117–18; Joseph J. Kruzel, "Military Alerts and Diplomatic Signals," Ellen P. Stern, ed., *The Limits of Intervention* (Sage Publications, 1977), pp. 83, 87–89; also see *Department of Defense Annual Report Fiscal Year 1980*, pp. 72–73.

46. *Department of Defense Appropriations for 1980*, Hearings before a Subcommittee of the House Appropriations Committee, 96 Cong. 1 sess. (GPO, 1979), pt. 3, pp. 476–77; Lambeth, *How To Think About Soviet Military Doctrine*, p. 17.

missile submarine force is deployed at sea.[47] While technical constraints partially explain the low levels of alert in the past, the continuing practice appears to be related to broader aspects of the Soviet operational philosophy.

Most important is the priority placed by Soviet leaders on the strict command and control of nuclear forces, evident in constrained alert rates, positive command arrangements, and associated operational practices.[48] This attitude probably accounts for the general Soviet disinclination to use changes in the alert status of its nuclear force as a means of sending political signals during crises.[49] The Soviet tradition of a highly centralized system of political and military control seems to reinforce the natural disinclination of any political leadership to devolve its authority over critical matters. Soviet military writings indicate that nuclear weapons have substantially increased the role of the top leadership in directing wartime operations.

Strict control of nuclear forces limits to some degree the USSR's ability to take decisive counteraction during the initial phase of a major conflict. The tension between these conflicting requirements is resolved (at least in theory) by the Soviet expectation that there would be strategic warning that war was imminent.[50] The USSR would expect to have enough time to bring its military forces to higher alert levels and to deploy its submarine force more advantageously. Soviet apprehensions concerning a surprise attack by the United States have probably diminished since the 1950s, while the survivability of Soviet strategic forces has improved, enabling the USSR to more confidently rely on receiving adequate strategic warning. The low alert rates of the Soviet nuclear forces are consistent with the Soviet Union's preference for conserving its military assets by limiting their peacetime operations and holding down the potentially high expense of maintaining a large military force, an effort that is reflected in the USSR's operation of its conventional forces as well.[51]

47. *United States Military Posture for FY 1979* (Office of the Joint Chiefs of Staff, 1978), pp. 27–28; *Department of Defense Appropriations for 1980*, Hearings, pt. 3, pp. 476–77.

48. Kruzel, "Military Alerts," pp. 87–89; Stephen S. Kaplan, ed., *Diplomacy of Power: Soviet Armed Forces as a Political Instrument* (Brookings Institution, 1981), pp. 54–55.

49. Kaplan, *Diplomacy of Power*, pp. 54–55.

50. Kruzel, "Military Alerts," pp. 88–89; *Allocation of Resources*, Hearings, pt. 4, pp. 67–68, 117–18.

51. *Allocation of Resources*, Hearings, pt. 4, pp. 67–68.

CHAPTER THREE

SOVIET STRATEGIC FORCE DEVELOPMENT

LONG-TERM missile programs have been the main factor in development of the Soviet strategic force posture since the end of World War II. New weapons and modifications of old ones have continually been introduced, as military requirements have changed. But at a few critical periods of military or political change, decisive turns in the evolution of the Soviet strategic forces can be discerned. During the 1950s regional strategic requirements were clearly dominant in decisions regarding the development of Soviet weapons. But in the early 1960s the intercontinental requirements of Soviet strategic forces increased so dramatically that they came to match regional requirements in importance and urgency. In its efforts to meet the needs of both forces defined during the 1960s, the Soviet Union alternately deployed new generations of intercontinental and regional nuclear missiles, and it sought to acquire variable-range missiles that could satisfy the requirements of both forces.

The military requirements that prompted development of the generation of Soviet intercontinental missile forces being deployed in the early 1980s were set initially during the early 1960s; in the intervening years Soviet intercontinental requirements appear to have changed only incrementally. Similarly, the development of Soviet regional forces being deployed in the early 1980s can be traced—though less clearly—to requirements set roughly fifteen to twenty-five years earlier. Perhaps the most visible of the critical periods was the early 1960s, when both the political and the military situation shifted suddenly. The redirections and ''quick fixes'' in Soviet strategic planning initiated then determined how Soviet strategic forces would develop for the next two decades.

The Initial Postwar Period

The experience of World War II reaffirmed the central role of Soviet Ground Forces as the ultimate guarantor of the survival of the Soviet state. Conventional forces continued to form the basis of Soviet strategic power through the early postwar years. The hegemony that these forces gave the Soviet Union over Eastern Europe served as a political and a military buffer against Western influence and incursion.

The Soviet Army's success in World War II reinforced the USSR's commitment to an all-arms approach centered on the Ground Forces. Although the Ground Forces were substantially demobilized in the late 1940s, many divisions remained active and were given new armor and mechanized equipment. This deterrent force appears to have provided an initial means for offsetting the American monopoly on nuclear weapons. Ironically, the perception at that time of Western Europe as hostage to a conventional Soviet invasion was based largely on inflated Western assessments of Soviet strength.

While the Ground Forces were suitable for supporting the USSR's traditional continental interests, American power posed a new challenge to Soviet security. The United States, as it had demonstrated during the war, was able to transport and sustain its conventional forces over great distances. This strength, underpinned by the American mobilization base, made the United States an important threat in Soviet military plans. Beyond that, improvements were being made in U.S. long-range bombers and nuclear weapons technology.

Despite Stalin's public expressions implying a lack of appreciation for the importance of modern weapons, the USSR was vigorously pursuing a variety of short- and long-term programs to improve its military position. By 1949 the Soviet Union had tested its first atomic device, and by 1953 a thermonuclear device had been detonated.[1] Experimental testing of short-range land- and sea-launched missiles was undertaken at the end of the war, and by 1950 design plans for developing medium- and intercontinental-range ballistic missiles (MRBMs and ICBMs) had been established.

In 1948, air defense forces were withdrawn from the command of the Soviet Army and reorganized into an independent service, the National Air Defense Forces. Their increasing autonomy signaled the USSR's first recognition that its security in the postwar world could no longer be based solely on the Ground Forces. At the start of the postwar period, the Soviet air defense forces comprised about 1,000 World War II vintage fighters. By 1953 these forces were equipped with about 2,000 modern

1. Maj. Gen. S. N. Kozlov, *The Officer's Handbook (A Soviet View)* (U.S. Government Printing Office, 1977), p. 142.

jet aircraft, large numbers of antiaircraft artillery, and electronic early-warning systems for the long-range detection of enemy bombers.[2] The new air defenses provided the capability to counter high-altitude, clear-weather, daytime bombing raids over the USSR, although by this time the West was already planning to acquire strategic bombers capable of strikes in adverse weather and at night.

To counter the possibility of amphibious assaults by Western naval powers, the USSR undertook a construction program after World War II to create a naval force capable of defeating a Western seaborne invasion. The program envisaged deployment of large numbers of surface ships, diesel submarines, and torpedo bombers for intercepting and destroying Western amphibious forces at sea.[3] Though the Soviet perception of the naval threat later changed and the program was modified, countering a direct naval threat to the Soviet homeland remained an important feature of Soviet strategic planning.

Also during the later 1940s, the USSR began deployment of its first strategic offensive system, the TU-4 Bull bomber. Although the TU-4 was copied from the American B-29 bomber, its production was nonetheless a major technical feat. The development of this bomber by the Tupolev design bureau[4] was the Soviet Union's first postwar effort to project its strategic power beyond the capability of its Ground Forces. By the time production ended in 1953, about 1,500 of these propeller-driven, medium bombers were being operated under the command of Long Range Aviation (LRA) and the Naval Air Force.[5] The upgraded priority accorded to long-range bombardment was dictated by the new Soviet requirement for regional-range strike systems that could support the USSR's growing political and military interests, protect the homeland, and support the operations of the Ground Forces in wartime. The TU-4 bombers could be used to counter new regional threats from Western conventional forces or from forward-deployed, nuclear-armed aircraft of the United States. The Soviet bombers, armed only with nonnuclear bombs, also could have been used to destroy or degrade the

2. Thomas A. Wolfe, *Soviet Power and Europe, 1945–1970* (Johns Hopkins Press, 1970), pp. 47–49; Marshal P. Batitskiy, "The National Air Defense (PVO Strany) Troops," in U.S. Foreign Broadcast Information Service, *Selected Translations: Voyennaya mysl' (Military Thought)*, November 1973, pp. 35–36 (hereafter, *Military Thought*).

3. Siegfried Breyer and Norman Polmar, *Guide to the Soviet Navy*, 2d ed. (Naval Institute Press, 1977), pp. 29–34.

4. William Green and Gordon Swanborough, *The Observer's Soviet Aircraft Directory* (London: Frederick Warne, 1975), p. 29.

5. Robert P. Berman, *Soviet Air Power in Transition* (Brookings Institution, 1978), p. 25.

relatively small number of Western air and naval bases, vital communication and transportation centers, and military storage sites. At the time, less than one hundred critical targets probably existed within Central Europe and Great Britain.

The Shift to a Modern Strategic Posture

After Stalin's death in 1953, Soviet political and military leaders began to grapple in earnest with the impact of nuclear and long-range weapons on military strategy and organization. By 1954, nuclear weapons started to be integrated into the Soviet armed forces and taken into account in military training.[6] The first Soviet nuclear strike forces became operational in this period, while longer-range missile programs continued in development.

The Transition to Nuclear Weapons

Among the first Soviet nuclear weapon systems was a series of tactical missiles—the SS-1 and SS-2—developed for the Ground Forces in the early 1950s. By 1955 an operational-tactical missile, the SS-3 Shyster, was assigned to support Ground Force operations. The missiles' limited range and their command under the Ground Forces suggest these nuclear missiles were seen as modern equivalents of traditional Soviet artillery in providing fire support for the Ground Forces.[7] In wartime such missiles probably would have been used to provide long-range barrages of nuclear or chemical explosives to pave the way for the Ground Forces' assaults. The importance of operational-tactical missiles grew through the 1950s as NATO's deployments of nuclear-capable artillery and tactical nuclear missiles expanded.

At about the time that the Soviet Union began assimilating nuclear systems in its force structure, important changes took place in the West's strategic forces that dramatically altered the USSR's regional require-

6. Lt. Gen. M. Gareyev, "Ever Guarding the Achievements of October," in U.S. Air Force, Directorate of Soviet Affairs, Air Force Intelligence Service, *Soviet Press Selected Translations,* no. 78-4 (April 1978), pp. 107–08.

7. Graham T. Allison, *Essence of Decision: Explaining the Cuban Missile Crisis* (Little, Brown, 1971), p. 114; Joseph D. Douglass, Jr., *The Soviet Theater Nuclear Offensive,* Studies in Communist Affairs, vol. 1, prepared for the Office of Director of Defense Research and Engineering and the Defense Nuclear Agency (GPO, 1976).

Table 3-1. Soviet Nuclear Forces, by Number of Delivery Systems and Warheads, 1955–80

Nuclear force and instrument	Number					
	1955	1960	1965	1970	1975	1980
	Delivery systems					
Regional forces	1,320	1,580	1,718	2,040	2,219	2,132
Bombers	1,296	1,296	880	724	660	655
Battlefield nuclear missiles[a]	24	48	28	54	72	72
Medium- and intermediate-range missiles	0	200	705	607	598	580
Variable-range missiles[b]	. . .	. . .	. . .	290	320	380
Sea-based missiles	0	36	105	365	569	445
Intercontinental forces	0	149	434	1,456	1,652	1,696
Land-based missiles	0	4	224	1,220	1,267	1,018
Sea-based missiles	0	0	15	41	196	522
Heavy bombers	0	145	195	195	189	156
All delivery systems	1,320	1,729	2,097	3,496	3,871	3,828
	Warheads					
Regional range	324	1,034	2,085	2,281	2,467	3,497
Intercontinental range	0	294	381	1,403	1,875	6,156
All warheads	324	1,328	2,466	3,684	4,342	9,653

Sources: International Institute for Strategic Studies, *The Military Balance* (London: IISS), selected years; *United States Military Posture for 1982* (U.S. Office of the Joint Chiefs of Staff, 1981), pp. 99, 100; Edward L. Warner III, *The Military in Contemporary Soviet Politics: An Institutional Analysis* (Praeger, 1977), pp. 187–200; "Statement of Secretary of Defense Robert S. McNamara before a Joint Session of the Senate Armed Services Committee and the Senate Subcommittee on Department of Defense Appropriations on the Fiscal Year 1966–70 Defense Program and the 1966 Defense Budget," declassified (U.S. Department of Defense, 1965), and statements for the budgets of 1967 and 1970; Robert P. Berman, *Soviet Air Power in Transition* (Brookings Institution, 1978), p. 25; *Department of Defense Annual Report Fiscal Year 1982*, p. 66.

a. Includes the SS-3 and SS-12 operational missiles.

b. Initially, nuclear weapon production lagged substantially behind the number of potential delivery systems. Additionally, the early TU-4 Bull bomber probably was only assigned to deliver nonnuclear weapons.

ments (see tables 3-1 and 3-2). As part of their determination to upgrade their defense position following the outbreak of the Korean War, the Western powers strengthened NATO's defense capability and began the rearming of West Germany, the traditional adversary of the USSR. After its failure to halt the trend toward Germany's rearmament and eventual entry into NATO, the USSR announced the formation of the Warsaw Pact.[8]

During this same period, the Eisenhower administration began to emphasize American willingness to rely on the U.S. nuclear advantage to deter communist threats around the world. The shift in the American military posture was manifested in the worldwide buildup of nonnuclear forces and tactical nuclear weapons and the spread of U.S. political and military commitments. Its most notable feature, however, was the deployment of regional-range nuclear systems in areas adjacent to the Soviet Union. From a few strategic bombers stationed in Europe or the

8. Wolfe, *Soviet Power and Europe*, p. 76.

Table 3-2. Strength of Western and Chinese Nuclear Forces, by Number of Delivery Systems and Warheads, 1950–80

Nuclear force and instrument	1950	1955	1960	1965	1970	1975	1980
	Number						
	Delivery systems						
Intercontinental forces (U.S. only)	520	1,309	1,809	2,157	2,171	2,159	2,016
Bombers[a]	520	1,309	1,735	807	501	489	428
Land-based missiles	0	0	42[b]	854	1,054	1,054	1,052
Sea-based missiles	0	0	32	496	616	616	536
Regional forces	116	441	772	782	668	802	853
United States							
Theater nuclear missiles[c]	0	114	128	252	108	108	108
QRA aircraft[d]	0	12	72	72	72	68	66
Forward-based bombers	45	135	0	0	0	0	0
Carrier-based aircraft	0	0	58	120	120	96	96
Sea-based missiles	0	0	0	40	40	40	40
European allies of the United States							
Theater nuclear missiles[c]	0	0	72	72	72	72	72
QRA aircraft[d]	0	56	96	110	92	48	34
Carrier-based aircraft	0	0	0	12	12	14	0
Medium- and intermediate-range missiles	0	0	105	0	0	18	18
Bombers	70	122	180	104	86	86	81
Sea-based missiles	0	0	0	0	48	112	128
China							
Bombers	0	0	0	12	18	60	90
Medium-range missiles	0	0	0	0	0	80	122
All delivery systems	636	1,750	2,581	2,939	2,939	2,961	2,869
	Warheads[e]						
Intercontinental range	n.a.	2,310	4,362	4,002	3,689	7,725	8,018
Regional range	n.a.	698	772	862	748	1,290	1,343
All warheads	n.a.	3,008	5,134	4,864	4,437	9,015	9,361

Sources: Stockholm International Peace Research Institute, *Tactical Nuclear Weapons: European Perspectives* (London: Taylor and Francis, 1978), pp. 16, 109–16, 124–34, 130–36; Bill Gunston, *The Illustrated Encyclopaedia of the World's Rockets & Missiles* (Crescent Books, 1979), pp. 34–41; George H. Quester, *Nuclear Diplomacy: The First Twenty-five Years* (Dunellen, 1970), p. 111; *Department of Defense Semi Annual Report and the Semiannual Reports of the Secretary of the Army, Secretary of the Navy, Secretary of the Air Force, January 1 to June 30, 1956* and the reports for 1957–61; *Aviation Week and Space Technology*, February 25, 1963, p. 105; Strategic Air Command, Office of the Historian, *Development of Strategic Air Command 1946–1976* (U.S. Air Force, 1976), pp. 20, 47, 81, 119, 148, 177; *United States Military Posture for FY 1979* (U.S. Office of the Joint Chiefs of Staff, 1978), p. 32; IISS, *The Military Balance 1965–1966, 1970–1971, 1975–1976, 1980–1981*.

n.a. Not available.

a. Does not include aircraft in storage. By the early 1960s many bombers were equipped to launch nuclear air-to-surface missiles (ASMs) such as the Hound Dog and, later, short-range attack missiles. In 1960, 54 ASMs were operational; in 1965, 542; in 1970, 345; in 1975, 1,759; and in 1980, 1,020. The flexibility of bomber operations increased as airborne tankers entered the air force. In 1950, 126 tankers were operational; in 1955, 761; in 1960, 1,094; in 1965 and 1970, 615; in 1975, 599; and in 1980, 515.

b. Includes 30 U.S. Air Force Snark intercontinental-range cruise missiles.

c. Includes the early Mace and Matador cruise missiles and the Redstone and Pershing ballistic missiles.

d. Quick-reaction alert aircraft.

e. Before the development of thermonuclear weapons, the number of nuclear weapons available for delivery was substantially less than the number of delivery systems.

Far East in 1952, the number of U.S. and NATO forward-based systems capable of nuclear strikes against the Soviet homeland had increased by 1955 to more than 500. These included B-47 medium-range bombers at forward bases, fighter-bombers on land and aboard aircraft carriers, and surface-to-surface cruise missiles.

The changes in the Western military threat coincided roughly with a serious Soviet effort to integrate strategic defense forces into the Soviet strategic posture. The constantly improving Western capability to deliver nuclear strikes led the USSR to increase the importance of its National Air Defense Forces. One indication of the Air Defense Forces' growing significance to the Soviet strategic posture was the upgrading of its commander in chief to deputy minister of defense in May 1954.[9] This first clear step away from the traditional military posture portended the later Soviet decision to supplant the Ground Forces with a force armed with modern weapons as the main means of providing Soviet military security.

During the mid to late 1950s the USSR upgraded its ground-based warning-and-control system, deployed surface-to-air missiles for the first time, and introduced high-speed interceptor aircraft capable of all-weather operations. Concentric circles of SA-1 missile launchers were deployed around Moscow, while SA-2 missiles provided a high-altitude defense of other vital targets.[10] Two special air defense districts were created to cover the Moscow and Baku areas, encompassing the political and economic heartland of the Soviet Union. And efforts began to integrate the Warsaw Pact countries into the Soviet Union's strategic air defense system.[11]

Stalin's plans to build a large navy of surface ships were abandoned as it became apparent that the primary naval threat to the USSR was not an amphibious invasion but nuclear-armed aircraft launched from aircraft carriers. Soviet leaders turned to missile-carrying submarines and land-based aviation as a more effective and less expensive solution to Soviet naval problems. Furthermore, submarines capable of firing nuclear torpedos at enemy harbors were among the first Soviet nuclear delivery systems.[12]

Since the primary means for delivering nuclear weapons over long distances was the manned bomber, Long Range Aviation achieved an

9. Col. Gen. V. D. Sozinov, "National Air Defense Forces," *Great Soviet Military Encyclopedia*, 3d ed., reprinted in U.S. Air Force, Intelligence, Directorate of Threat Applications, *Soviet Press Selected Translations*, November 1975, pp. 2–3.

10. William F. Scott, "Troops of National Air Defense," *Air Force Magazine*, March 1978, pp. 57–58.

11. Wolfe, *Soviet Power and Europe*, pp. 43, 49, 148.

12. Raymond L. Garthoff, *Soviet Strategy in the Nuclear Age* (Praeger, 1958), pp. 203–04. This point is developed in detail in Michael MccGwire, "The Rationale for the Development of Soviet Seapower," *Naval Review 1980*, May 1980, p. 158.

unprecedented importance in Soviet defense planning by the mid-1950s. The bomber's ability to deliver nuclear attacks against enemy targets, at regional as well as intercontinental ranges, gave the USSR certain political and military benefits it had lacked. In particular, it probably enhanced the Soviet political position vis-à-vis the United States and its allies in the continuing tension over Berlin.

With the deployment of jet-engined TU-16 Badger medium bombers in 1954[13] the USSR had its first nuclear-strike force capable of reaching targets throughout Europe and in most of the Far East. This bomber force also offered a means for countering the growing Western nuclear threat along the USSR's periphery. It could attack forward-deployed bombers, aircraft carriers, and tactical nuclear weapons and support systems at fixed sites. But the bombers were vulnerable to the expanding Western air defense systems and ineffective against mobile targets.

By the mid-1950s the Soviet Union's first intercontinental bombers, the MYA-4 Bison and TU-20 Bear, became operational.[14] Only about two hundred of these heavy bombers were eventually deployed, significantly fewer than the large Soviet medium bomber force of TU-16 Badgers and, later, TU-22 Blinders. Their targets were undoubtedly U.S. military bases, nuclear production facilities, and strategic bomber bases (aerial refueling and the longer-range B-52 bomber made the bomber bases particularly valuable targets). The eight to ten hours necessary to reach their targets curtailed the effectiveness of Soviet bombers. Nonetheless, they may have been valued for their political effect by starting to offset the intercontinental threat posed by the United States to the Soviet homeland and its regional security objectives. The strategic bombers were also probably seen as a useful hedge against failure or delay in the development of strategic missiles.

Establishing the Strategic Rocket Forces

By the late 1950s Soviet military doctrine had begun to shift in recognition that the advent of long-range, nuclear-armed missiles had created a "revolution in military affairs."[15] The USSR conducted the

---

13. Berman, *Soviet Air Power*, p. 25.
14. Ibid.
15. Col. Gen. M. Povaliy, "Development of Soviet Military Strategy," *Military Thought*, February 1967, p. 69; Harriet Fast Scott and William F. Scott, *The Armed Forces of the USSR* (Westview, 1979), pp. 40–42.

world's first full-range test of an intercontinental ballistic missile—the SS-6—in August 1957, followed two months later by the dramatic launch of the *Sputnik* satellite into orbit using a similar SS-6 booster.[16] About the same time, the USSR's first regional-range strategic missile, the SS-4, entered into flight testing. As these strategic missiles neared deployment in 1958–59, difficult questions undoubtedly arose concerning their wartime role and who would command them. These momentous events foreshadowed important changes in the Soviet Union's military force structure and international political position. With strategic missiles, the USSR acquired a technology that could support its regional political and military objectives and directly offset American intercontinental strategic might. Nikita Khrushchev seized on these same developments to help transform the Soviet defense posture into one more consistent with his own defense views and national priorities.

Organizationally, the major result of the shift in doctrine was the establishment in December 1959 of the Strategic Rocket Forces, with responsibility for both the regional and intercontinental missile forces. The SRF was declared in Soviet writings to be the preeminent service in wartime, displacing the Ground Forces. Similarly, Soviet industrial resources shifted from strategic bomber to missile production. Development of the heavy bomber ended with the MYA-50 Bounder, which was first flown in 1957[17] and never produced; the Bounder may have been developed only as a hedge against the failure of the ICBM program.

The decisions required for this basic alteration in strategic doctrine were probably taken some time around the Twenty-first Party Congress in January 1959. Khrushchev's internal political position was very strong during this period when secret General Staff seminars were concluding that nuclear missiles compelled basic revision in Soviet defense concepts.[18] The party leadership was attributed an important role in modernizing the Soviet strategic posture, and Khrushchev's belief that nuclear missiles reduced the need for large numbers of conventional forces, and even such weapons as strategic bombers,[19] was instrumental in orienting the Soviet military posture increasingly toward nuclear

16. William H. Schauer, *The Politics of Space: A Comparison of the Soviet and American Space Programs* (Holmes and Meiers, 1976), p. 14.

17. Green and Swanborough, *Observer's Soviet Aircraft Directory*, p. 34.

18. Carl A. Linden, *Khrushchev and the Soviet Leadership, 1957–1964* (Johns Hopkins Press, 1966), pp. 72–81.

19. Edward L. Warner III, *The Military in Contemporary Soviet Politics: An Institutional Analysis* (Praeger, 1977), pp. 138–45.

missiles. Many in the military resisted these trends, stressing that victory in war required a more balanced, all-arms capability.[20]

Although the change in the Soviet strategic posture was quite apparent, the motivations and methods involved were not. Those who sought both an independent and a central role for the strategic missile forces undoubtedly held complex and even conflicting aims. The serious strategic challenge posed by Western regional nuclear forces and the prospect of growing U.S. intercontinental forces could probably best be countered by nuclear missiles. The ballistic missile's ability to reach enemy targets over almost any distance in a relatively short time made it far more appealing than strategic bombers, with their lengthy flight times and vulnerability to air defenses.[21] And the missile was more compatible with Soviet military tradition and institutional interests. Many Soviet military leaders may have viewed missiles as a modern means of performing the artillery's traditional counter-battery role through decisive strikes against the enemy's main forces.[22] Land-based missiles probably also appealed to both political and military leaders because of their more economical operating requirements and the possibility they afforded of tight command and control.

The Soviet leadership was disposed to play down the importance of the strategic bomber in part as a way of undercutting the significance of the substantial American advantage in intercontinental bomber forces. And Khrushchev, to enhance the Soviet strategic deterrent and to extract concessions in political negotiations over critical issues such as Berlin, was able to sustain the image of a growing Soviet lead in missile technology through frequent misleading claims on Soviet missile strength.[23] The continuing credibility for Soviet claims of technological superiority, however, rested on a series of spectacular achievements in the Soviet space program, not on the less visible ICBM program.[24] As a result of

20. Ibid.

21. Marshal of the Soviet Union V. D. Sokolovskiy, *Soviet Military Strategy,* 3d ed., ed. Harriet Fast Scott (Crane, Russak, 1975), pp. 252–53.

22. Ibid., pp. 241–42; Warner, *Military in Contemporary Soviet Politics,* pp. 136–37, 189–90. Also see John Erickson, "The Soviet Military System: Doctrine, Technology, and 'Style,' " in John Erickson and E. J. Feuchtwanger, eds., *Soviet Military Power and Performance* (Archon Books, 1979), pp. 25–28.

23. Wolfe, *Soviet Power and Europe,* pp. 84–85; Arnold L. Horelick and Myron Rush, *Strategic Power and Soviet Foreign Policy* (University of Chicago Press, 1965), pp. 35–38.

24. James E. Oberg, *Red Star in Orbit* (Random House, 1981), pp. 35–38.

escalating Soviet claims, a gap increasingly developed between the perceived image and the actuality of Soviet intercontinental strength.

The motivations for the changes probably went beyond strategic considerations. Khrushchev and his supporters seemed convinced that reductions in the Soviet conventional forces were necessary in order to fulfill their promises for domestic economic progress.[25] They probably believed that the USSR could not afford to undertake an expensive modernization program based on nuclear weapons and long-range missiles while also maintaining large conventional forces. And Khrushchev may have wished to dilute the substantial political power of the Soviet Army by overshadowing it with the new missile command created under his personal patronage.

Yet even Khrushchev could not simply order the Strategic Rocket Forces into existence. Assigning control of the strategic missile program to Long Range Aviation during testing and the initial year of deployment may have offered an interim solution to the problem.[26] Clearly, however, the creation of the SRF depended on elements within the defense establishment that had an interest in the formation of an independent rocket command or at least agreed with the need for it. Among the elements that provided the means for establishing the SRF, the political leadership appears to have drawn heavily on the artillery branch for the expertise to man the new service.[27] Support may have come also from groups involved in the development of long-range missiles who were seeking to lessen the domination of the Ground Forces.

For several years after the Strategic Rocket Forces were established, they were armed predominantly with regional-range strategic missiles. In part, this resulted from the technical difficulties associated with the early Soviet ICBM program. But it also reflected the priority the USSR continued to accord to political and military objectives in the regional

25. Increasing the manpower available for the domestic economy was quite consistent with Khrushchev's overall domestic priorities. There are no signs of a direct conflict between domestic and defense priorities, however. See Karl F. Spielmann, *Analyzing Soviet Strategic Arms Decisions* (Westview, 1978), pp. 131–34; Wolfe, *Soviet Power and Europe*, pp. 160–64.

26. William T. Lee, "Soviet Targeting Strategy and SALT," *Air Force Magazine*, September 1978, p. 121.

27. Warner, *Military in Contemporary Soviet Politics*, pp. 27, 189–90. The artillery branch's link with Soviet missile development is often noted in the annual commemoration of Missile Forces and Artillery Day on November 19. U.S. Foreign Broadcast Information Service, *Daily Report: Soviet Union*, November 26, 1975, p. V-7, notes that the first SRF commander, M. I. Nedelin, was also a chief marshal of artillery.

theaters surrounding it. The strategic missiles deployed during the late 1950s and the early 1960s were effective means of meeting Soviet regional military requirements that had evolved through the 1950s. The SS-4, a medium-range ballistic missile with about twice the range of the Ground Forces' SS-3 missile, was first deployed in late 1958. By the mid-1960s nearly 600 SS-4 launchers were deployed. The SS-4s were eventually supplemented by about 100 SS-5 intermediate-range ballistic missile (IRBM) launchers, which first became operational in 1961. Together, these missiles could attack a wide range of military and industrial targets throughout Europe and over much of the Far East. Priority targets probably included Western air bases, Thor and Jupiter missile sites, and nuclear storage sites. At the same time, the Soviets probably underestimated the pace of the U.S. ICBM program which got off to a slow start. Using concurrent development programs, the United States rapidly advanced to the deployment of advanced ICBMs, including the solid-fuel Minuteman missile.

By comparison with U.S. missiles, the first generation of Soviet intercontinental missiles did not provide an adequate military capability for the USSR. Despite its worldwide notoriety, the SS-6 Sapwood ICBM was never deployed in more than token numbers.[28] As a military system, it suffered from a series of shortcomings.[29] But as the main booster for the early Soviet space program, it performed quite well. Hundreds of the SS-6 or its derivatives were produced for the space program,[30] in part because the design bureau headed by S. P. Korolev, a pioneer of modern Soviet rocketry, was most closely associated with that program.[31] The space achievements through the early 1960s were clearly valuable to Khrushchev in his political campaign against the West.

By the late 1950s a number of new strategic missiles were in process of development—the SS-7, SS-8, and SS-9, all large ICBMs suitable for covering area targets such as bomber bases and early missile sites in the U.S. mainland. Design plans for other missiles were probably being set.

---

28. Only four were deployed, although they probably remained in service into the 1970s. *Fiscal Year 1976 and July–September 1976 Transition Period Authorization for Military Procurement, Research and Development, and Active Duty, Selected Reserve, and Civilian Personnel Strengths,* Hearings before the Senate Armed Services Committee, 94 Cong. 1 sess. (GPO, 1975), pt. 4, p. 1745.

29. The missile's nonstorable, liquid propellant hampered its launching, and its radio guidance could be disrupted by electronic interference. Schauer, *Politics of Space,* p. 13.

30. Ibid., p. 22; Spielmann, *Analyzing Soviet Strategic Arms Decisions,* p. 117.

31. Spielmann, *Analyzing Soviet Strategic Arms Decisions,* p. 117.

These included the smaller SS-11, under design by the Chelomei bureau and probably intended for use against maritime targets;[32] the USSR's first solid fuel ICBM, the SS-13; and the Yankee-class submarine and its ballistic missiles. The great achievement in Soviet strategic affairs, however, was the transition from a military posture centered around conventional military forces to one based on nuclear forces. A major outcome of this long and difficult process was the formation of the Strategic Rocket Forces. The SRF represented a major step toward providing the basis for a modern strategic posture. Combined with the strategic bomber force, the SRF's regional-range missiles could defend the Soviet homeland and provide effective support for Soviet interests in adjoining regions that were of primary political and military concern to its leaders. At the time, the bulk of the nuclear forces facing the USSR were either based in these areas or would be engaged there in wartime. Intercontinental forces retained only a supplementary strategic role through the 1950s, and it was not until the early 1960s that a dramatic combination of political and military events would alter this situation.

Changing Requirements and Expedient Solutions

Development of the Soviet intercontinental missile force began in earnest in the 1960s. Changes in the military requirements of Soviet intercontinental and regional forces as well as technical shortfalls in key missile programs compelled the USSR to redirect many of its programs and devise expedient measures. Important among these was the reorientation of the SS-11 ballistic missile from an antinaval role to that of a system flexible enough to perform both regional and intercontinental strategic missions.

The rapid expansion and alterations in the United States' plans for its intercontinental strategic forces that occurred during 1961 radically affected the U.S.-Soviet military balance. Having entered office claiming that a missile gap existed favoring the USSR and that a greater range of military options was needed, the Kennedy administration promptly accelerated and redirected several major defense programs in its first year.[33] Authorizations for the Polaris program leapt from nineteen to

32. "Russian Missile Bureaus," *Aerospace Daily*, January 22, 1979, p. 100; Walter Pincus, *Washington Post*, June 26, 1980.

33. Desmond Ball, *Politics and Force Levels: The Strategic Missile Program of the Kennedy Administration* (University of California Press, 1980), pp. 107–26.

forty-one submarines, with delivery schedules significantly advanced; the number of Minuteman ICBMs planned for deployment in hardened silos nearly tripled and plans for a rail-mobile system were canceled; a new push for civil defense began; and emphasis on strategic bombers disappeared with the cancellation of the B-70 high-altitude-bomber program. In less than a year's time, it became evident for the USSR that it was being rapidly outpaced—both qualitatively and quantitatively— by the United States in terms of intercontinental strike forces.

The USSR suddenly faced a serious threat from American forces that could not be directly countered by either its growing regional missile force or its strategic defensive forces. The initial burden of responding to the American ICBM force would fall on the second-generation Soviet ICBMs, the SS-7 Saddler and SS-8 Sasin, which would not be available for deployment until 1962–63. Their relatively poor accuracy and high vulnerability to counterattack made them an inadequate counter, how- ever, to the new Minuteman generation of missiles.[34] Furthermore, the low production rate of these large Soviet ICBMs would permit the United States to open up an expanding lead in number of missiles deployed. Beyond that, Soviet antisubmarine and ballistic-missile defenses were of limited utility. By 1961 the Soviet political and military leadership undoubtedly realized that its planned strategic posture was inadequate to meet the evolving American strategic threat.

The seriousness of the changing military balance was driven home by an even more sudden change in the Soviet Union's political position in dealing with the West. The widespread belief in a missile gap favorable to the USSR rapidly disappeared when the United States made public— most pointedly in the October 1961 speech by the deputy secretary of defense[35]—its new assessment of the U.S.-Soviet strategic balance, presumably based on information from its photoreconnaissance satel- lites. Soviet leaders had to face the disturbing possibility that the United States realized not only that it had never been inferior in intercontinental striking power but that it now held a significant strategic advantage. The sudden coincidence of these political and military events may well have convinced Soviet leaders that dramatic changes in their strategic arms

---

34. Lawrence Freedman, *US Intelligence and the Soviet Strategic Threat* (Westview, 1977), p. 99; "Statement of Secretary of Defense Robert S. McNamara before a Joint Session of the Senate Armed Services Committee and the Senate Subcommittee on Department of Defense Appropriations on the Fiscal Year 1965–69 Defense Program and 1965 Defense Budget," declassified material (Department of Defense, February 3, 1964), pp. 49–50.

35. Ball, *Politics and Force Levels*, pp. 96–97.

plans were necessary if the USSR was to acquire an adequate intercontinental capability for directly offsetting U.S. intercontinental might.

The change in attitude did not, however, occur overnight. Under increasing internal stress concerning his views on defense, and in the midst of a tense political campaign over the Berlin issue, Khrushchev made a series of concessions during mid-1961 allowing plans for troop reductions to be suspended and accepting the necessity for a more balanced mix of defense forces. The growing intensity of statements by Soviet military leaders warning of the danger of surprise attack suggests an internal struggle to undertake a new, more ambitious defense program.[36] The reorientation of Soviet defense plans probably occurred by October 1961 as the Twenty-second Party Congress was meeting and the Berlin crisis was being resolved to the disfavor of Khrushchev.[37]

The pressure on the Soviet leadership to eliminate the American strategic advantage and the stretch of years before a new generation of strategic missiles could be deployed apparently led Khrushchev to gamble on placing Soviet regional-range missiles on the island of Cuba. By September 1962 the first strategic missiles had been sent to Cuba in cargo ships. The Soviet plan apparently was to deploy some twenty-four SS-4 medium-range and sixteen SS-5 intermediate-range missile launchers (each with one reload) to ten separate sites.[38] Consistent with Soviet all-arms thinking, the missiles would be only part of a package including air defenses, Soviet ground forces, and local security forces.[39] Soviet MRBMs and IRBMs based in Cuba could cover a variety of important U.S. strategic targets, such as ICBM and bomber bases as well as command-and-control sites, although the soft basing sites of the Soviet missiles were vulnerable to attack in wartime.

This forward deployment of its strategic missiles probably offered the USSR its only means of quickly improving its strategic position relative to the United States. But it was a very high risk venture and it ended in a major confrontation with the United States.[40] During the course of the October 1962 crisis the United States backed its demands for the withdrawal of the missiles with a naval quarantine of Cuba and compelled

36. Wolfe, *Soviet Power and Europe,* pp. 95–96.
37. Ibid.
38. Allison, *Essence of Decision,* pp. 104–05; interviews.
39. Ibid.
40. Wolfe, *Soviet Power and Europe,* pp. 96–99; Alexander L. George and Richard Smoke, *Deterrence in American Foreign Policy: Theory and Practice* (Columbia University Press, 1974), pp. 459–81.

the USSR to dismantle and withdraw its nuclear missile launchers. The failure of Khrushchev's gambit in Cuba meant that the Soviet Union's response continued to rest on its long-term intercontinental force program.

Searching for Expedient Solutions

Most of the Soviet ICBMs deployed or under development in 1961 were designed to destroy area targets, such as bomber bases, early U.S. ICBM sites, or administrative and economic centers. The U.S. Minuteman, then under development, was not only to be deployed in hardened, underground silos, but it had a relatively high degree of accuracy which made it a formidable threat to the early Soviet missile forces.

Given the years it would require to develop new strategic weapons more appropriate to countering the U.S. forces, the USSR had to rely on its existing missile programs. Shortcomings in its ballistic-missile defenses (see appendix D) placed the entire burden on its offensive forces. The third generation of Soviet ICBMs, to be deployed in the mid-1960s, offered the only solution. It included three new ICBMs (the SS-9, the SS-10, and the SS-13), each produced by a different design bureau.[41] The USSR apparently turned to the SS-9 and the SS-13 ICBMs (the SS-10 was later canceled).

The SS-9 Scarp, produced by the Yangel design bureau to replace the SS-7 and to cover large area targets, possessed greater accuracy and a larger yield than the SS-7, thus making it well suited for attacking hardened, point targets such as Minuteman missile silos or underground launch-control centers. But the size and expense of the SS-9 probably precluded production at levels needed to match the high deployment rate of the Minuteman force. Consequently, the USSR was compelled to diversify its approach to the problem. It apparently planned to deploy enough SS-9s to neutralize the U.S. Minuteman force through attacks on the one hundred very hard launch-control centers critical to its operation[42] while counting on the deployment of substantial numbers of SS-13 ICBMs to politically match (and perhaps militarily counter) the Minuteman missile-for-missile.

41. The nonstorable liquid-fuel SS-10 was designed by the Korolev bureau, the storable liquid-fuel SS-9 by the Yangel bureau, and the solid-fuel SS-13 by the Nadiradize bureau.

42. "Remarks Prepared for Delivery by the Honorable Harold Brown, Secretary of Defense, at the U.S. Naval Academy, Annapolis, Maryland," news release, Office of the Assistant Secretary of Defense (Public Affairs), May 30, 1979, p. 3.

The SS-13 Savage program represented a significant departure from the earlier Soviet ICBM series designed for attacking large area targets. Unlike its predecessors, the SS-13 utilized solid-fuel propellants and carried a small nuclear warhead. In many respects this missile, developed by the Nadiradize design bureau which specialized in solid-fuel missiles,[43] appears to have been intended as the Soviet counterpart to the American Minuteman I; it was similar in size and propellant type and started development about the same time as the Minuteman in the late 1950s. The smaller size of the SS-13 could have allowed it to be produced more rapidly and cheaply than the larger Soviet missiles. The SS-13 seems to have been intended to serve as a strategic reserve for the Soviet land-based missile force. Its propulsion system made it feasible to be deployed as a mobile missile, difficult to locate and destroy in wartime. The long-standing interest of the USSR in mobile missiles and its claims to have developed a mobile ICBM during the mid-1960s[44] suggest that a mobile SS-13 was expected to serve as a hedge against a U.S. first strike and as a secure strategic reserve in the event of a prolonged nuclear conflict.

Serious technical problems associated with the SS-13's guidance system and solid-fuel motor apparently hampered its development. Only sixty of the ICBMs were deployed, all of them in silos.[45] One of the important repercussions of this failure may have been Soviet rethinking of the nature of the future strategic reserve force. The immediate response, however, was the search for a replacement.

The Soviet leadership found its substitute by turning to a new source, the missile design bureau of V.N. Chelomei. One of its products, the SS-11 Sego, eventually would satisfy the Soviet need for an ICBM that could be deployed promptly enough to match the U.S. Minuteman missiles in number. Like the SS-13, the SS-11 was relatively small, with modest accuracy and a small warhead, but it used storable liquid fuel. The SS-11 seems also to have been a program that was redirected to meet the new military requirements. Certainly its development was unexpected from a design bureau whose work had been mainly focused on producing naval missiles.[46] And the SS-11 was the only ICBM at the

43. Freedman, *US Intelligence*, p. 113; "Russian Missile Bureaus," *Aerospace Daily*, January 22, 1979, p. 100.

44. Wolfe, *Soviet Power and Europe*. p. 434.

45. Doug Richardson, "Soviet Strategic Nuclear Rockets Guide," *Flight International*, December 11, 1976, p. 1732.

46. Walter Pincus, *Washington Post*, June 26, 1980.

time that had a variable-range capability,[47] which enabled it to strike targets at less than its full intercontinental range.

The many anomalies associated with the program suggest that relatively late in its development cycle the SS-11 was selected as a means for matching U.S. Minuteman deployments. Given the naval heritage of its design bureau, it is possible that the SS-11 was originally designed in the mid-1950s as a land-based ballistic missile for use against enemy naval forces at long distances. Statements and technical developments at the time provide evidence of Soviet interest in developing a weapon to counter the significant threat posed by nuclear-armed, carrier-based aircraft in the American strategic strike force.[48] The difficulty of redirecting the development of the SS-11 was probably eased by the fact that the U.S. program that created the need for the missiles also downgraded the role of the aircraft carrier as American ballistic-missile submarines became operational. The combined failure of the SS-13 program and the rapid change in the nature of the strategic threat in the early 1960s were only the first in a series of new requirements that affected the development of Chelomei's SS-11 missile.

Evolving Roles for the Sea-based Forces

Important decisions were also made during the early 1960s concerning the strategic missions of the Soviet Navy. With the formation of the Strategic Rocket Forces, the Navy apparently lost any major role in conducting strategic strikes[49] (less than one hundred sea-based ballistic missiles were operational through the mid-1960s).

The changing American strategic posture, marked by the accelerated deployment of Polaris submarines, dramatically affected the Soviet Navy's ability to perform its strategic defense mission against enemy sea-based nuclear forces.[50] Beginning in 1962, several of the U.S. submarines were committed to the NATO nuclear strike plan, thus posing a serious threat to the Soviet homeland as well as to targets in the

47. William Beecher, *New York Times,* February 11, 1970; Raymond L. Garthoff, "SALT and the Soviet Military," *Problems of Communism,* vol. 24 (January–February 1975), p. 31.

48. Wolfe, *Soviet Power and Europe,* p. 434.

49. Norman Polmar, "Soviet Nuclear Submarines," *United States Naval Institute Proceedings,* vol. 107 (July 1981), p. 34.

50. "Remarks by Secretary McNamara, NATO Ministerial Meeting, 5 May 1962, Restricted session," declassified material, Department of Defense, p. 24.

Warsaw Pact countries. Countering this threat had supplanted defending against aircraft carrier strike forces as the Soviet Navy's main defense mission by the mid-1960s.[51] Its prospects, however, for effectively carrying out the new assignment were fairly low.

In many respects, the Western sea-based strategic missiles posed the Soviet Union's most difficult defense problem, particularly given the absence of defenses against ballistic missiles.[52] Antisubmarine warfare (ASW) was a challenging problem for any nation in an age of nuclear-powered submarines that were able to patrol continuously concealed in the ocean's depths. The Soviet Navy was especially handicapped by the lack of either the equipment or the experience for conducting ASW operations in the open oceans.[53] Its problems were compounded by the fact that the USSR's routes to the open oceans generally require its naval forces to go through narrow straits—choke points—controlled by the United States and its allies and by the Soviet Union's lack of major overseas bases. Finally, Soviet submarines were significantly more vulnerable to detection than those of the United States, which has maintained a critical edge in passive sonar systems and relatively silent-running submarines.[54]

Nonetheless, the Soviet Union responded to the Polaris threat by reorienting its naval construction program to emphasize antisubmarine warfare.[55] By the late 1960s growing numbers of Soviet surface ships, aircraft, and helicopters were available for this mission. However, during this same time, improvements in the range of the U.S. Polaris missile nearly tripled the potential patrol area of Polaris submarines to almost 4 million square miles.[56]

Eventually convinced of the futility of attempting to counter the U.S.

51. James M. McConnell, "Strategy and Missions of the Soviet Navy in the Year 2000," in James L. George, ed., *Problems of Sea Power As We Approach the Twenty-First Century* (Washington: American Enterprise Institute for Public Policy Research, 1978), pp. 47–48.

52. During the early 1960s the USSR started to deploy an ABM system around Leningrad. However, it was terminated and dismantled by 1964 (see appendix D).

53. Norman Polmar, "Thinking About Soviet ASW," *United States Naval Institute Proceedings: Naval Review 1976*, vol. 102 (May 1976), pp. 111–12.

54. George C. Wilson, *Washington Post*, May 28, 1978; "Excerpts of a Breakfast Group Meeting with Secretary of Defense Harold Brown," Sheraton Carlton Hotel, Washington, D.C., September 11, 1980, p. 4.

55. Polmar, "Thinking about Soviet ASW," pp. 119–21.

56. Alton H. Quanbeck and Archie L. Wood, *Modernizing the Strategic Bomber Force: Why and How* (Brookings Institution, 1976), p. 72.

force with existing means, the USSR turned away from mass production of such important ASW forces as the large Moskva-class helicopter cruiser and the high-speed Alpha-class attack submarine. It appears to have chosen to develop less direct means of countering the Polaris, such as by degrading its operational effectiveness. American command-and-control links could be attacked with ballistic missiles, and Soviet antisatellite systems (which were first tested in the late 1960s) could be directed against U.S. space-based navigational aids for the Polaris submarines (see appendix E).

In the late 1960s the USSR also began expanding its own sea-based ballistic-missile forces. In 1968 Yankee-class submarines were armed with the SS-N-6 Sawfly missile.[57] While addition of the SS-N-6 generally enhanced the Soviet Union's overall strategic position, the Yankee-class submarine apparently was assigned only a limited role in intercontinental strike missions against targets located in U.S. coastal areas, probably in part because its survivability in wartime is questionable. Nonetheless, deployment of these submarines signaled the beginning of a period in which the role of Soviet sea-based ballistic-missile forces would increase, especially in the intercontinental theaters of operations. Construction of strategic-missile submarines had the highest priority in the Soviet naval program, thus signifying the Soviet leaders' sense of urgency in enhancing the sea-based missile force and matching the U.S. sea-based forces.[58]

Despite the growing importance of the nuclear-armed submarine within the Soviet force structure and the belated recognition of its usefulness in strategic strikes, there is reason to believe that the original requirement for the Yankee-class nuclear-powered ballistic-missile submarine (SSBN) was to defend against enemy naval forces. A combination of changing national requirements and technical difficulties altered its role as it approached deployment. When this submarine entered development in the late 1950s, the Soviet Navy's primary mission was to defend against Western sea-based nuclear forces.[59] With the creation of the SRF, the Navy's role in the USSR's strategic-strike plans was tentative at best. Shortly after work began on the Yankee SSBN, a tactical ballistic missile—the SS-NX-13—apparently began being devel-

57. U.S. Office of the Chief of Naval Operations, *Understanding Soviet Naval Developments*, 4th ed. (GPO, 1981), p. 98.

58. Claude R. Thorpe, "Mission Priorities of the Soviet Navy," in Paul J. Murphy, ed., *Naval Power in Soviet Policy* (GPO, 1978), pp. 163–64.

59. McConnell, "Strategy and Missions," p. 47.

oped. This missile could have been launched from the Yankee.[60] The SS-NX-13, with a 400-mile range and a terminal guidance system, would have been suitable for use against Western carrier task forces, and possibly even against Polaris submarines.[61]

Soviet Navy plans to deploy the Yankee SSBN in this role appear to have been altered by the technical difficulties that plagued development of the SS-NX-13 and precluded its deployment. But the Yankee program was most affected by the changes in intercontinental requirements that Soviet leaders began to confront in 1961. They were apparently convinced of the need to expand the Soviet sea-based strategic capability and politically match the growing U.S. SSBN force. Sea-based missiles not only would improve the survivability of the strategic forces but also could serve as a strategic reserve.

Initial evidence of this shift in Soviet thinking was the regular assignment by 1964 of older Soviet ballistic-missile submarines to patrol in the open ocean. Within a few years the first Yankee-class SSBNs were deployed, carrying the SS-N-6, a missile with a range of 1,300 nautical miles designed by the Chelomei bureau from existing components. By 1970, patrol areas for the Yankee submarines were established off both U.S. coasts, thereby giving the USSR sea-based coverage of a wide range of targets. Nevertheless, during this period the Soviet SSBNs apparently were limited to covering U.S. SSBN support and communication facilities, large ports, and major U.S. home fleet centers such as Norfolk, Virginia. Soviet writings indicate that nuclear strikes against such targets would be considered an extension of the Soviet Navy's wartime missions of combating the enemy's fleet and disrupting his sea-lanes of communication. Institutional interests of other services, such as the SRF, probably prohibited any further expansion in the Navy's strategic strike mission through the 1960s.

The ability of Yankee-class SSBNs to serve as a strategic reserve was probably questionable. Unlike American submarines, which were considered highly survivable when at sea, the Yankee SSBN had a doubtful chance of surviving long in a U.S.-Soviet conflict. The Soviet submarines

60. *United States Military Posture for FY 1978* (U.S. Office of the Joint Chiefs of Staff, 1977), p. 16.

61. K. J. Moore, Mark Flanigan, and Robert D. Helsel, "Developments in Submarine Systems, 1956–76," in Michael McGwire and John McDonnell, eds., *Soviet Naval Influence: Domestic and Foreign Dimensions* (Praeger for the Centre for Foreign Policy Studies, Department of Political Science, Dalhousie University, 1977), p. 172.

had to slip through Western-controlled choke points to reach their patrol areas and because they were relatively noisy were vulnerable to detection.[62] In addition, the relatively short range of the SS-N-6 missiles limited the ability of these submarines to perform deep-strike missions against all U.S. strategic targets without risking detection. But the SS-N-6s were probably quite useful for covering regional targets; since only a small part of the Yankee SSBN force was normally on patrol near U.S. coasts, many of these submarines could have been on call in home waters for regional support.

Problems for the Regional Nuclear Force

The shift of Soviet resources in the mid-1960s to building up the intercontinental force did not signal a decline in the importance of the regional-range forces. Instead, it reflected the immediacy of the need to offset the expanding American intercontinental threat. In the mid to late 1960s, new threats to the survivability of the Soviet regional forces prompted the USSR to turn to variable-range weapons to ensure the effectiveness of its regional strategic posture. By the mid-1960s, about seven hundred SS-4 and SS-5 ballistic missiles had been deployed in the Soviet Union, most of them in clusters at soft sites. When the silo hardening program ended in 1964 with the shift in emphasis to the ICBM force, much of the Soviet regional nuclear forces was left highly vulnerable. Previously the primary threat to these forces had been from strategic aircraft or nuclear cruise missiles, which were relatively slow and could be intercepted by Soviet air defense, or possibly even preempted by a nuclear missile strike. This situation changed dramatically when the United States deployed long-range ballistic missiles—in particular, the quick-reacting and highly survivable Polaris missiles could effectively strike both Soviet regional nuclear missiles and strategic bomber bases. As early as May 1963 the United States had committed five Polaris submarines to NATO's defense,[63] and in 1964 the Polaris A-3, with its greater accuracy and multiple warheads, became operational. The long-range Mace surface-to-surface cruise missile deployed in Germany could also reach Soviet regional forces.[64] Beyond that, in the early 1960s the

62. William Beecher, *New York Times,* October 9, 1969.
63. William W. Kaufmann, *The McNamara Strategy* (Harper and Row, 1964), pp. 126–27.
64. The Mace missile had an operational range of about 1,200 nautical miles.

Soviet Union faced the prospect that the United States and its NATO allies might deploy a land-mobile, medium-range ballistic missile.[65]

The USSR undoubtedly planned to protect its regional nuclear forces by deploying mobile ballistic missiles. By the mid-1960s testing began on two such missiles, the medium-range SS-14 and the intermediate-range SS-15.[66] Soviet defense planners probably envisaged them as a more survivable replacement or supplement to the increasingly vulnerable SS-4s and SS-5s. However, technical problems arose with the development of these expensive, solid-fuel missiles, and only a few SS-14s were deployed for a brief time. To compound these problems, a new set of targets for the Soviet regional forces emerged in the form of China. Sino-Soviet relations had fully deteriorated by the mid-1960s, and the Soviet military—presumably for the first time—received new requirements to cover Chinese targets. By 1969 additional Soviet nuclear forces (including some SS-14 and SS-15 missiles) were arrayed close to the border.[67]

With the survivability of its forces decreasing and its target requirements expanding, the Soviet Union apparently again turned to the SS-11 missile. From a regional-range missile for striking naval targets, it had been redirected to help meet intercontinental requirements. Just as it neared deployment as a long-range weapon, the SS-11 system was probably drawn upon once more to serve as a more survivable system for Soviet regional forces.[68] With its variable range, and deployed in hardened silos, the SS-11 was well suited for its expanded role. The first SS-11s became operational in 1966; by 1968, deployment had begun with 120 missile launchers at sites in western Russia previously used only for regional missiles,[69] while other SS-11s deployed near the Sino-Soviet border probably were assigned to cover targets in the Far East. The significant contribution of this new component of the regional strike forces meant that the USSR gave up little in 1970–71 when it dismantled about seventy of the more vulnerable SS-4 and SS-5 launchers in the Far

65. Bill Gunston, *The Illustrated Encyclopaedia of the World's Rockets & Missiles* (Crescent Books, 1979), p. 68.

66. "Statement of Secretary of Defense Robert S. McNamara before the House Armed Services Committee on the Fiscal Year 1968–72 Defense Program and 1968 Defense Budget," declassified material (U.S. Department of Defense, 1967), p. 47.

67. Harrison E. Salisbury, *New York Times,* May 24, 1969.

68. When it was upgraded for the intercontinental strike mission, the SS-11 probably retained the technical capability for flexible targeting.

69. Freedman, *US Intelligence,* pp. 158–59.

East.[70] In combination with the submarine-launched SS-N-6, the SS-11 would have made a critical contribution to the overall survivability and target coverage of the Soviet regional forces at a time when they were under great stress.

The Contemporary Period

With the deployment of the fourth generation of regional and intercontinental missiles in the 1970s, substantial improvements were made in the Soviet strategic force posture. The USSR's third-generation missile deployments had matched the U.S. missile force in number, and in the following generation significant advances were made in the overall effectiveness and survivability of the force.[71] Paradoxically, the USSR had attained a significant degree of success in fulfilling its political aims in the buildup of its strategic force in the 1960s but had generally failed to meet its military requirements. It was this unusual combination of circumstances that set the stage for the initiation of serious U.S.-Soviet strategic arms limitation talks (SALT I) which resulted in 1972 in the signing of the Antiballistic Missile (ABM) Treaty and an interim agreement limiting strategic offensive arms.

Both the defensive and the offensive strategic forces of the USSR fell far short of meeting Soviet doctrinal requirements vis-à-vis the United States in the 1960s. Yet Soviet missile deployments were viewed as an effective deterrent to the American use of (and the threat to use) strategic nuclear forces. The USSR's second-strike capability gave it a credible deterrent, at least in the eyes of the West, that immeasurably improved the basis for Soviet political and military security.

Another of the Soviet Union's objectives in building up its intercontinental force was to achieve nuclear parity with the United States and thereby gain recognition as a global superpower. The USSR considered attaining nuclear parity an important factor in shifting the global "correlation of forces" against the United States and in reducing the United States' willingness to exercise its political and military power abroad.

70. Beecher, *New York Times,* March 3, 1972.
71. The Soviet decision for deployment of fourth-generation ICBMs appears to have included a rough balance of four to one between the SS-11 and the larger SS-9. Over 1,100 SS-11 launchers were deployed, along with about 300 SS-9 launchers. The numbers reflect a temporary suspension of deployments and a modest cutback during the SALT I negotiations. Garthoff, "SALT and the Soviet Military," pp. 29–31.

A similar combination of broad security objectives and specific military problems is reflected in the Soviet approach to the SALT I negotiations. The negotiations and the resulting agreements served to codify the new status of the USSR as a political and military equal of the United States.[72] The negotiations also offered the USSR an alternate means for dealing with military problems. One Soviet motivation in agreeing to the 1972 treaty limiting ABM deployments appears to have been to prevent the military advantage that one nation (the United States) possessing an effective ABM system along with missiles carrying multiple warheads could acquire over its adversary.[73] Soviet leaders may have been convinced that the USSR's security requirements could best be served by avoiding a disadvantageous competition with the United States in ABM systems while moving ahead with development of Soviet missiles with multiple warheads. Soviet military planners may have similarly concluded that in light of the uncertainty of providing an effective ABM defense of Soviet urban centers, combined with the undoubted difficulty of attacking U.S. strategic forces protected by ABM systems, an ABM Treaty would offer a net advantage to the Soviet Union.

With the deployment of the fourth generation of land- and sea-based missiles in the mid-1970s, the USSR finally made major steps toward matching the capability of the U.S. intercontinental force. The relatively slower rates of deployment of fourth-generation ICBMs, coupled with the high-paced flight-testing program, are evidence of the increasing confidence of the USSR in the quality of its strategic forces. The shift is best reflected in the differences between the 1972 SALT I agreements and the proposed SALT II Treaty, signed in 1979. The Soviet Union's willingness to give up the quantitative advantages it held in the SALT I agreement on offensive arms limitations may have reflected a new-found confidence in its ability to compete with the United States in the more important arena of qualitative arms competition.

Creating a Strategic Reserve Force at Sea

At some point in the mid to late 1960s the Soviet leadership apparently decided to diversify its intercontinental strategic strike forces by the

72. Samuel B. Payne, Jr., *The Soviet Union and SALT* (MIT Press, 1980), pp. 68, 76–80.

73. See, for instance, Maj. Gen. N. Vasendin and Col. N. Kuznetsov, "Modern Warfare and Surprise Attack," *Military Thought*, June 1968, p. 43; Maj. Gen. V. Zemskov, "Wars of the Modern Era," *Military Thought*, May 1969, pp. 60–61.

development of long-range sea-based missiles. This national decision to augment the silo-based ICBM force with a substantial strategic reserve at sea eventually required major alterations in the role and character of the Soviet Navy. Coupled with the deployment of Delta-class SSBNs armed with long-range sea-launched ballistic missiles (SLBMs), such a decision meant that the Soviet submarine force was finally to share in the deep-strike (or strategic intercontinental strike) mission against a wide range of targets in the United States. To ensure the survivability of its SSBN force, the Soviet Navy added a new mission, the strategic support of the SSBN force.[74] Surface ships and other forces would be used to defend the force in wartime against Western threats.

Beyond the inherent advantages of a sea-based ballistic missile, the failure of the SS-13 program to furnish a land-mobile ICBM during the critical years of the mid-1960s probably caused the Soviet leadership to decide to enlarge the sea-based missile force. The timing of the SS-N-8 SLBM's development and the nature of its progressively lengthened flight test series suggest that it was somewhat of a "quick fix" measure.[75] So does the fact that the missile is launched from a Delta-class SSBN, which is simply a modification of a Yankee-class hull rather than a new design.[76] (In 1978 a much improved missile with multiple warheads—the SS-N-18—was deployed on the Delta-III-class SSBN.)[77]

The deployment of submarines with longer-range missiles beginning in the early 1970s reflected an evolution in the Navy's mission as well as the Soviet Union's decision to move a large part of its strategic forces to sea. Soviet writings increasingly attributed to the Soviet SLBM force the capability to destroy land targets both on the enemy's seaboard and deep in his rear.[78] Until the early 1970s the SLBM force was probably not recognized as being prepared to perform the full strategic strike role against the enemy—a mission the American SSBN force has been dedicated to from its inception.

74. For a discussion of this concept of actively ensuring the survivability (or "combat stability" in Soviet terms) of strategic missile submarines in wartime, see *Understanding Soviet Naval Developments,* p. 10; Fleet Adm. S. G. Gorshkov, *The Sea Power of the State* (Naval Institute Press, 1979), p. 189.

75. The increased range of the SS-N-8 came as a surprise to U.S. analysts. *Department of Defense Appropriations Fiscal Year 1974,* Hearings before the Senate Appropriations Committee, 93 Cong. 1 sess. (GPO, 1973), pt. 1, p. 46.

76. Ibid., p. 607.

77. "Soviets Deploying MIRVed SS-N-18 on Submarines, U.S. Sources Say," *Aerospace Daily,* August 1, 1978, p. 141.

78. See A. A. Grechko, *On Guard for Peace and the Building of Communism,* JPRS-54602 (Springfield, Va.: National Technical Information Service, U.S. Department of Commerce, 1971), p. 37.

The decision to move part of the intercontinental strike forces to the sea would have occurred at about the time that the Soviet Navy was realizing how ineffective its efforts would be against the U.S. Polaris submarines and how potentially vulnerable Soviet submarines were to Western ASW forces.[79] Thus, a combination of military deficiencies and national requirements may have resulted in the Soviet Union's turn to the sea for a survivable, strategic reserve force and the consequent redirection of the wartime roles of the Soviet Navy.

The technological superiority of Western forces in submarine warfare that made even those Soviet submarines near the homeland vulnerable led the Soviet Union to formulate a strategic-support mission for its Navy. Surface ships, attack submarines, and ASW aircraft are to be used in combined operations aimed at protecting Soviet SSBNs from Western ASW forces. It became clear during the early 1970s that the Navy was placing a high priority on protecting its own submarines.[80] By 1975 it was evident that the new Delta-class SSBNs would patrol primarily in the Barents and Norwegian Sea waters relatively near their home areas rather than in the open oceans like the Yankee-class SSBNs.[81] The Soviet Union seems to have chosen to trade off the greater operating area made possible by long-range SLBMs for potentially safer deployments near its own shores. Soviet naval writings emphasized the need for active support of strategic missile submarines to ensure their "combat stability" or resilience against enemy threats,[82] and Soviet weapons developments and annual exercises revealed that priority was being put on the ASW mission.[83]

To perform its new mission of strategic support of the SSBN force, the Soviet Navy reoriented its ASW forces from attack operations to defense. What was a force with a marginal offensive capability became a substantial defensive force. By in effect creating protected sanctuaries

---

79. MccGwire, "Rationale for the Development of Soviet Seapower," pp. 166–67.

80. Various Soviet military writers referred to the active protection of strategic-missile submarines in the 1960s; for instance, see Sokolovskiy, *Soviet Military Strategy*, p. 254.

81. George C. Wilson, *Washington Post*, April 28, 1975. At about the same time the USSR began to actively protect its forward-deployed Yankee-class SSBN by assigning nuclear-powered attack submarines (SSNs), such as the Victor-class SSNs, to operate with the SSBN. William Beecher, *Boston Globe*, December 19, 1975.

82. Sergei G. Gorshkov, *Red Star Rising at Sea*, trans. Theodore A. Neely, Jr. (U.S. Naval Institute, 1974), p. 131.

83. Polmar, "Thinking about Soviet ASW," pp. 120–21; Donald C. Daniel, "Trends and Patterns in Major Soviet Naval Exercises," *Naval War College Review*, vol. 30 (Spring 1978), p. 37.

or bastions for its strategic submarines in its home waters, the USSR turned the natural choke points to its own advantage and gave its submarines closer support from land-based aircraft and its fleets' bases. Its innovative use of various naval forces to actively defend its SSBNs against Western ASW forces[84] helps to assure the survivability of a critical component of the Soviet intercontinental strike force.

Major Advances with Fourth-Generation Deployments

With the deployment of its fourth-generation ICBMs during the 1970s, the Soviet Union made impressive gains in the overall capability of its land-based missile force. These ICBMs, designed in the mid-1960s to replace existing missiles, were expected to meet the SRF's diverse targeting requirements and to enhance the force's survivability. The new deployments offered an increasingly effective, and redundant, capability for countering the U.S. ICBM force. The large SS-18, a product of the Yangel bureau put in operation in late 1974,[85] was capable of attacking very hard targets. One version of the SS-18 with a single, large warhead was suitable for attacking such targets as U.S. Minuteman launch-control centers, while other SS-18 ICBMs carrying multiple warheads made it possible for the USSR to effectively extend its target coverage to the Minuteman silos for the first time.

The Minuteman force was not the SRF's only targeting responsibility against the United States. The SS-17, with four independently targeted, large-yield warheads, probably supplanted the SS-7 in coverage of air bases and other area targets.[86] Both the new SS-19 ICBM and the third modification of the SS-11, which carried multiple warheads, were missiles capable of covering various targets in regional and intercontinental theaters. The SS-19 also was accurate enough to threaten hardened targets[87] and thus provided a backup to the SS-18 force. A variety of modifications to these systems, such as single-warhead missiles, improved the Soviet capability against special kinds of targets in very hard silos or that were not easy to locate.

84. This development is confirmed by *Understanding Soviet Naval Developments,* p. 10.

85. *United States Military Posture for FY 1979,* p. 22.

86. It is a noteworthy coincidence that the SS-7 ICBM remained in the Soviet operational inventory until about 1975 when the SS-17 ICBM first became operational.

87. "Soviets' Nuclear Arsenal Continues to Proliferate," *Aviation Week and Space Technology,* June 16, 1980, p. 69.

In terms of improving ICBM survivability, the USSR undertook a vigorous program to harden its silos, probably in expectation that the United States would deploy a new ICBM by the late 1970s. Public reports suggested the United States might develop a more accurate missile, with a large throw weight, known as the WS-120A which would become operational soon after deployment of the Soviet fourth-generation missiles.[88] The continuing threat to the land-based missile force, as well as the institutional interests involved, also probably accounts for initiation of the SS-X-16 mobile missile program in the fourth generation of Soviet ICBM development. The SS-X-16 was lighter than its contemporaries and like its predecessor, the solid-fuel SS-13, could deliver only a relatively small payload. By the early 1970s it became clear that the United States would not deploy a new ICBM for another ten years and that the Soviet silo-based ICBM force was sufficiently survivable to preclude the need for a mobile ICBM. Given the SS-X-16's limited capability and reported testing difficulties, the USSR had little incentive to deploy more than a small force at the expense of its silo-based ICBMs. Consequently, it agreed to prohibition of the SS-X-16 in the SALT II negotiations because of its similarity to the intermediate-range SS-20.[89] It may have seemed preferable to the USSR to delay deployment of a solid fuel mobile ICBM until a more effective model could be developed.

By the late 1970s the USSR also had modernized many of the initial weapon systems assigned to its regional nuclear forces. One of the first new systems was the TU-22M Backfire bomber (replacing the aging Badger bombers) that became operational in 1974.[90] The Backfire is effective against both land and sea targets because it can fly at low altitudes as well as high speeds and thus reduce the amount of time that enemy air defense systems have to react. It has the flexibility to perform both nuclear and nonnuclear missions.[91] Deployment of the SS-19 and SS-20 land-based ballistic missiles added substantially to the capability of regional nuclear forces. The SS-19, with its variable range,

88. Although the WS-120A project was never started, the U.S. Air Force later initiated an advanced ICBM program that resulted in the MX ICBM. Donald C. Winston, "Nixon Delays Advanced ICBM Development," *Aviation Week and Space Technology*, May 12, 1969, p. 26.

89. U.S. Department of State, Bureau of Public Affairs, *SALT II Agreement, Vienna, June 18, 1979*, Selected Document 12A (GPO, 1979), pp. 15–16, 34.

90. *Department of Defense Authorization for Appropriations for Fiscal Year 1979*, Hearings before the Senate Armed Services Committee, 95 Cong. 2 sess. (GPO, 1978), pt. 9, p. 6554.

91. Phillip A. Petersen, "Flexibility: A Driving Force in Soviet Strategy," *Air Force Magazine*, March 1980, p. 96.

provided a relatively secure, land-based reserve force for covering regional as well as intercontinental targets. The SS-20 IRBM—a long overdue follow-on to the vulnerable SS-4 and SS-5 missiles—with its multiple warheads greatly increased the regional forces' target effectiveness and coverage. Its solid-fuel propulsion system enables the SS-20 to be deployed as a mobile missile, which improves its survivability and makes this missile a major addition to the Soviet regional nuclear capability.

The regional forces' flexibility has been significantly improved with deployment of a series of new shorter-range missiles (the SS-21, SS-22, and SS-23) that can attack battlefield targets with nuclear or advanced nonnuclear munitions.[92] Increasingly, other new systems are capable of performing missions similar to those of the Soviet regional strike forces. The SU-24 Fencer, for example, is an attack aircraft that can adequately perform nonnuclear and nuclear attacks which previously only medium bombers could undertake. With technological improvements of this kind, the earlier delineation of roles between Soviet tactical and regional forces has steadily diminished.

Prospects for the Next Generation

Forecasting strategic force trends depends critically on underlying assumptions. Those deployments that the USSR makes to meet the military requirements established in the 1970s will reflect needs identified even earlier. The fifth-generation Soviet missile deployments seem likely to feature improvements in accuracy and to attempt to deal with long-term threats to missile survivability. The new designs and modifications to current ICBMs nearing the flight-testing stage[93] include both liquid-fuel missiles and solid-fuel missiles. One of the solid-fuel missiles, believed to be medium-sized, is probably intended as a replacement for the USSR's silo-based SS-13 and SS-11 ICBMs. Another may serve as a follow-on to the mobile SS-X-16 ICBM (prohibited by the SALT II agreement).

The new ICBMs are likely to have the accuracy necessary to afford a

92. *Department of Defense Annual Report Fiscal Year 1982*, p. 64; "New Russian War Plans," *Newsweek*, August 14, 1978, p. 15.

93. Clarence A. Robinson, Jr., "Soviets Testing New Generation of ICBM," *Aviation Week and Space Technology*, November 3, 1980, p. 28.

high probability of destroying a hardened enemy target with only a single warhead. While it involves some risk of technical failure or delay, Soviet transition to solid-fuel missiles could offer greater missile efficiency, safer handling, and lower operating costs. The fact that large numbers of liquid-fuel missiles will remain in the SRF inventory for some time helps minimize the risks associated with attempts to deploy solid-fuel missiles, an area that has proved difficult for the USSR.

During the 1980s the USSR also must be concerned with the growing capability of U.S. strategic missiles (the planned MX ICBM, the Trident II SLBM, and the long-range cruise missile) to threaten the survivability of its land-based ICBM force. With one exception, few major changes are likely to occur in the Soviet Union's ICBM deployment patterns. The USSR apparently has been taking measures to mitigate the vulnerability of its ICBMs. As part of that continuing effort it will have to harden its new launchers to estimated levels of 6,000 pounds per square inch,[94] if they are to be adequately protected.

The deployment of long-range SLBMs on Delta-class ballistic-missile submarines is a major contribution to the survivability of the Soviet missile force. This helps to explain the Soviet willingness to agree in SALT I to dismantle the older SS-7 and SS-8 ICBM launchers of the Strategic Rocket Forces in exchange for additional SLBM deployments.[95] Since the Soviet Union has already made the decision to move to the sea, it is unlikely that it will deploy many more SLBMs even if the vulnerability of its silo-based ICBMs should increase in the future.

Improvements in Soviet early-warning systems and missile alert rates since the late 1960s raise the possibility that launch under attack has become a basic element of Soviet operational doctrine in the event of a U.S.-Soviet nuclear conflict. Nevertheless, the silo hardening program continues, suggesting that the Soviet leadership is not content to simply rely on this operational option.

The one new development that is likely for improving Soviet ICBM survivability is the deployment of mobile ICBMs, as a supplement to a larger silo-based force. The U.S. cancellation of plans for an improved replacement for the Minuteman III ICBM (in addition to possible

94. Ibid.

95. Raymond Garthoff, executive secretary and senior State Department adviser on the U.S. SALT delegation from 1969 to 1973, told us that he believed the Soviet delegation to the SALT I negotiations was under instructions to specify "land-based ICBMs" in any reference to ICBMs in the SALT I agreements—clearly suggesting a Soviet view by the early 1970s that there also could be sea-based ICBMs.

technical problems in the SS-X-16 program) probably enabled the USSR to forgo deployment of mobile ICBMs, in accordance with the SALT II agreement. The requirement for deploying mobile ICBMs in the next generation of missiles, however, will be more compelling. They can serve as a hedge against an unexpected vulnerability in other components of the strategic missile forces. While mobile ICBMs are expensive to maintain, Soviet deployments are likely to avoid complicated basing schemes and to be limited in number because of Soviet reluctance to give up the close control of the silo-based force.

The USSR is also likely to upgrade its strategic reserves in the early 1980s. Currently it is testing a long-range, solid-fuel SLBM, the SS-NX-20, which will probably be more effective than the SS-N-8 and the SS-N-18 sea-based missiles. Deployed on the large Typhoon-class SSBN, the SS-NX-20 is a major step toward a highly survivable strategic reserve, which the USSR has been seeking since the late 1960s. The Typhoon-class SSBN, along with other naval developments such as the Kirov-class battle cruiser and the Oscar-class attack submarine, should significantly enhance the Soviet ability to sustain a sanctuary in home waters for its submarines in wartime.

CHAPTER FOUR

CRITICAL DECISIONS
IN THE 1980s

THE MILITARY requirements that prompted development of the generation of Soviet missile forces to be deployed in the early 1980s appear to have changed only incrementally since they were set two decades ago. Yet the testing and deployment of the fifth-generation missiles, long in development, are likely to receive wide attention in the West. And their appearance is likely to overshadow a far more important event—a reevaluation of Soviet strategic force posture. The crucial political and military decisions on requirements that could set the course of development for both Soviet regional and intercontinental forces for another twenty years probably will be made by the mid-1980s.

A new set of requirements seems inevitable because the current generation of Soviet deployments has made large steps toward meeting the earlier requirements. More important, a series of new strategic conditions appears to be developing that Soviet planners must consider. In the 1980s the United States and the nuclear weapons states on the Soviet periphery will probably deploy new types of nuclear weapons. The United States is planning to deploy the MX intercontinental ballistic missile (ICBM), possibly in a new, more survivable basing system. Given its potential to deliver large numbers of highly accurate reentry vehicles, this new U.S. system could significantly upgrade the threat to the survivability of Soviet land-based missile forces. Additionally, the United States intends to deploy a Trident II submarine-launched ballistic missile (SLBM) that is capable of striking key military targets. Because of the potential increase in the Trident's range, the amount of ocean area that Soviet forces must cover will significantly increase. Modernization of the U.S. bomber force is likely to provide not only large numbers of air-launched cruise missiles, but also a new penetrating bomber during the 1980s.

Soviet regional forces face the prospect of NATO deployment of large numbers of long-range cruise missiles as well as an upgraded version of the Pershing surface-to-surface missile that can reach key targets located in the Soviet homeland. These new systems may result in important changes in the Soviet regional forces' requirements. A notable expansion in the nuclear offensive capability of the USSR's regional neighbors, China, France, and Great Britain, is also planned or expected.

Currently, the USSR appears to be in the process of reassessing its political and military relations with the United States. While the political succession within the Soviet leadership is being resolved, a central factor will undoubtedly be a decision as to whether the USSR should continue adherence to the strategic arms control agreements or return to unconstrained arms competition with the West. Finally, by the mid-1980s it may be clearer whether technologies for achieving effective strategic defensive forces (such as ballistic missile defenses) are feasible. For all of these reasons the early 1980s is likely to be a period for determining critical new requirements.

The outcome of Soviet decisions taken during this time will not become evident for several years. However, if both regional and intercontinental forces face new requirements, the competition for weapon design and production resources could push the USSR toward even greater reliance on flexible strategic systems capable of performing regional as well as intercontinental missions. Furthermore, the USSR might choose to deploy fewer new strategic systems, instead emphasizing modifications and improvements in components of existing systems.

In the absence of continuing strategic arms limitations, Soviet missile deployments would be unrestricted and the USSR would not have to retire its older weapon systems. Undoubtedly the desirability of deploying antiballistic missile defenses will be a major question in the 1980s. While U.S. deployment of ABM defenses would seriously complicate Soviet defense planning, the continuing growth of regional nuclear capabilities is likely to encourage Soviet interest in future missile defenses.

The Responsiveness of Soviet Strategic Posture

The responsiveness of the Soviet posture to changing doctrinal and military requirements is one of the distinctive features of both its regional and its intercontinental strategic force. The USSR has not attempted simply to replicate the American strategic posture, nor are its strategic responses free from its own traditions or the influences of its institutional process. Rather, such factors as the basic geographical and political situation of the USSR, its distinctive military traditions and strategic doctrine, its particular institutions and technological base are all elements in the process that shapes Soviet strategic responses.

In the past, Western actions have created or affected many of the basic requirements that have determined how the Soviet strategic forces would develop. In the early 1960s U.S. actions appear to have presented certain force level requirements that substantially influenced Soviet strategic forces development for two or three generations of weapon systems. Changes in particular American weapon systems or their employment (such as the shift of the B-52 bomber to low-altitude penetration missions) tend to elicit fairly obvious and specific responses in the Soviet strategic force posture. Often, however, these changes are not appreciated in the West; for instance, the redirection of the SS-9 ICBM to target launch-control centers for U.S. ICBMs and the Soviet creation of a naval doctrine to actively defend its strategic missile submarines against a serious Western threat were belatedly recognized in the West. Clearly, the Soviet strategic force posture has developed not only in response to special Soviet security requirements but also in response to strategic developments in the United States and the countries adjoining the USSR. As part of a complex and interactive process, the USSR has sought to take account of external developments and develop a capability to counter them while attempting to fulfill its long-standing security requirements.

Implications for U.S. Security

The distinctions between the American and Soviet strategic postures raise important questions about the American strategic force posture and doctrine. The greatest challenge presented by the Soviet strategic forces may be in compelling the United States to clarify its own choices.

Indeed, U.S. strategic doctrine appears to have been slowly changing for more than a decade, in part because of the push of Soviet strategic developments. The Carter administration's ''countervailing strategy'' was an attempt to maintain a credible deterrent against the USSR by

STUDIES
IN
DEFENSE
POLICY

★ ★ ★ ★ ★

Soviet
Strategic Forces
Requirements
and Responses

ROBERT P. BERMAN
AND JOHN C. BAKER

THE BROOKINGS INSTITUTION

making victory in wartime appear improbable as "seen through Soviet eyes." As part of that doctrinal shift, the United States began to emphasize the value of targeting conventional forces and command and control structures, both presumably targets of great value to the Soviet leadership. In contrast, the criterion for an adequate deterrent as expressed in U.S. strategic doctrine during the late 1960s was the "assured destruction" of urban and industrial wealth. In retrospect, the belief that this was a sufficient measure of the requirement to deter a "rational" enemy was clearly a projection of U.S. thinking and values.

Within the course of a decade the United States made the transition from a Western basis for attempting to deter Soviet attack to seeking deterrence in terms of the Soviet Union's own approach and values. The question now is just how far this process will go. To what degree can the United States account for the distinctiveness of the Soviet strategic posture without attempting simply to replicate it? As the United States faces a series of critical questions concerning its strategic weapon programs and its approach to nuclear arms control, a clearer understanding of what shapes the Soviet strategic force posture will aid U.S. efforts to make the best choices possible on these difficult issues.

The Process of Missile Design and Development

THE CHARACTER of Soviet strategic forces is in part a reflection of the Soviet system of technological development and industrial production. The distinctive structure of the Soviet defense industry and its system of incentives have instilled certain characteristics in the Soviet process of acquisition of strategic weapons.

Like all other acquisition programs for weapon systems in the USSR, the development of strategic weapons is directed by the minister of defense through the Council of Ministers and, in the case of missiles, the Ministry of General Machine Building (GMB).[1] The ministry was established in 1965 and took over missile development from the Aviation Ministry. Until the economic reform of 1965 the ministries of Defense, Aviation, Shipbuilding, Radio Industry, Electronics, Machine Building, and Medium Machine Building were state committees under the State Defense Committee. The State Committee on Aviation, in addition to running part of the Radio Ministry, had organized two missile design bureaus headed by S. P. Korolev and M. K. Yangel, which produced all of the Soviet Union's medium-range, intermediate-range, intercontinental, and submarine-launched ballistic missiles (MRBMs, IRBMs, ICBMs, and SLBMs). In the late 1950s the committee had presumably retooled the factories that were producing Bison bombers (designed by the Myasishchev design bureau) in order to handle missiles from the Yangel design bureau.[2]

1. David Holloway, "Soviet Military R & D: Managing the 'Research-Production Cycle,' " in John R. Thomas and Ursula M. Kruse-Vaucienne, eds., *Soviet Science and Technology: Domestic and Foreign Perspectives* (George Washington University for the National Science Foundation, 1977), p. 197. Arthur J. Alexander, *Decision-Making in Soviet Weapons Procurement*, Adelphi Papers 47 and 48 (London: International Institute for Strategic Studies, 1978), p. 22.

2. Karl F. Spielmann, *Analyzing Soviet Strategic Arms Decisions* (Westview, 1978),

Aviation Roots

The close historical relation between aviation and missile development is apparent in the organization of the two industries. The Soviet minister of aviation (in the 1970s P. V. Dementiev) is a member of the Council of Ministers; he directs the Ministry of Aircraft Production, whose main departments are the Central Aerohydrodynamic Institute, the Central Design Office, the Central Engine Research Office, the Scientific Research Institute for Airplane Equipment, and the All-Union Institute of Aviation Materials.[3] Both the military and the civil aviation ministries submit their requirements for new aircraft to the Ministry of Aircraft Production. Any technical disagreements about requirements are settled by the Central Aerohydrodynamic Institute.[4] Once approved, the requirement is passed to the Central Design Office which issues the design concept to the design bureaus. A review committee of representatives from the Ministry of Aircraft Production, the Air Force, Aeroflot, and the Central Aerohydrodynamic Institute then selects the best of the preliminary designs. A number of prototypes are built and tested by one or more design bureaus. In time, prototypes are subjected to flight tests conducted by another committee, and the winning prototype is put into production. Recently the competition has often been resolved on paper, possibly because of the cost of building prototypes. In any event, there is roughly a four-year lag between design inception and the first flight test.[5] The Central Design Office, controlled by the chief designer, is responsible for all the aircraft design bureaus and has the power to close down unsatisfactory ones.[6] The nine active bureaus, each run by a chief designer, are Antonov, Beriev, Ilyushin, Kamov, Mikoyan, Mil, Sukhoi, Tupolev, and Yakovlev.[7] They are engaged in designing helicopters, flying boats, light and training aircraft, military and civil transports, bombers, and fighters.[8]

---

p. 93. In addition see Nikita Khrushchev, *Khrushchev Remembers: The Last Testament,* ed. and trans. Strobe Talbott (Little, Brown, 1974), p. 39.

   3. Robert D. Archer, *The Russian Approach to Aircraft Design,* report 1-1022 (McDonnell Douglas Corporation, 1969), p. 11.

   4. Ibid., p. 12.

   5. Our estimate.

   6. Archer, "Russian Approach to Aircraft Design," p. 14.

   7. Ibid., p. 15.

   8. Ibid., p. 17.

The Missile Development Process

With the establishment of the Ministry of General Machine Building in 1965, the Soviet missile program was removed from the control of the State Committee on Aviation. The ministry, directed by S. A. Afanasev, has four major departments—a Central Design Office where design requirements are assigned to the design bureaus (headed by M. K. Yangel, V. N. Chelomei, and V. N. Nadiradize), a Central Missile Engine Design Office and a Missile Engine Design Bureau (both once run by V. P. Glushko), a Central Guidance Development Office, and a Central Construction Office responsible for construction of launch-control centers and silos.[9] The ministry also associates with a number of research institutes[10] and various military staff schools such as the Dzerzhinskiy Military Engineering Academy which have supported missile research since the mid-1950s.[11]

The Soviet Union, by and large, appears to rely on single sources for developing missile prototypes. Development requests are established by the Ministry of Defense, a research institute, or the political leadership, and only rarely by design bureaus themselves.[12] The best example of the political leadership's interjection of its priorities into the system is Stalin's crash program for ICBM development that was initiated in the late 1940s.[13]

Any request for a new missile is submitted to the Ministry of General Machine Building, which has authority to question the missile requirement. Once the requirement is approved, it is put under the control of the chief designer, who issues the technical specifications to an appropriate design bureau to construct the missile as well as to departments responsible for such development tasks as engine tests (before full-scale testing) and programs to improve guidance aboard older missile frames.

The Central Missile Design Office appears to be directly responsible

9. John A. McDonnell, "The Soviet Weapons Acquisition System," in David R. Jones, ed., *Soviet Armed Forces Review Annual*, vol. 3: *1979* (Gulf Breeze, Fla.: Academic International Press, 1979), pp. 179, 197.

10. Ibid., p. 178. See also V. P. Glushko, *Development of Rocketry and Space Technology in the USSR* (Moscow: Novosti Press, 1973).

11. McDonnell, "Soviet Weapons Acquisition System," p. 178.

12. Ibid., p. 19. Most of the tactical and technical requirements are set by the military. However, development requests for SS-6 missiles appear to have come from the Korolev bureau for use in the space program, and the Chelomei bureau apparently suggested modifying the regional-range SS-11 for intercontinental tasks.

13. Ibid., p. 187.

for the supervision and operation of the missile design bureaus—the Yangel bureau (presumably with two ballistic-missile design teams), the Chelomei bureau (probably with a design team for cruise missiles and one each of land- and sea-based ballistic missiles), and the Nadiradize bureau with one design team.

Once the design is complete and a prototype is built, about ten flight tests are conducted as a preliminary evaluation by the design bureau.[14] At every stage the Strategic Rocket Forces (SRF) participate in the process. If the preliminary tests are successful, another ten to fifteen tests are conducted by the SRF before the missile either enters production or is rejected (production can include missiles for crew training and for reloads).

Production of the Soviet missiles is a large-scale and diverse operation. It may involve over sixty facilities located at Dnepropetrovsk, Plesetsk, and Bisk.[15] These factory complexes, because of long production runs, may be semiautonomous affiliates of the Yangel, Chelomei, and Nadiradize bureaus, respectively. Undoubtedly, however, the SRF maintains close contact with the production plants in order to insure quality control.

Each of the factory complexes may be capable of producing some 1,000–1,500 metric tons of missiles annually. The addition of 18 million square feet of floor space and the general modernization of factories in the early 1970s, probably undertaken to support simultaneous production of the SS-17 and the SS-18 by the Yangel bureau,[16] made it possible by 1976 for some 38,000 metric tons of ballistic missiles to be produced annually.[17]

The Design Bureau

The critical link in the acquisition process is the missile design bureau which brings together the design and development functions within the Ministry of GMB.[18] Soviet design bureaus tend to center on one man

14. *The SALT II Treaty,* Hearings before the Senate Foreign Relations Committee, 96 Cong. 1 sess. (U.S. Government Printing Office, 1979), pt. 2, p. 242.

15. *Aerospace Daily,* January 15 and 22, 1979; and *Allocation of Resources in the Soviet Union and China—1980,* Hearings before the Joint Economic Committee, 96 Cong. 2 sess. (GPO, 1980), pt. 6, p. 98.

16. *Allocation of Resources,* p. 26.

17. Reported in William L. Perry, "Research, Development, Testing, and Engineering FY 1979 Posture Statement" (U.S. Department of Defense, 1978).

18. Ibid.; McDonnell, "Soviet Weapons Acquisition System," pp. 181–84.

and to instill stability by their focus on steady improvement of existing systems and constant planning for follow-on systems. Thus while a missile design may be new, many of its components may already have been used in other weapons.

The design bureau itself will not necessarily engage in theoretical research on the tactical and technical requirements of a missile. Rather, it develops the specifications laid out by the Ministry of Defense or the research institutes supervised by the Ministry of GMB. While this somewhat limits the design bureau's definition of its own role in the acquisition process, it gives the bureau great freedom to find solutions. It is in this role that the design bureau is preeminent.

Because the Soviet system for acquiring missiles has developed a somewhat regular pattern, it is possible to reconstruct the set of military requirements that probably initiated the development of each missile. A typical cycle for acquisition of a missile may run fifteen years. It may take seven years just to turn a specific requirement request into a missile prototype. Two years of flight testing are likely to follow before deployment occurs. Finally, the production run is likely to take six years, with missile modifications made along the way.[19] By determining these phases it is possible to construct a general life cycle for the various missile systems.

Soviet Missile Designers

Each of the missile design bureaus represents the attempt of the Soviet defense industry to satisfy military requirements through long-term development and production cycles. Because of the nature of the Soviet weapon acquisition process, the importance of the design bureaus and their directors is magnified. Even today, the activity of the missile design bureaus reflects the influence of a handful of chief designers.

The leading figure in modern Soviet rocketry, regarded as the most brilliant of the Soviet rocket designers, is S. P. Korolev.[20] His main interest was in space exploration, although in order to attract support for his research, he was instrumental in developing military rockets for the army before World War II. A victim of Stalin's prewar purges,

19. Our estimates, based on our projections of the cycle of missile development and production.
20. Khrushchev, *Khrushchev Remembers,* p. 45.

Korolev resided in a special prison during the war and continued his rocket research.[21] After the war, he headed a design bureau that developed long-range rockets based on the V-2.

For several years Korolev was aided in this endeavor by M. K. Yangel, another Soviet rocket scientist.[22] By 1945 Yangel formed his own design bureau, based on other rockets the Germans had built. Both linked the German rocket legacy with Soviet missile development. It was Yangel's design bureau that produced the series of large ICBMs necessary to meet Soviet military requirements where Korolev failed.

Korolev's status as the chief designer of Soviet missiles, conferred in 1966, was confirmed by his role in developing the SS-6, the first ICBM, and the booster for the 1957 *Sputnik* launch.[23] Although never seriously deployed as a military weapon, the SS-6 was a very capable space booster when additional booster rockets were strapped to it.[24] Subsequent missiles designed by Korolev—the SS-8, the SS-10, and the G-class lunar rocket—were also relatively unsuccessful attempts to field military and space systems.[25] After Korolev's death in 1966, the post of chief designer shifted to Yangel until his death in 1971.

One of the more interesting missile designers is V. N. Chelomei whose reputation in Soviet rocketry has been mixed.[26] Chelomei and his designers have been responsible for a broad range of Soviet weapon systems, including cruise missiles and satellites. Although Chelomei's original expertise was in aviation propulsion,[27] he reportedly was introduced to rocket development by Korolev during the latter's time in prison.[28] During the course of his career in missile design, Chelomei apparently was in competition with Korolev to some degree for the leading role in rocket design. Chelomei's success was undoubtedly facilitated by his political connections (Khrushchev's son was one of his engineers)[29] and his flexibility in administering several successful missile

21. Leonid Vladimirov, *The Russian Space Bluff,* trans. David Floyd (London: Tom Stacey, 1971), p. 17.

22. Ibid., p. 43; James E. Oberg, *Red Star in Orbit* (Random House, 1981), pp. 45–46.

23. Khrushchev, *Khrushchev Remembers,* pp. 46–47.

24. Vladimirov, *Russian Space Bluff,* pp. 77–80.

25. Twenty-three SS-8 launchers were deployed while no SS-10s are believed to have become operational. Lawrence Freedman, *US Intelligence and the Soviet Strategic Threat* (Westview, 1977), pp. 100, 208.

26. Vladimirov, *Russian Space Bluff,* pp. 41, 60, 82.

27. Ibid., pp. 41, 46; Khrushchev, *Khrushchev Remembers,* p. 43.

28. Vladimirov, *Russian Space Bluff,* p. 41.

29. Ibid., p. 53; Khrushchev, *Khrushchev Remembers,* p. 43.

programs. The appointment of Chelomei to the Academy of Sciences in 1962 signified his growing importance and may have marked the shift of his design bureau's work into strategic missile development.[30] The prominence of Chelomei and his design teams has probably increased in recent years along with the expansion of their work on land- and sea-based strategic missile systems.

Although a modest amount of information about the early Soviet missile designers exists, relatively little is known about their successors, or of the head of the solid-fuel design bureau, V. N. Nadiradize. While the influence of contemporary designers may not rival that of their predecessors, the Soviet weapon acquisition process probably ensures that it continues to be substantial.

Missile Design Support

Another obvious indication of activity related to new missile work is nuclear weapon tests. These are the responsibility of the Ministry of Medium Machine Building which was established in 1953 and is run by Ye. P. Slavskiy.[31] The ministry, whose development cycle is probably very similar to that of the Ministry of GMB probably includes a central design office, a design bureau, and applied laboratories. Its military testing program is likely to be directed toward the same requirements as the Ministry of General Machine Building's missile programs.

While testing has occurred regularly since 1953 (except during the moratorium in 1959 and 1960), there have been surges in the test program that seem to indicate that new weapons or warheads are being readied for deployment. These surges have occurred roughly two to four years before flight testing of new missiles.[32]

The first surge, in 1956–58, may have included development of warheads that corresponded to the SS-4, SS-5, SS-6, and SS-7 missiles. The next series of tests, in 1961–62, was more extensive and may have included weapons for the SS-8, SS-9, SS-10, and SS-11, and possibly for

30. David S. Sullivan, "Evaluating U.S. Intelligence Estimates," in Roy Godson, ed., *Intelligence Requirements for the 1980's: Analysis and Estimates* (Washington: National Strategy Information Center, 1980), p. 59.

31. Karl F. Spielmann, "Defense Industrialists in the USSR," *Problems of Communism,* vol. 25 (September–October 1976), pp. 54–55.

32. Based on data in Stockholm International Peace Research Institute, *World Armaments and Disarmament: SIPRI Yearbook 1980* (London: Taylor and Francis, 1980).

the large Proton space booster. The next phase, in 1971–72, undoubtedly included warheads for the SS-16, SS-17, SS-18, SS-19, and SS-20, the Soviet Union's first missiles with multiple warheads capable of independent reentry. The testing in 1974 may have been for modifications of the SS-17, SS-18, and SS-19 to include single-warhead reentry vehicles. All of these testing cycles probably included tests for other systems such as submarine-launched ballistic missiles (SLBMs). The testing that began in 1978 may well have included warheads for the generation of ICBMs and SLBMs expected to begin testing in the early 1980s.

The Missile Development Approach

Broadly viewed, the Soviet missile development process is characterized by both diversity and continuity. Its diversity results from the varied military requirements it must meet as well as the several design bureaus it involves. Its continuity stems from the regularity of its modernization programs and from the stability offered by long-standing design bureaus. The process serves as a valuable register of the impact of important events in the evolution of the Soviet strategic force posture. The preeminence accorded to the strategic missile narrows the field of inquiry. And the categorization of missiles by design bureau, which indicates the distinctive priorities of each bureau, helps explain certain characteristics through successive missile generations.

Figure A-1 is a chronological reconstruction of the probable development of Soviet nuclear missiles by the major design bureaus. It was the first step in the construction of the life cycles of Soviet missile programs for this study. Initially there were two main missile design bureaus, headed by Korolev and Yangel. By the 1960s these had diversified into four bureaus. Korolev's bureau dropped out of military missile design, and a separate bureau appears to have been created out of Chelomei's bureau to develop long-range sea-based missiles. Missiles with common characteristics are assumed to have come from the same design bureau and to reflect the major focus of the bureau and its chief designer, as follows:[33]

33. Based on Khrushchev, *Khrushchev Remembers; Aerospace Daily,* January 15 and 22, 1979; Walter Pincus, *Washington Post,* January 7, 1979, June 26, 1980; Edward L. Warner III, *The Military in Contemporary Soviet Politics: An Institutional Analysis* (Praeger, 1977); Oleg Penkovskiy, *The Penkovskiy Papers,* trans. Peter Deriabin (Avon,

Figure A-1. Development of Soviet Ballistic Missiles, by Design Bureau, 1945–80

Figure A-1. Development of Soviet Ballistic Missiles, by Design Bureau, 1945–80

Korolev

Yangel

Nadiradize

Chelomei

Chelomei derivative

○ Begin design △ Flight Test ▷ Enter Service □ Space test and service ▮ Terminate development

▲ Shared technical characteristics (direction of arrow indicates technical flow)

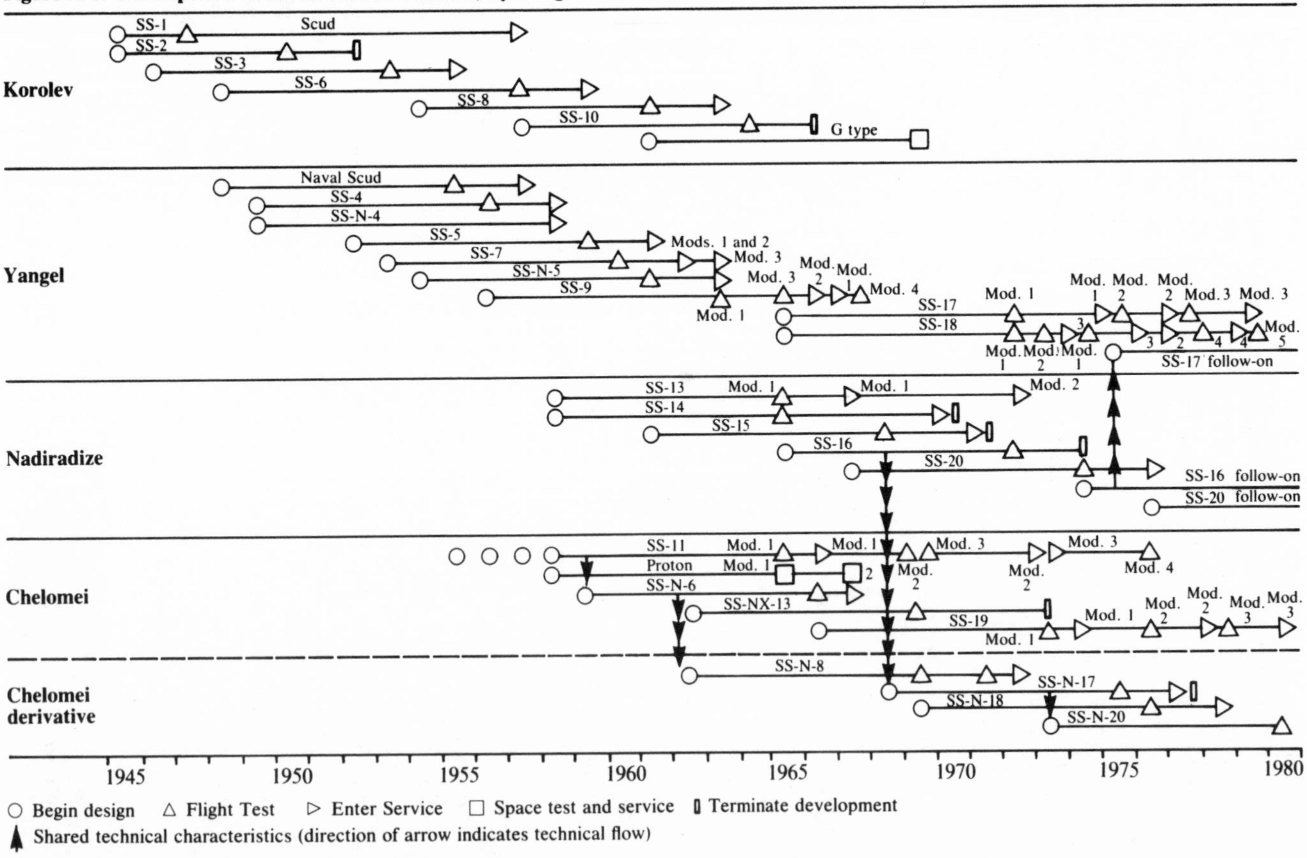

Chief designer	Major focus	Common characteristics
S. P. Korolev	Space boosters and global rockets	Nonstorable liquid fuel; large missiles
M. K. Yangel	Land-based ICBMs and MRBMs	Storable liquid fuel; large missiles
V. N. Nadiradize	Land-based military missiles	Solid fuel; small missiles
V. N. Chelomei	Cruise missiles, naval missiles, space boosters, and variable-range ICBMs	Storable liquid fuel; sea-based and variable-range missiles

Most of a missile's life cycle can be established from published data on its initial flight tests, its initial operational deployment, and its rate of deployment (or number of launchers in operation). Recasting such evidence makes it possible to estimate the date of initiation of missile development programs. Requirement studies and analysis—or program engineering—probably would begin about seven years before the missile's first flight test. Establishing the period when the missile's initial design requirements were set and predicating the characteristics of the missile on the presumed military requirements facing the USSR at the time provide a useful means of examining the evolution of the Soviet strategic force posture.

The life cycle of a Soviet strategic missile system from design initiation to retirement can extend twenty-five years. Almost inevitably, a tension develops between the missile's initial characteristics and its evolving mission assignments as military requirements change over time. To mitigate this problem, variants of a missile are often deployed as an interim measure until a totally new missile becomes available. The modifications are presented as part of each missile's development in figure A-1.

The deviations from normal patterns of Soviet missile development,

1965). See also Oberg, *Red Star in Orbit;* Vladimirov, *Russian Space Bluff;* Michael Stoiko, *Soviet Rocketry: Past, Present, and Future* (Holt, Rinehart and Winston, 1970); Matthew P. Gallagher and Karl F. Spielmann, Jr., *Soviet Decision-Making for Defense: A Critique of U.S. Perspectives on the Arms Race* (Praeger, 1972); William H. Schauer, *The Politics of Space: A Comparison of the Soviet and American Space Programs* (Holmes and Meier, 1976); U.S. Department of Defense, *Soviet Military Power* (GPO, 1981), p. 56; *Aviation Week and Space Technology,* March 31, 1969, December 7, 1970, June 25, 1979, June 16, 1980, November 3, 1980.

testing, or deployment often indicate that there have been important problems or redirections in Soviet strategic development. Sometimes, serious technical problems have hindered or even prevented deployment of missiles. At other times, changes have coincided with major shifts in Soviet military requirements, suggesting that high-level decisions had been made to redirect a missile's development. These deviations are a guide to important decision points for the Soviet strategic posture.

Examining the production of Soviet missile design bureaus provides a limited view of the development of Soviet strategic forces. It ignores important areas such as strategic bombers, missile-carrying submarines, and defenses, and it does little to reveal how the missiles were assigned or redirected once they were deployed. Nevertheless, focusing on the products of the Soviet missile design bureaus over time provides a useful baseline for charting the evolution of the Soviet strategic force posture since 1955.

Design and Operating Characteristics of Missiles

SOVIET missile designs since the end of World War II can be divided into five general categories, mainly based on the missiles' range capability. The Soviet military defines tactical missiles (with ranges up to 300 nautical miles) as those weapon systems operated by combat maneuver units that are in direct contact with the enemy. Operational-tactical missiles (with ranges of 300–600 nautical miles) are part of the weaponry to be used in combat missions of theater or front-level forces. Medium, intercontinental, and global missiles are all categorized as strategic missiles capable of destroying installations deep in enemy rear areas (medium range is 600–3,000 nautical miles, intercontinental 3,000–6,000 nautical miles, and global more than 6,000 nautical miles).[1] The history and capability of the missiles in each of the strategic categories is shown in tables B-1, B-2, B-3, and B-4, at the end of this appendix.

Given the USSR's strong emphasis on the advantages of ballistic missile systems at all levels of warfare, the development of these systems can be assumed to reflect both the operational requirements of the Soviet military and the technological advances within the missile development programs.

Design Characteristics

The Soviet Union has produced four generations of land-based ICBMs. By the mid-1980s it is likely to be producing a fifth. Each missile system seeks to match the best available technology with broad operational requirements. Thus changes in the military requirements that a

1. *Dictionary of Basic Military Terms: A Soviet View* (U.S. Government Printing Office, 1976), p. 192.

missile is expected to meet can cause dramatic shifts in a design program. Changes in performance characteristics are primarily based on advances in propulsion, guidance, and warhead development.

Propulsion Systems

Soviet missile designers have relied on nonstorable liquid, storable liquid, and solid fuel systems for rocket propellants and motors.[2] Nonstorable liquid fuels, mostly derivatives of liquid oxygen mixtures, had the advantage immediately after World War II of being produced by a still-active wartime industry while other propellant systems were in the development stage. Because the fuel, with its corrosive chemicals, could be kept aboard a missile for only a short time, the missile was kept unfilled and thus had a long operational life. Further, it was comparatively easy to predict the rate at which the fuel would burn and thus the range and accuracy of the missile. However, the volatility of the fuel and the militarily significant amount of time required to fuel the missile for launch limited the usefulness of such missiles for combat deployment. These characteristics did not affect space flight efforts, however. The Korolev design bureau based its early short-range systems (SS-1, SS-2, SS-3) as well as its intercontinental ballistic missiles (ICBMs)(SS-6, SS-8, SS-10) on this technology.[3]

Storable liquid fuels have some of the advantages of pure liquids. Their rate of burn, and the missile's accuracy, can be fairly well predicted. Because the fuels can be stored on the missile, they can be circulated frequently with a relatively low danger of explosion and without reducing the missile's longevity. Missiles fueled with storable liquids can be launched on short notice—perhaps within four to eight minutes. And those with large payloads can be fired without incurring the cost penalties that highly refined solid fuels may impose. The Yangel design team first introduced this technology in 1954 when it started production efforts for the SS-4 and SS-5 medium-range ballistic missiles (MRBM) and the SS-7 ICBM. In addition, V. N. Chelomei adapted this technology to the missiles designed by his bureau.[4]

2. Bill Gunston, *The Illustrated Encyclopaedia of the World's Rockets & Missiles* (Crescent Books, 1979), pp. 16, 50–56.

3. Nikita Khrushchev, *Khrushchev Remembers: The Last Testament,* ed. and trans. Strobe Talbott (Little, Brown, 1974), pp. 43–48.

4. Ibid., pp. 52–53.

Solid fuels have raised entirely different problems for Soviet missile designers. They have been used successfully in short-range offensive and defensive missile systems, but the technology apparently has not been readily transferred to long-range ICBMs. Solid fuels offer the advantage that they allow missiles to be launched at the turn of a key. Moreover, a given volume of solid fuel is more efficient and powerful than the same volume of storable liquids.[5] But the unpredictable rate of burn of the fuel means that a missile's accuracy depends on its guidance system being nearly perfect. This may have been a major constraint on Soviet plans to utilize solid fuels. The USSR has also found it difficult to refine, package, and mass produce the fuel grains that make up a solid fuel system. Unless all ingredients can be precisely measured and uniformly produced, the rocket motors' overall reliability and range are uncertain. Solid fuels may limit the service lifetime that the USSR has come to expect from storable liquid fuel missiles and that its acquisition and retirement practices are based on. Only the Nadiradize bureau has deployed missiles fired with solid fuel. The Yangel bureau seems likely to move into solid fuels and the Chelomei bureau derivative has used them in its experimental sea-based missile, the SS-NX-20.

Guidance Systems

Four basic types of missile guidance (beyond simple free flight) have been used or tested by the USSR—autopilot guidance, much like that the German V-2 used; radio-command guidance, where ground-control stations continually track the missile to correct its flight path; fly-the-wire guidance, a simple form of inertial guidance based on calculations made before the flight; and inertial guidance, where an onboard computer keeps the missile on course. Additionally, the missile's warhead may employ a terminal guidance system that uses a sensor to zero in on the target.[6]

Early Soviet ballistic missiles used autopilot guidance systems or were even unguided. All of the algorithmic calculations for estimating range, azimuth, and so forth, for the autopilot system used an artillery-like firing table. These techniques would not have been acceptable for missiles of medium or intercontinental ranges.

5. For instance, see the relative yields and weight ratios of various missiles. This may also increase with the size of the missile.
6. Gunston, *Rockets & Missiles,* pp. 17, 48.

Radio-command guidance, from ground stations located every 250 miles along a missile's initial flight path, greatly improved the accuracy of long-range missile flights.[7] Once the missile left Soviet airspace, however, its accuracy depreciated rapidly. The USSR deployed large numbers of SS-4 and SS-5 medium-range missiles which would not be so handicapped by radio guidance as ICBMs. A more direct problem than that of guidance for radio-command missiles is their high susceptibility to electronic jamming by the enemy. In addition, only one missile at each base can be launched at a time. All of these factors would play havoc with the flight and eventual impact of missiles as well as foreclosing the possibility of a coordinated strike.[8]

One way to overcome these problems is to use inertial guidance. Yet as late as development of the SS-15 intermediate-range ballistic missile (IRBM), the Soviet Union was unable to mass produce the sophisticated mechanical and electrical components of an advanced inertial-guidance system.

The technical shortcomings of the Soviet production system may have caused a variety of problems. For example, the USSR's inability to maintain, without great expense, a large number of missiles on combat alert arose from the fact that the gyroscope in its guidance systems—necessary to induce stability in the missile—rotated on metal ball bearings, not on the gas-actuated bearings found on U.S. missile systems. The guidance system thus needed some time to warm up before a missile could be launched. And in any sustained period of holding a missile ready for immediate launching, the entire guidance system would fail because the ball bearings, which were mass produced to less than perfect tolerances, would fail under such continuing stress.[9] If guidance systems could not be held on alert for more than 12 hours, and 10 percent of a force of ICBMs had to be put on alert each day, 20 percent of the guidance systems would have to be replaced on the first day and the entire force of ICBMs would be incapacitated after five days. Clearly, as its reliance on ICBMs increased, the USSR could not afford lengthy alert rates.

Deficiencies in the military industrial research and development base also delayed introduction of a sophisticated computer-driven inertial-

7. Khrushchev, *Khrushchev Remembers*, p. 48.
8. Ibid.; *New York Times*, July 26, 1962.
9. Interview with Defense Secretary Harold Brown in "Could Russia Blunder into Nuclear War?" *U.S. News and World Report*, September 5, 1977, p. 18.

guidance system on Soviet missiles. There was a moderately effective substitute, however, in fly-the-wire guidance, a simpler but less reliable type of onboard inertial-guidance system. Inertial guidance allows a missile to respond to changes automatically, while fly-the-wire guidance must be planned before launch. Unanticipated errors cannot be corrected in flight, and accuracy can decrease correspondingly.

By 1973 a first-generation onboard, inertial computer system, still using fly-the-wire commands, had been approved for use and deployment. It allows Soviet missiles to continually monitor and correct deviations from flight path and it is less inaccurate than earlier systems. In the short term, the USSR will probably seek to improve the accuracy of this system by improving computer parts and such subcomponents as ball bearings. Over the long term it might add terminal guidance, which would allow a reentry vehicle to compare a live radar return from a target area with a stored radar image of the area and adjust its flight until the images matched. Early terminal-guidance techniques may have been tested on the Chelomei bureau's SS-NX-13, a tactical missile produced for the Navy.

Warhead Design

Another factor that influences a missile's effectiveness is its reentry vehicle, which contains the warhead. The characteristics of the reentry vehicle determine whether the warhead will be less accurate than the missile itself was during its flight. Soviet reentry vehicles may use heavy shielding designed to protect the warhead against the many indirect effects of nuclear detonation, whether induced by defensive or other offensive vehicles. And to insure against unplanned detonation, the reentry vehicles probably carry complicated arming and fusing mechanisms.[10] The accuracy of the warhead is influenced by the combination of its weight and size and the amount of aerodynamic drag on it when it enters the earth's atmosphere. These three factors—represented as the reentry vehicle's "beta" value—determine its reentry speed. The higher the beta value the less subject the reentry vehicle is to atmospheric forces such as wind and rain that can degrade its accuracy. Also, the higher the beta value the less time the reentry vehicle is exposed to the

---

10. Stephen A. Garrett, "Détente and the Military Balance," *Bulletin of the Atomic Scientists,* April 1977, p. 15.

risk of antiballistic missiles (ABMs) while it travels through the atmosphere.

Patterns of Missile Deployment

Over the past twenty years, steady and impressive advances in the Strategic Rocket Forces' missile basing system and in Soviet deployments of sea-based missiles have increased the survivability of the Soviet strategic forces. The deployment of its strategic missiles is one of the important indicators of the Soviet Union's strategic priorities and concerns. At times, survivability may have been a more important and achievable objective of Soviet strategic planning than strike capability.

Land-based Missiles

Land-based missiles have been deployed aboveground on unprotected launching pads, on protected sites, and in mobile systems, and underground in hardened silos. Though harder and better constructed fixed sites and a high degree of mobility have increased the survivability of the Soviet missile force, they have forced the USSR to sacrifice some of its earlier, notable ability to reload missile launchers.

The first Soviet strategic missiles, the regional-range SS-4 and SS-5, were deployed aboveground in the early 1960s in clusters of three or four relatively soft launchers, each with a reload missile.[11] From 1963 to 1966, 135 of these missiles were placed in hardened shelters. The hardening program then ceased,[12] probably because of the priority placed on construction of silos for the SS-9 and SS-11, which began to be deployed in 1964, and a desire to retain the reload capability that softer sites provided.

The SS-4 and SS-5 force continued to be relatively vulnerable to attack by Western nuclear forces, a problem the USSR appeared to be planning to alleviate by deploying mobile missiles. Soviet military writings in the 1960s frequently noted the ability of mobile missiles to evade enemy surveillance. In the mid-1960s the Soviet Union started

11. See Graham T. Allison, *Essence of Decision: Explaining the Cuban Missile Crisis* (Little, Brown, 1971), p. 104.

12. "Statement of Secretary of Defense Robert S. McNamara before the House Armed Services Committee on the Fiscal Year 1968–72 Defense Program and 1968 Defense Budget," declassified material (U.S. Department of Defense, 1967), p. 47.

testing the SS-14 medium-range and the SS-15 intermediate-range missiles, which employed mobile launch systems. However, because of problems with their solid-fuel propellants, neither was deployed in large numbers for any length of time.

During the 1960s the USSR substantially improved the survivability of its growing intercontinental-range missile force, although improvements in the U.S. Minuteman ICBMs continued to keep a large portion of the SRF's missile force vulnerable. Yet, by the end of the decade, the overall survivability of the Soviet intercontinental missile force had been substantially upgraded.

The early Soviet deployments of the SS-6 at soft, aboveground launch pads were vulnerable by any standards. Both launch areas and support facilities had to be exposed because of the awkwardness and volatility of the missile's nonstorable liquid fuel. As the second-generation SS-7 and SS-8 were deployed, greater attention was given to their protection and concealment, but like the SS-4 and SS-5 force, most of them were deployed in soft, concentrated clusters with two launchers per site.[13]

One advantage of basing missile launchers in a cluster was to ease their reloading once they had been fired. And clustered launchers were probably easier than single missiles to defend with surface-to-air missiles (SAMs) against enemy bomber attack. By the early 1960s, however, the major U.S. threat was shifting from bombers to missiles; with ICBMs, warning time was minimal and defenses nonexistent. Even a nominal, one-megaton blast delivered by an ICBM detonating as far away as one-half mile would have an excellent chance of disabling an entire cluster and obviating any reload advantage. Consequently, beginning in 1962, the Strategic Rocket Forces began placing their ICBMs in separate coffin-like revetments, with three launchers per site,[14] and later in first-generation underground silos. The priority on survivability and ability to reload would be affirmed in succeeding generations.

With deployment of the third-generation SS-9 and SS-11, the clustering of launchers ceased and ICBMs were deployed in separated, underground silos, hardened to withstand blasts of about 200–400 pounds per square inch (psi).[15] The USSR's priorities shifted to emphasize missile protection over ability to refire rapidly.

13. Hanson W. Baldwin, *New York Times,* July 26, 1962.

14. Ibid.

15. "Statement of Secretary of Defense on the Fiscal Year 1966–70 Defense Program and 1966 Defense Budget," p. 50; International Institute for Strategic Studies, *Strategic Survey 1977* (London: IISS, 1978), p. 116; John Erickson, *Soviet–Warsaw Pact Force Levels,* USSI Report 76-2 (Washington, D.C.: U.S. Strategic Institute, 1976), p. 27.

In the fourth-generation deployments the Soviet Union made major strides in survivability. All of the new SS-17, SS-18, and SS-19 ICBMs and modifications of the SS-11 were emplaced in very hard silos estimated to be capable of withstanding approximately 4,000 psi in blast overpressure.[16] In addition to a tremendous amount of concrete, the missile was given internal cushioning; support equipment was removed from the lip of the silo, where it was highly vulnerable to attack, and placed in the silo itself.[17] Soviet interest in a reload capability resurfaced in the SS-17 and SS-18, which could be launched cold, holding engine ignition until after the ICBM was propelled out of the silo, which meant that the silo could be more easily refurbished and reloaded with reserve missiles.[18] With these deployments the USSR can be reasonably confident that at least in the near future the United States is unlikely to have large enough numbers of very accurate warheads to effectively neutralize its hardened missile force.

The Soviet motivation for undertaking these expensive hedges against ICBM vulnerability could have been the reported U.S. interest in the late 1960s in developing a much more accurate, large throw-weight ICBM known as the WS-120A. Soviet expectations that such a weapon would be deployed during the lifetime of its fourth-generation ICBMs may have persuaded the USSR to devote substantial resources to insuring its missiles' survivability, including the development of mobile missile systems. This interest was initially manifested in the mid-1960s with the SS-14 and SS-15 mobile systems. Western analysts had expected the solid-fuel SS-13 ICBM to be mobile,[19] but because of technical problems it was only deployed in small numbers in silos.

16. "Soviets' Nuclear Arsenal Continues to Proliferate," *Aviation Week and Space Technology,* June 16, 1980, p. 67.

17. *United States Military Posture for FY 1978* (U.S. Office of the Joint Chiefs of Staff, 1977), p. 17; William Beecher, "SIG: What the Arms Agreement Doesn't Cover," *Sea Power,* December 1972, pp. 8–9.

18. Serious debate exists over the USSR's ability to reload silos rapidly (within 24 hours) and over whether it has stockpiled ICBMs for the reload mission. See Clarence A. Robinson, Jr., "Soviet SALT Violations Feared," *Aviation Week and Space Technology,* September 22, 1980, pp. 14–15; Henry S. Bradsher, *Washington Star,* April 12, 1979.

19. Lawrence Freedman, *US Intelligence and the Soviet Strategic Threat* (Westview, 1977), p. 135. While there are apparently no U.S. reports concerning the testing of the SS-13 ICBM as a mobile missile, Soviet statements have alluded to a solid-fuel, mobile ICBM. See Lt. Col. V. M. Bondarenko, "Military-Technical Superiority: The Most Important Factor of the Reliable Defense of the Country," in William R. Kintner and Harriet Fast Scott, eds. and trans., *The Nuclear Revolution in Soviet Military Affairs* (University of Oklahoma Press, 1968), pp. 357–58.

In the 1970s the USSR developed two new solid-fuel mobile missiles, the intermediate-range SS-20 and the intercontinental SS-X-16. The SS-20 was put into operation but the USSR, in adherence with the proposed SALT II treaty, chose not to deploy the SS-X-16 in order to avoid verification problems with the technically similar SS-20.[20]

The SS-20, which is replacing the SS-4 and SS-5 force, is the SRF's first operational mobile missile. It is not likely, however, to travel randomly in search of concealed firing areas. Probably, an SS-20 regiment will be garrisoned at a central base and dispersed at various times to designated areas to await firing instructions.[21] The dispersion would increase the missiles' survivability. They would still enjoy air defense cover, offer economy in operation, and retain the reloading capability in the garrison area.

The generation of Soviet land-based missiles to be deployed in the 1980s is likely to continue both trends of greater hardening and more mobility. Whether a silo hardened up to 6,000 psi[22] will be able to offset U.S. advances in missile accuracy is open to question; indeed, once certain accuracy thresholds have been crossed, confidence in silo hardness would become fairly low. The USSR is thus more likely to place emphasis on a new mobile solid-fuel ICBM that is under development.[23]

Sea-based Missiles

Unlike land-based ICBMs, the sea-based strategic missile force has relied on missile range and factors other than the launch platform to enhance its survivability. Postwar exploration of the feasibility of German experiments to launch ballistic missiles from sea-going containers towed by submarines convinced the USSR early in the 1950s to shift its efforts to developing a missile that could be launched from the submarine itself. The USSR's first-generation sea-launched ballistic missile, the SS-N-4 Sark, was deployed in 1958 on six medium-range, diesel-powered patrol submarines converted to carry two missile launchers in their conning towers. The missiles could only be launched while

20. U.S. Department of State, Bureau of Public Affairs, *SALT II Agreement, Vienna, June 18, 1979*, Selected Document 12A (GPO, 1979), pp. 15–16, 34.

21. William Beecher, *Boston Globe*, September 5, 1976.

22. Clarence A. Robinson, Jr., "Soviets Testing New Generation of ICBM," *Aviation Week and Space Technology*, November 3, 1980, p. 28.

23. Ibid.

the submarine was on the surface and they had a relatively limited range of 350 nautical miles.[24] But the handful of these Zulu-V-class submarines provided the USSR with its initial sea-based ballistic missile force as well as a prototype system for training crew members and developing more advanced systems (see table B-5).

The Zulu-V class was soon followed by the Golf-class diesel-powered and the Hotel-class nuclear-powered submarines. Twenty-three G-class submarines were originally deployed (one sank in the Pacific in 1968) and eight H-class.[25] Both types of submarine were originally deployed with the surface-launched SS-N-4 ballistic missile, but in 1963 they were refitted with the more advanced SS-N-5 missile that could be launched from a submerged submarine.[26]

In 1967 the third-generation Soviet Yankee-class submarine went to sea, and the next year it became operational.[27] This submarine, a significant improvement over its predecessors, carried the SS-N-6 missile which some analysts contend was actually a "quick fix" substituted for the tactical SS-NX-13 (which was tested but never deployed).[28] Thirty-four Yankee-class submarines were deployed between 1966 and 1974.[29] They began to be dismantled in accord with SALT I (the Strategic Arms Limitation Talks), as newer Delta-class submarines became available. One Yankee II has been converted into a platform for testing the solid-fuel SS-NX-17 missile.[30]

The first Delta-class submarine, armed with the deep-strike SS-N-8 missile, became operational in July 1973.[31] The Delta II differed from

24. *Fiscal Year 1972 Authorization for Military Procurement, Research and Development, Construction and Real Estate Acquisition for the Safeguard ABM, and Reserve Strengths,* Hearings before the Senate Armed Services Committee, 92 Cong. 1 sess. (GPO, 1971), pt. 4, p. 3447.

25. Ibid.; U.S. Office of the Chief of Naval Operations *Understanding Soviet Naval Developments,* 4th ed. (GPO, 1981), p. 92. Official Defense Department statements in recent years credit the USSR with having built eight Hotel-class SSBNs, while Defense Department reports prior to the *United States Military Posture for FY 1977* statement state that the Soviets constructed nine Hotel-class submarines. *Understanding Soviet Naval Developments,* p. 93.

26. *United States Military Posture for FY 1979,* p. 28.

27. Ibid., pp. 27, 30.

28. *United States Military Posture for FY 1978,* p. 16; K. J. Moore, Mark Flanigan, and Robert D. Helsel, "Developments in Submarine Systems, 1956–76," in Michael MccGwire and John McDonnell, eds., *Soviet Naval Influence: Domestic and Foreign Dimensions* (Praeger for the Centre for Foreign Policy Studies, Department of Political Science, Dalhousie University, 1977), p. 172.

29. *United States Military Posture for FY 1978,* p. 17.

30. *Understanding Soviet Naval Developments,* p. 98.

31. *Department of Defense Appropriations for 1977,* Hearings before a Subcommittee of the House Appropriations Committee, 94 Cong. 2 sess. (GPO, 1976), pt. 2, p. 7.

the Delta I only in its greater length, which accommodated a larger number of launchers.[32] The range of the SS-N-8 missiles allows the Delta-class submarines to cover their targets in the United States from safer, home waters.

The next submarine-launched missile, the SS-N-18 with multiple warheads, was deployed on Delta-III submarines. The USSR's latest submarine, the large Typhoon-class, is probably intended to carry the new SS-NX-20 missile, if it is successfully tested and deployed.[33]

The Soviet ballistic-missile submarine force has gradually expanded its deployments, so that by 1980 it was active in three of the four main fleets of the Soviet Navy. About 70 percent of the submarines are assigned to the Northern Fleet based at Murmansk on the Kola Peninsula;[34] they are deployed to regular patrol areas in the Barents, Norwegian, and Greenland seas, as well as forward to stations off the eastern coast of the United States. Most of the others are stationed with the Pacific Fleet at the submarine base at Petropavlovsk on the Kamchatka Peninsula. The USSR reportedly is constructing another base in the Far East in the Kuril Islands.[35] Six Golf II submarines were deployed to the Baltic Fleet for the first time in 1976.[36]

The early generation of ballistic-missile submarines, the Z-V, G, and H classes, were probably not deployed beyond Soviet home waters until the mid-1960s. After an extensive ocean survey, the USSR began to regularly patrol Golf- and Hotel-class submarines in the open ocean areas by 1966.[37]

In early 1966, the USSR undertook its first underwater, around-the-world cruise by nuclear powered submarines.[38] The regular patrol areas of the G- and H-class submarines at this time were west of the Azores

---

32. *United States Military Posture for FY 1979,* p. 22.

33. *Understanding Soviet Naval Developments,* p. 96.

34. *Fiscal Year 1979 Arms Control Impact Statements,* Joint Committee Print, Statements Submitted to the House International Relations Committee and the Senate Foreign Relations Committee, 95 Cong. 2 sess. (GPO, 1978), p. 167.

35. "Soviets Deploy SS-N-18," *Aviation Week and Space Technology,* November 13, 1978, p. 58.

36. *Understanding Soviet Naval Developments,* p. 11.

37. Michael Getler, "Soviet Missile Subs Patrol Off U.S.," *Missiles and Rockets,* April 4, 1966, p. 12; Charles C. Petersen, "Trends in Soviet Naval Operations," in Bradford Dismukes and James M. McConnell, eds., *Soviet Naval Diplomacy* (Pergamon, 1979), pp. 77–84.

38. For reference, see Robert Waring Herrick, "The USSR's 'Blue Belt': A Unified Military Plan for Defense Against Seaborne Nuclear Attack by Strike Carriers and Polaris/Poseidon SSBNs," in Paul J. Murphy, ed., *Naval Power in Soviet Policy* (GPO, 1978), pp. 169–71.

and east of Nova Scotia in the Atlantic and west of Hawaii in the Pacific.[39] Not until late 1969 did the first Yankee-class submarines initiate continuous patrols along the Atlantic coast of the United States, one deployed north of Bermuda and the other south of Bermuda.[40] A Hotel-class nuclear-powered submarine continued to be maintained east of Nova Scotia and a Golf-class diesel-powered submarine west of the Azores. Yankee-class submarines began continuous patrols in the northeast Pacific by 1970 with one submarine stationed west of Hawaii.[41]

By 1974 Delta-class submarines carrying the long-range SS-N-8 or SS-N-18 missiles had initiated regular patrols. They remain close to home waters and are able to cover most U.S. targets, while Yankee-class submarines continue on patrol off the East and West coasts of the United States.[42]

Operating Characteristics

Soviet design bureaus seem to specialize in missiles that fall into range groups. The longer-range weapons capable of striking enemy targets of strategic importance can be subdivided into medium-range, intercontinental, and global missiles. Improvements in the design and operating characteristics of strategic missiles show a logical progression within these categories.

The foundation for the development of the USSR's entire ballistic-missile fleet rests on work on tactical-range missiles that began immediately after World War II. Work by the S. P. Korolev bureau based on German V-2 technology provided the operational know-how for much longer range missiles. The bureau's SS-1 and SS-2 missiles, tested in 1947 and 1950,[43] are believed to have served only as research and

39. Getler, "Soviet Missile Subs," p. 12.
40. William Beecher, *New York Times,* April 24, 1970; George C. Wilson, *Washington Post,* November 6, 1970; Neil Sheehan, *New York Times,* October 4, 1970; Robert G. Weinland, "The State and Future of the Soviet Navy in the North Atlantic," in MccGwire and McDonnell, *Soviet Naval Influence,* pp. 411–12.
41. Orr Kelly, *Washington Star,* April 20, 1973; "Soviet Y-class Submarine Off Hawaii," *Aviation Week and Space Technology,* May 10, 1971, p. 14; Petersen, "Trends in Soviet Naval Operations," pp. 77–84.
42. George C. Wilson, *Washington Post,* April 28, 1975; Petersen, "Trends in Soviet Naval Operations," pp. 77–84; *Department of Defense Annual Report Fiscal Year 1980,* p. 72; *United States Military Posture for FY 1982,* p. 100.
43. Ray Bonds, ed., *The Soviet War Machine: An Encyclopaedia of Russian Military Equipment and Strategy* (London: Chartwell, 1976), pp. 202–03.

development test beds and crew training platforms. The third version of the SS-1 had two and one-half times more thrust than the original V-2, as did the SS-2 which had extra fuel tanks and a longer range than the SS-1.

Operational-tactical missiles, which are assigned to the higher Soviet command echelons (front level), have a range that falls between those of tactical and strategic missiles. These missiles offer a certain flexibility to Soviet tactical planners since they are more likely to survive the initial phases of a conflict than aircraft are. Their response time and the size of their nuclear warheads (or special nonnuclear munitions) make them well suited for use by higher commands hundreds of miles away from the tactical operations of Soviet divisions or naval formations.

Operational-tactical missiles have received only modest attention from Soviet designers, possibly because those already deployed appear to be adequate for tactical purposes or because other weapon systems, such as cruise missiles, can do the job.

The SS-3 Shyster was a logical next step from the SS-1 and SS-2 tactical missiles toward longer-range missile systems.[44] Its major drawback was the vulnerability in combat of the simple rail and pad from which it was launched. Its replacement, the SS-12 Scaleboard, deployed on wheeled trucks, eliminated that liability. The new SS-22 missile, expected to replace the SS-12, is also mobile.

Soviet sea-based missiles have a mobility that enables them to perform in a variety of wartime roles. For instance, short-range missiles such as the SS-N-4 launched from submarines are deployed to cover intercontinental targets such as U.S. naval bases. Therefore, the submarine-launched missile cannot be strictly categorized by range capability. Initial development of these missiles began in the early postwar years as the Soviets explored the feasibility of such German experiments as the launching of V-2 ballistic missiles from sea-going containers, towed underwater by a submarine and uprighted before launching.[45] Tests in the early 1950s of the Golem missile, an advanced Soviet version of the V-2, proved this launching system to be infeasible and led to development of a missile that would be launched from the submarine itself. In the first launch of a ballistic missile from a submarine, in September 1955, a

44. The range of the SS-3 was about 600 miles, twice that of the SS-2 and four times that of the SS-1. The SS-3 could have carried a 200-kiloton warhead.

45. Siegfried Breyer and Norman Polmar, *Guide to the Soviet Navy,* 2d ed. (Naval Institute Press, 1977), pp. 62–63.

short-range ground force weapon, the Scud, was launched while the submarine was on the surface.[46]

The first-generation sea-launched ballistic missile, the SS-N-4 Sark, was deployed on Golf-class diesel-powered submarines in 1958 and on Hotel-class nuclear-powered submarines in 1959. A third-generation operational-tactical missile, the SS-NX-13, which was probably never deployed, apparently was intended for use as a defense against aircraft carriers or even other nuclear-powered submarines.[47]

Medium-range Missiles

Development of the Soviet Union's medium-range missiles has reflected the evolution of its military requirements in the regions surrounding it. Along with medium bombers, these missiles are responsible for covering a wide range of targets in Europe, the Middle East, and Asia.

In many respects the medium-range missiles (table B-1) are distinct from other Soviet strategic missiles. The initial models of the SS-4 and SS-5 were deployed aboveground in soft bases so that they could be reloaded. Missiles in the medium-range category are the only land-based, mobile ballistic missiles that the USSR has deployed. The SS-14 and SS-15 were never assigned to regular missile units, but their follow-on, the SS-20, is a successful mobile system.

The medium-range force is also notable because certain of its missile systems—the SS-11 and its follow-on, the SS-19—are capable of striking regional and intercontinental targets. At least one field of SS-11 and SS-19 intercontinental-range missiles, comprising 180 silos, appears to be assigned to covering a variety of regional Western targets in wartime.[48] Others, closer to China, could be considered targeted at that country. One missile that appears to have drawn on the SS-11 for components is the SS-N-6. Some analysts believe it was an interim system to be deployed on Yankee-class submarines while the SS-NX-13 was being developed.

Intercontinental-range Missiles

Intercontinental-range missiles have been one of the most challenging areas and highest priorities in the postwar development of Soviet weapon

46. Moore, Flanigan, and Helsel, "Developments in Submarine Systems," p. 153. Breyer and Polmar, *Guide to the Soviet Navy*, pp. 62–63.

47. *United States Military Posture for FY 1978*, p. 16.

48. Ibid.

systems. These weapons are dedicated to covering large numbers of different types of targets located primarily in the U.S. mainland. Until the late 1970s intercontinental ballistic missiles were the predominant means for covering such targets, and a small number of heavy bombers and sea-based nuclear forces was available to help in the task. Since the late 1960s the USSR has produced significant numbers of long-range, submarine-launched ballistic missiles capable of striking these targets. The sea-based missiles deployed on Delta-class submarines (table B-4) may be (in operational terms at least) merely an extension of the Soviet land-based ICBM force.

Given the importance of the ballistic missile in the Soviet strategic force posture, the USSR has attempted to build into its missile force the kind of flexibility manifested by the U.S. strategic bomber force. Some of the medium-range missiles that are capable of attacking targets at intercontinental ranges were merely upgraded to that range, while flexibility was part of the original design of other missiles.

The world's first ICBM was the SS-6 Sapwood (table B-2). Because of many problems with its fueling system, such as reaction times as long as twelve hours, and the high susceptibility of its guidance system to electronic jamming, its success as an ICBM was limited. But as a booster rocket the SS-6 eventually became the workhorse of the Soviet Union's space program. The SS-7 Saddler, the first Soviet ICBM to be mass produced, was also the first Soviet ICBM to employ storable liquid fuel.[49] Another second-generation ICBM, the SS-8 Sasin, was at one time thought to have emphasized electromagnetic pulse (EMP) rather than blast for its destructive effect.[50]

In the third modification of the SS-9 Scarp a fractional orbital bombardment system (FOBS) was introduced and in the fourth the USSR's first multiple-reentry-vehicle (MRV) system. The fifth modification of the SS-9 is a space booster for the Soviet antisatellite systems launched from above-ground pads in Tyuratam.

The SS-11, notable for its ability to strike targets at regional as well as intercontinental ranges, was the first light ICBM developed by the USSR and as such reflected a change in Soviet targeting requirements. The first modification may have had initially a range of only 3,000 nautical miles, commensurate with its origins as a naval or regional strike system. The second modification was the first Soviet ICBM to carry penetration

49. Gunston, *Rockets & Missiles,* p. 52.
50. Freedman, *US Intelligence,* p. 100.

aids such as chaff or decoys.[51] The third modification, the first operational MRV system in the Soviet inventory, carries three 350-kiloton warheads; it operates on a rail dispensing system rather than a post-boost vehicle reentry bus. The fourth modification of the SS-11, which is also an MRV system, has warheads that reportedly reenter the atmosphere simultaneously and at a very low speed;[52] they may have been designed for such specialized missions as chemical strikes against aircraft carriers or possibly even as antisubmarine weapons. All told, some 1,030 SS-11 launchers were constructed in modestly hard underground silos, including over 300 launchers in missile fields near Europe and China.

The SS-13 Savage, the first Soviet ICBM to use solid fuel, represented a shift away from large missiles. The SS-13 was first tested in 1965 and was deployed in 1967–69. Only sixty were ever deployed, probably because of problems encountered with the last-stage rocket motor. At one time the United States had estimated that as many as 300 might be deployed both in silos and mobile launchers to fill a pressing Soviet requirement for a survivable strategic reserve. The SS-X-16, a direct follow-on to the SS-13, was never deployed because of limitations in the proposed SALT II treaty. However, by 1977 over 100 reportedly had been produced for test purposes.[53]

The SS-17 fulfills SS-7 mission requirements, although it is replacing SS-11 missiles in their silos. Along with the SS-18 and SS-19 ICBMs, the SS-17 was capable of delivering the more accurate multiple, independently targeted reentry vehicle (MIRV) warheads. It can be launched cold, being ejected from the silo before its engine ignites.

The SS-18 is a follow-on design and replacement for the SS-9. The second modification of the SS-18, with two combinations of multiple warheads, encountered development problems that the fourth modification appears to have remedied.

The SS-19, a direct follow-on in design and mission to the SS-11, proved so successful in flight tests (with reliability values of 90 percent reportedly) that it immediately began to be deployed in very hard underground silos formerly occupied by the SS-11.

Soviet intercontinental-range submarine-launched missiles appear to

51. "Statements of Secretary of Defense on the Fiscal Year 1967–71 Defense Program and 1971 Budget," p. 57; "DIA Official Notes Uncertainty About 'MOD 4' of Soviets SS-11 ICBMs," *Aerospace Daily,* December 18, 1979.

52. *Aerospace Daily,* December 18, 1979.

53. Bernard Weintraub, *New York Times,* November 3, 1977; "SS-16 Deployment Raises Senate Questions," *Aviation Week and Space Technology,* September 24, 1979, p. 24.

be distinguished from their shorter-range predecessors by their greater dedication to the role of intercontinental strategic strike. Their many similarities to land-based ICBMs suggest that in wartime they would be directly controlled by the Supreme High Command. The first of these missiles was the SS-N-8, whose strategic reserve mission was to include deep strikes against U.S. mainland targets. A direct product improvement of the SS-N-8, the SS-N-18, was the first Soviet submarine-launched ballistic missile (SLBM). This missile, with its long range, will significantly enhance Soviet sea-based coverage of targets deep in the U.S. homeland.

The fifth-generation SS-NX-20, which uses solid-fuel propellant, would be a major improvement to the Soviet Union's sea-based strategic reserve.

Global Missiles

Global missiles, which are readily adaptable to changes in targeting doctrine as well as to supporting the Soviet space program, are assigned area targets such as U.S. Strategic Air Command bases or economic centers (table B-3). They have also had some interesting military roles outside the range of ICBMs. For instance, military configurations of the Proton space booster were introduced in the mid-1960s; after that the trend toward increasingly larger warheads in the SRF inventory ended. The later G-class space booster with its enormous payload was clearly built without the constraints of the military development program. Its design work (probably by the Korolev bureau) began about the same time the Soviets were engaged in a determined space program with the Kosmos series.

The third modification of the SS-9, a fractional orbital bombardment system (FOBS), was capable of global strikes, attacking either around the South Pole or in depressed-trajectory shots over the North Pole. The first FOBS was developed for the SS-10 but that missile was never deployed, probably for political and military reasons. In the fourth generation of ICBMs, only the third modification of the SS-18 approaches global range. It allows coverage of potential adversaries of the USSR, such as South American countries and South Africa, that have an interest in or are capable of producing nuclear weapons. The fifth modification has sufficient range to strike U.S. naval forces almost anywhere on the high seas. It may be that the USSR's new long-range SLBMs will be a feasible means of global coverage.

Table B-1. Characteristics of Soviet Land-based, Medium-range Missiles

Generation and missile[a]	Design bureau	Year design began	First flight test	Propulsion system	Guidance system	Warhead type
First generation						
SS-4 Sandal (medium range)	Yangel	1949–50	1957	Liquid fuel	Radio command; later, inertial	Single
SS-5 Skean (intermediate range)	Yangel	1952–53	1959–60	Liquid fuel	Radio command; later, inertial	Single
Second generation						
SS-11 Sego, mod. 1 (variable range)	Chelomei	1955–58	1965	Liquid fuel	Fly-the-wire, inertial	Single
SS-14 Scapegoat (medium range)	Nadira-dize	1958	1965	Solid fuel	Inertial	Single
SS-15 Scrooge (intermediate range)	Nadira-dize	1958–61	1968	Solid fuel	Inertial	Single
Third generation						
SS-19 (variable range)	Chelomei	1966	1973	Liquid fuel	Fly-the-wire, onboard digital computer	Multiple or single
SS-20 (intermediate range)	Nadira-dize	1965–68	1974–75	Solid fuel	Inertial	Multiple

Sources: *Department of Defense Annual Report Fiscal Year 1974* and reports for 1975, 1980, 1981, 1982; *United States Military Posture for 1973* (Office of the Joint Chiefs of Staff, 1972), and for 1975–81; "Statement of Secretary of Defense Robert S. McNamara before a Joint Session of the Senate Armed Services Committee and the Senate Subcommittee on Department of Defense Appropriations on the Fiscal Year 1966–70 Defense Program and 1966 Defense Budget," declassified (U.S. Department of Defense, January–February 1965), and statements for the budgets of 1967–72; Department of Defense, *Soviet Military Power* (U.S. Government Printing Office, 1981); Lawrence Freedman, *US Intelligence and the Soviet Strategic Threat* (Westview, 1977); *U.S.-U.S.S.R. Strategic Policies,* Hearing before the Subcommittee on Arms Control, International Law, and Organization of the Senate Foreign Relations Committee, 93 Cong. 2 sess. (GPO, 1974); *Hearings on Military Posture and H.R. 1872 [H.R. 4040] Department of Defense Authorization for Appropriations for Fiscal Year 1980,* Hearings before the House Armed Services Committee, 96 Cong. 1 sess. (GPO, 1979), bk. 1, pt. 3; Chief of Naval Operations, Department of the Navy, *Understanding Soviet Naval Developments,* 4th ed. (GPO, 1981); *Jane's Weapon Systems, 1980–81,* Ronald T. Pretty, ed. (London: Jane's, 1980); Kenneth W. Gatland, "Soviet Missiles," in Ray Bonds, ed., *The Soviet War Machine: An Encyclopaedia of Russian Military Equipment and Strategy* (Chartwell, 1976); Bill Gunston, *The Illustrated Encyclopaedia of the World's Rockets & Missiles* (Crescent Books, 1979); International Institute for Strategic Studies, *The Military Balance 1980–81* (London: IISS, 1980);

Basing mode	Year opera-tion began	Number of war-heads	Yield, per warhead (megatons)	Accuracy (nautical miles)	Range (nautical miles)	Number of missiles deployed
Soft site, with 4 launchers and ability to refire; hard site, with 4 launchers	1958	1	2.0	1.5	1,100	100
Soft site, with 4 launchers and ability to refire; hard site with 3 launchers	1961	1	4.0–6.0	1.0	2,200	600
Hardened silo	1970	1	0.95	0.76	5,900	320
Mobile	n.a.	1	0.6	0.8–1.0	1,500	n.a.
Mobile	n.a.	1	0.6	0.8–1.0	3,000–4,000	n.a.
Hardened silo	1975	6	0.55	0.14–0.19	5,200–5,450	120
Mobile	1977	3	0.15–0.50	0.16	2,700	180

Department of Defense Authorization for Appropriations for Fiscal Year 1979, Hearings before the Senate Armed Services Committee, 95 Cong. 2 sess. (GPO, 1978), pt. 9; Elizabeth Pond, *Christian Science Monitor*, November 27, 1981; Doug Richardson, "Soviet Strategic Nuclear Rockets Guide," *Flight International*, December 11, 1976; *Soviet Aerospace*, March 24, 1975; *Aviation Week and Space Technology*, March 31, 1969, December 7, 1970, June 25, 1979, June 16, 1980, November 3, 1980; *New York Times*, March 21, 1973; William H. Schauer, *The Politics of Space: A Comparison of the Soviet and American Space Programs* (Holmes and Meier, 1976); Nikita Khrushchev, *Khrushchev Remembers: The Last Testament*, ed. and trans. Strobe Talbott (Little, Brown, 1974); James E. Oberg, *Red Star in Orbit* (Random House, 1981); Desmond Ball, *Politics and Force Levels: The Strategic Missile Program of the Kennedy Administration* (University of California Press, 1980); *Fiscal Year 1976 and July–September 1976 Transition Period Authorization for Military Procurement, Research and Development, and Active Duty, Selected Reserve, and Civilian Personnel Strengths*, Hearings before the Senate Armed Services Committee, 94 Cong. 1 sess. (GPO, 1975), pt. 4.; William Beecher, "SIG: What the Arms Agreement Doesn't Cover," *See Power*, December 1972.

n.a. Not available.

Mod. Modification.

a. Missile numbers are those used by U.S. military services; names are those used by NATO forces.

Table B-2. Characteristics of Soviet Land-based, Intercontinental-range Missiles

Generation and missile[a]	Design bureau	Year design began	First flight test	Propulsion system	Guidance system	Warhead type	Launching mode
First generation							
SS-6 Sapwood	Korolev	1949–50	1957	Non-storable liquid fuel	Radio command	Single	n.a.
Second generation							
SS-7 Saddler							
Mods. 1 and 2 }	} Yangel	} 1954	} 1961	} Liquid fuel	} Radio command	} Single	} n.a.
Mod. 3							
SS-8 Sasin	Korolev	1954	1961	Non-storable liquid fuel	Radio command	Single	n.a.
Third generation							
SS-9 Scarp							
Mod. 1			1964			Single	
Mod. 2	} Yangel	} 1957	1964–65	} Liquid fuel	} Fly-the-wire, inertial	Single	} Hot
Mod. 3			1965			Single	
Mod. 4			1968			Multiple	
SS-11 Sego							
Mod. 1			1965			Single	
Mod. 2	} Chelomei	} 1955–58	1969	} Liquid fuel	} Fly-the-wire, inertial	Single	} Hot
Mod. 3			1969			Multiple	
Mod. 4			1974			Multiple	
SS-13 Savage							
Mod. 1	} Nadiradize	} 1958–62	1965–69	} Solid fuel	} Fly-the-wire, inertial	Single	} Hot
Mod. 2			1970			Single	
Fourth generation							
SS-X-16	Nadiradize	1965	1972	Solid fuel	Fly-the-wire, onboard digital computer	Single	Hot
SS-17							
Mod. 1			1972		Fly-the-wire,	Multiple	
Mod. 2	} Yangel	} 1965	1976	} Liquid fuel	onboard digital	Single	} Cold
Mod. 3			n.a.		computer	Multiple	
SS-18							
Mod. 1			1972		Fly-the-wire,	Single	
Mod. 2	} Yangel	} 1965	n.a.	} Liquid fuel	onboard digital	Multiple	} Cold
Mod. 3			n.a.		computer	Single	
Mod. 4			n.a.			Multiple	
SS-19							
Mod. 1			1973		Fly-the-wire,	Multiple	
Mod. 2	} Chelomei	} 1966	n.a.	} Liquid fuel	onboard digital	Single	} Hot
Mod. 3			n.a.		computer	Multiple	

Sources: See table B-1.
n.a. Not available.
Mod. Modification.
a. Missile numbers are those used by U.S. military services; names are those used by NATO forces.
b. Another 60 in preparation.

Base	Year operation began	Number of war-heads	Yield per warhead (mega-tons)	Accuracy (nautical miles)	Range (nautical miles)	Throw weight (pounds)	Number of missiles deployed
Fixed site	1959–61	1	5.0	2.0	3,200	7,000–9,000	4
}Fixed site	1962	1	3.0	1.5	}5,900	}3,000–4,000	}197
	1963	1	6.0	1.0			
Fixed site	1963	1	3.0	1.0	5,400	2,500–4,000	23
}Hardened silo	1967	1	20.0	0.5	}6,500	}9,000–11,000	}288
	1966	1	20.0	0.5			
	1969	1	20.0	n.a.			
	1971	3	3.5	1.0			
}Hardened silo	1966	1	0.95	0.76	5,900	}1,000–2,000	}1,030
	1973	1	1.10	0.59	6,500		
	1973	3	0.35	0.59	5,700		
	n.a.	3–6	n.a.	n.a.	n.a.		
}Hardened silo	1967–69	1	0.6	1.0	}5,075	}1,000	} 60
	1972	1	0.6	0.82			
Mobile and hardened silo	. . .	1	0.65	0.26	4,970	2,000	. . .
}Hardened silo	1975	4	0.75	0.24	5,400	}8,000	}150
	1977	1	3.6	0.23	5,900		
	1979	4	0.75	n.a.	n.a.		
}Hardened silo	1974	1	24.0	0.23	6,500	}16,000	}308
	1976	8–10	0.9–0.55	0.23	5,900		
	1976	1	20.0	0.19	8,640		
	n.a.	10	0.55	0.14	5,400		
}Hardened silo	1975	6	0.55	0.19	5,200	}8,000	}300[b]
	1978	1	4.3	0.21	5,450		
	1979	6	0.55	0.14	5,200		

Table B-3. Characteristics of Soviet Global-range Missiles

Missile[a]	Design bureau	Year design began	First flight test	Propulsion system	Guidance system	Warhead type
SS-9 Scarp, mod. 3	Yangel	n.a.	1965	Liquid fuel	Fly-the-wire, inertial	Single
SS-X-10 Scrag	Korolev	1957–58	1964–65	Non-storable liquid fuel	Fly-the-wire inertial	Single
SS-18, mod. 3	Yangel	n.a.	1975	Liquid fuel	Fly-the-wire, onboard digital computer	Single

Sources: See table B-1.
n.a. Not available.
Mod. Modification.

Table B-4. Characteristics of Soviet Sea-based Missiles

Generation and missile[a]	Design bureau	Year design began	First flight test	Propulsion system	Guidance system	Warhead type
First generation SS-N-4 Sark	Yangel	1949–50	n.a.	Liquid fuel	Inertial	Single
Second generation SS-N-5 Serb	Yangel	1954–55	n.a.	Liquid fuel	Inertial	Single
Third generation SS-N-6 Sawfly						
Mod. 1	Chelomei	1960	1967	Liquid fuel	Inertial	Single
Mod. 2			1972			Single
Mod. 3			1973			Multiple
Fourth generation SS-N-8						
Mod. 1	Chelomei derivative	1962	1969	Liquid fuel	Stellar inertial	Single
Mod. 2			1976			Single
Fifth generation SS-NX-17	Chelomei derivative	1969	1976	Solid fuel	n.a.	Single, post boost vehicle
SS-N-18						
Mod. 1	Chelomei derivative	1969	1976	Liquid fuel	Stellar inertial	Multiple, independently targeted
Mod. 2			n.a.			Single
Mod. 3			n.a.			Multiple, independently targeted
Sixth generation SS-NX-20	Chelomei derivative	1973	1980	Solid fuel	n.a.	Multiple, independently targeted

Sources: See table B-1.
n.a. Not available.
Mod. Modification.

Basing mode	Year operation began	Number of warheads	Yield, per warhead (mega-tons)	Accuracy (nautical miles)	Range (nautical miles)	Throw weight (pounds)	Number of missiles deployed
Hardened silo	1969	1	20.0	1.0–2.0 / 1.5–3.0	Depressed trajectory / FOBS[b]	9,000–11,000	18
n.a.	. . .	1	20.0	1.0–2.0 / 1.5–3.0	Depressed trajectory / FOBS[b]	9,000–11,000	. . .
Hardened silo	1976	1	20.0	0.19	8,600	16,000	n.a.

a. Numbers are those used by U.S. military services; names are those used by NATO forces.
b. Fractional orbital bombardment system.

Submarine assignment[b]	Year operation began	Number of warheads	Yield, per warhead (megatons)	Accuracy (nautical miles)	Range (nautical miles)
Golf I; Hotel I	1958	1	2.0–3.5	2.0	350
Golf II; Hotel II	1963	1	4.0	1.5	750
} Yankee I; Golf IV for testing	1968	1	0.7	1.0	1,300
	1973	1	0.65	1.0	1,600
	1973	2–3	0.35	1.0	1,600
} Delta I and II; Hotel III; Golf III	1973	1	n.a.	n.a.	4,200
	n.a.	1	0.8	0.84	4,900
Yankee II for testing	n.a.	1	n.a.	n.a.	2,100
} Delta III	1978	3	0.2	0.76	3,500
	n.a.	1	0.45	0.76	4,300
	n.a.	7	n.a.	n.a.	3,500
Typhoon	n.a.	12	n.a.	n.a.	4,500

a. Missile numbers are those used by U.S. military services; names are those used by NATO forces.
b. See table B-5.

Table B-5. Development of Soviet Ballistic Missile Submarines, 1955–80

Submarine class[a]	Year operation began	Propulsion type	Surface displacement (tons)	Number of launch tubes	Missile carried	Number of submarines In operation in 1980	Number of submarines Built as of 1980
Zulu V	1955	Diesel-electric	1,950	2	SS-N-4[b]	1	5
Golf I	1958	Diesel-electric	2,300	3	SS-N-4	0	23[c]
II	. . .		2,300	3	SS-N-5	13	
III	. . .		2,900	6	SS-N-8	1	
IV	. . .		2,900	5	SS-N-6	1	
Hotel I	1959	Nuclear	5,000	3	SS-N-4	0	8
II	1963		5,000	3	SS-N-5	7	
III	. . .		5,000	6	SS-N-8	1	
Yankee I	1968	Nuclear	8,000	16	SS-N-6	28[d]	34
II	. . .		8,000	12	SS-NX-17	1	
Delta I	1973	Nuclear	9,000	12	SS-N-8	18	33
II	1976		10,000	16	SS-N-8	4	
III	1978		10,500	16	SS-N-18	11	
Typhoon	1980	Nuclear	25,000	20	SS-NX-20	0	1

Sources: *Department of Defense Annual Report Fiscal Year 1982*, p. 46; Chief of Naval Operations, *Understanding Soviet Naval Developments*, 4th ed., pp. 83–99; IISS, *The Military Balance 1980–81*, pp. 9, 89; DOD, *Soviet Military Power*, pp. 9, 57–59; *Aviation Week and Space Technology*, June 16, 1980, pp. 75–76; *Fiscal Year 1977 Authorization for Military Procurement, Research and Development, and Active Duty, Selected Reserve and Civilian Personnel Strengths*, Hearings before the Senate Armed Services Committee, 94 Cong. 2 sess. (GPO, 1976), pt. 1, p. 85.

a. Names are those designated by NATO.

b. The original missile carried was the Naval Scud.

c. One sank in the Pacific Ocean in 1968; one Golf I has had its missiles removed and has been converted to serve as a command-and-control platform.

d. In order to stay within the limits established by the 1972 SALT I accords, the USSR has dismantled the launchers on five Yankee-class ballistic-missile submarines which the U.S. Navy now classifies as attack submarines.

Regional and Intercontinental Targeting

THE SOVIET UNION'S targeting requirements are based on diverse wartime objectives. The important targets presumably are the enemy's nuclear weapon forces, the bases and deployments of his general-purpose force, military and civilian command-and-control systems, and economic assets closely related to war production.

The target sets facing the USSR are always changing as the West deploys more survivable strategic forces; occasionally the number of targets has mushroomed, as it did when the USSR's relations with China broke down. When military requirements change unexpectedly or unforeseen technical failures disrupt planned weapon programs, Soviet planners are compelled to devise "quick fixes" or accept shortfalls in fulfilling targeting requirements. At times, doctrinal shifts in Soviet strategic planning—like that in the "revolution in military affairs"—alter requirements.

Some of the Soviet targets—military, political, economic, in regional and intercontinental theaters of military operations—can be classified as fixed area or point targets, and others—the most difficult to attack—as mobile targets. The vast majority of targets continue to be fixed; they are characterized as soft or hard, depending on their ability to withstand the effects of a nearby nuclear detonation. Large area targets, such as airfields or industrial facilities, are considered soft since only a small amount of overpressure (measured in pounds per square inch, or psi) is usually required to neutralize their operations. Effective nuclear strikes against these targets would require a single, large-yield weapon or a cluster of smaller-yield weapons. Point targets can be either hard or soft—a hardened, underground missile silo, or an early-warning radar site. Efficient strikes against point targets depend usually on a high degree of accuracy, and against hardened targets on direct hits by several weapons.

In developing its targeting options—deciding how to use its strategic forces to meet perceived threats—the Soviet Union appears to follow the traditional concepts of its Ground Force. The various levels of effectiveness designated for destroying enemy forces or plants with modern weapons resemble traditional wartime concepts of success and attrition.[1] At times Soviet writings have indicated the damage expected from a Soviet attack as annihilation if 60 percent or more of the enemy target or force is destroyed, military neutralization if 30 percent is destroyed, and harassment if only 10 percent is destroyed. These are high standards for annihilation and even for neutralization if they include allowances for unreliability and inaccuracy in the firing of a single shot. Whatever the damage expectancies assigned, however, this categorization suggests that the traditional criterion of mission success or failure applies even in the age of nuclear weapons. The American focus on cost-effectiveness, by contrast, tends to discourage military programs that cannot achieve a high level of effectiveness.

The USSR's approach to defense problems is also to seek multiple means for addressing them. In setting targeting options the USSR might aim at neutralizing an enemy system either by destroying the weapon itself or by disrupting or degrading its support system.[2] Indirect attacks might be aimed at vital command-and-control systems linking strategic forces to decisionmakers or perhaps at navigational aids that sea-based missile forces depend on for determining an accurate launch location. Significant improvements in the flexibility, endurance, and effectiveness of the Soviet strategic forces over the past twenty years have made it possible for them to fulfill their basic targeting requirements. This appendix reviews the development of Soviet targeting options. Tables C-1–C-12 at the end of the appendix provide the detailed analysis on which the interpretations are based.

Regional Forces: Targeting Requirements and Options

The regional-range targets that the Strategic Rocket Forces (SRF) must cover (figure C-1 and table C-2) have always been numerous and relatively vulnerable to low levels of nuclear blast and overpressure.

1. The practice of differentiated levels of damage expectancy is also consistent with Soviet artillery practice; see Christopher Donnelly, "Modern Soviet Artillery: Doctrine and Practice," *NATO's Fifteen Nations*, vol. 24 (June–July 1979), p. 53.
2. For a fuller discussion of this point, see Floyd D. Kennedy, Jr., "Attacking the

Hence the early assignment of SS-4s and SS-5s, with their large-yield warheads and ability to refire, to cover adversary forces in Europe, Asia, and the Middle East (see table C-3). The medium-range SS-4 could be targeted against NATO's air bases, radar installations, and weapon depots, against U.S. bases in the Far East, and against U.S. intermediate-range ballistic missile (IRBM) sites in Turkey and Italy. It may also have served as a transitional system for use in preplanned strikes in support of Ground Forces maneuvers. Those targets that posed a nuclear threat that fell outside the range of the SS-4—command-and-control centers, air bases, IRBM sites, industrial targets in Great Britain, and American strategic bomber bases in Spain and North Africa—could easily be covered by the intermediate-range SS-5.

By 1965 the Soviet regional strike force had over 1,300 on-line and reload missiles which were adequate for meeting the earlier targeting requirements of the regional force (see table C-4). However, French plans to deploy IRBMs and China's addition to the target list had changed the USSR's overall objectives. More significantly, the soft basing of the missile force made it vulnerable to preemption.

With the introduction of 120 SS-11 ICBMs into the medium-range ballistic-missile (MRBM) fields in the late 1960s, the regional force gained a variable-range missile with improved survivability. The SS-11s offered a means of countering the French IRBM deployment and provided surplus launchers to strike naval forces in the northern and Mediterranean seas.

A small training deployment of SS-14 and SS-15 missiles was assigned to the Far East, probably as a supplement to the SS-11 ICBM regiments in the Far East which, as part of a more flexible targeting policy, were focused on China rather than the United States. As the need for quick response in other regions diminished, the SRF probably was able to turn some of the SS-4 and SS-5 force toward China.[3] When the SS-19 was added to the regional force in the 1970s, it was installed in the missile fields that housed the western-based variable-range SS-11s. Other SS-11s in the Far East were probably targeted at China.

Most of the regional-range requirements are increasingly being met

Weakest Link: The Anti-Support Role of Soviet Naval Forces,'' *Naval War College Review,* vol. 32 (September–October 1979), pp. 48–55.

3. In 1966 the USSR began to add SS-4s in the Far East. Edward L. Warner III, ''Soviet Strategic Force Posture: Some Alternative Explanations,'' in Frank B. Horton III, Anthony C. Rogerson, and Edward L. Warner III, eds. *Comparative Defense Policy* (Johns Hopkins University Press, 1974), p. 316.

Figure C-1. Development of Soviet Strategic Weapons to Meet Regional Targeting Requirements, 1945–80

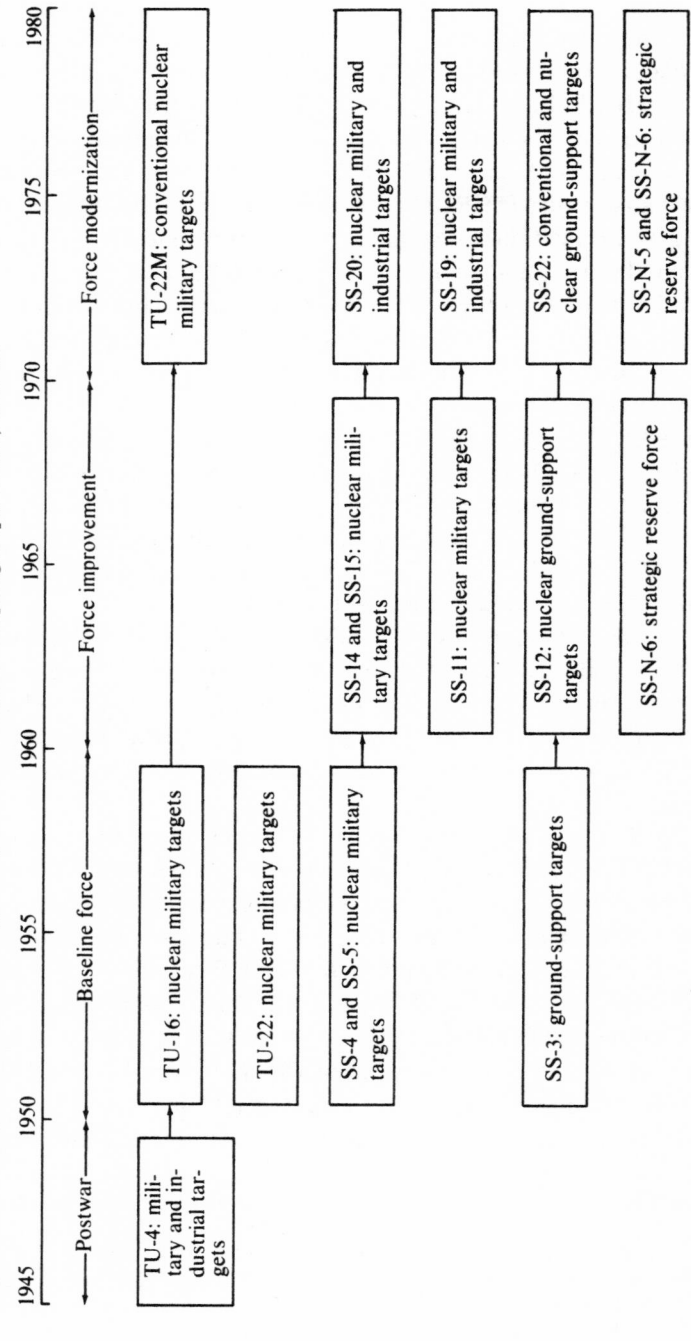

by the SS-20 which is a replacement for the SS-4 and SS-5. The SS-20 is a mobile missile with multiple warheads. Its wide coverage and ability to refire provide a greater chance of survival than the SS-4 and SS-5 had.

Intercontinental Forces: Targeting Requirements and Options

The predominant intercontinental targeting requirements of the USSR in the 1950s and early 1960s (figure C-2) were military and administrative and economic complexes that covered large areas and had a low resistance to blast. The most effective way of striking these targets was with large-yield (megaton-range) nuclear weapons. From the lethal area of the explosion, Soviet planners could calculate the amount of mega-tonnage required to saturate the U.S. target system. Hence there was a premium on heavy payload missiles.

Soft and Area Target Assignments

The SS-7 and SS-8 missiles, conceived in the early 1950s, were large-yield weapons that offered some degree of capability against soft, area targets—the early generation of U.S. Atlas and Titan missiles deployed in relatively unhardened and concentrated sites, and U.S. bomber bases, military bases with nonnuclear forces, and administrative and economic centers. By the time this force was being deployed, in the early 1960s, the number of soft, area targets they had to cover was double what it had been in the 1950s.

The immediate successor of the SS-7, the SS-9, had a warhead capable of three times the destructive force of the SS-7. This would have produced greater confidence among Soviet planners in the ability of the strategic forces to destroy soft, area military and economic targets. However, by the time the SS-9 began to be deployed, Soviet targeting requirements had changed to encompass a new threat. Nearly 500 SS-9 launchers along with the earlier SS-7 force would have satisfied earlier soft area targeting requirements.[4]

If this early baseline oriented to soft area targets had continued, much larger delivery vehicles with increased payloads would probably have been deployed to replace the SS-7 and SS-8 force. (A space booster

4. The SS-7 deployments may also have been curtailed by the development of the SS-9. The SS-9s were deployed in groups of 48; exact numbers would have to be in multiples of 48.

Figure C-2. Development of Soviet Strategic Weapons to Meet Intercontinental Targeting Requirements, 1950–80

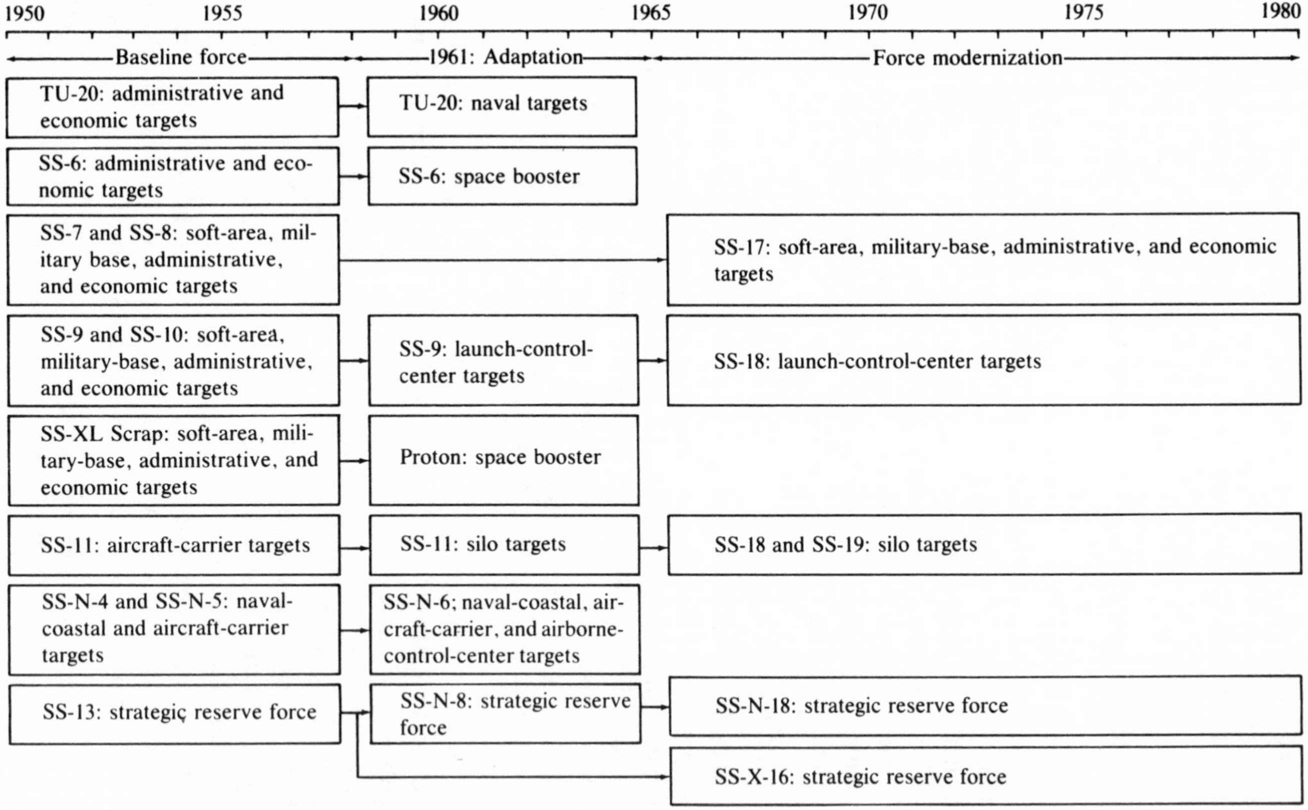

1950	1955	1960	1965	1970	1975	1980

←————————Baseline force————————→←————1961: Adaptation————→←————————————Force modernization————————————→

Baseline force	1961: Adaptation	Force modernization
TU-20: administrative and economic targets	TU-20: naval targets	
SS-6: administrative and economic targets	SS-6: space booster	
SS-7 and SS-8: soft-area, military base, administrative, and economic targets		SS-17: soft-area, military-base, administrative, and economic targets
SS-9 and SS-10: soft-area, military-base, administrative, and economic targets	SS-9: launch-control-center targets	SS-18: launch-control-center targets
SS-XL Scrap: soft-area, military-base, administrative, and economic targets	Proton: space booster	
SS-11: aircraft-carrier targets	SS-11: silo targets	SS-18 and SS-19: silo targets
SS-N-4 and SS-N-5: naval-coastal and aircraft-carrier targets	SS-N-6; naval-coastal, aircraft-carrier, and airborne-control-center targets	
SS-13: strategic reserve force	SS-N-8: strategic reserve force	SS-N-18: strategic reserve force
		SS-X-16: strategic reserve force

called Proton was first tested in 1965; its military equivalent, which we call SS-XL Scrap, could have carried the very large yield nuclear weapons the USSR had been testing in 1961.[5] The SS-9 was probably chosen because it offered enough flexibility to shift targeting assignments.)

Scrambling to Meet New Requirements

In 1961 a series of events dramatically and quickly changed the nature of U.S.-USSR political and military affairs.

Between 1961 and 1962 there was a rapid transformation and augmentation of the American threat facing the Soviet Union. Having entered office believing in the possibility of a missile gap favoring the USSR, and advocating the necessity for a greater range of military options, the Kennedy administration promptly expanded and redirected many U.S. defense programs. Most important were the substantial increases in the production rates and overall force goals of the U.S. strategic missile programs. Between Eisenhower's proposed budget for fiscal 1962 and Kennedy's budget for fiscal 1963, American plans for the Polaris fleet increased the number of nuclear-powered ballistic-missile submarines (SSBNs) to be built from 19 to 41 and accelerated their delivery schedule. The following changes took place in the proposed numbers of submarine-launched and intercontinental ballistic missiles (ICBMs and SLBMs) to be built:

Missiles	Eisenhower FY 1962 budget message	Kennedy March 1961 message	Kennedy FY 1963 budget message
Atlas ICBM	126	126	126
Titan ICBM	126	108	108
Mobile Minuteman ICBM	90	Canceled	Canceled
Fixed Minuteman ICBM	450	600	1,200
Polaris SLBM	304	464	656
Total number of missiles	1,096	1,298	1,964
Other weapons			
Refitting of USS *Long Beach*	Recommended	Canceled	Canceled
B-70 bomber	Research and development recommended	Canceled	Canceled

5. We believe that the Proton may have been the outgrowth of a large surface-to-surface missile that did not go beyond the experimental stage; we call it the SS-XL Scrap.

The number of Minuteman ICBMs to be deployed in hardened silos was more than doubled and plans to deploy the Minuteman in a mobile system were canceled.[6]

For the Soviet Union these new American forces posed a serious threat that could not be directly affected by either regional offensive or defensive strategic forces. The initial burden of countering the planned American strategic forces would fall on the Soviet SS-7 and SS-8 ICBMs. Their low accuracy and prelaunch survivability would eliminate them as an effective military counter to the more accurate and securely based Minuteman ICBM forces. Furthermore, the slow production rate of the large Soviet ICBMs would enable the United States to open up an expanding lead in numbers of deployed ICBMs. The Soviet Navy, despite its growing capability against Western carriers, was incapable of meeting the threat posed by Polaris missiles to the Soviet homeland. Unless serious changes in the Soviet posture were undertaken, Soviet strategic forces would be inadequately prepared to deal with the evolving American strategic threat.

The sudden growth and redirection of the American strategic force posture in the early 1960s led to a series of new targeting requirements for the Soviet Union's strategic forces that were both significantly different from the previous ones and demanding of an immediate response. The Soviet Union undertook a series of quick fixes for the 1960s but also initiated longer-term solutions for the next decade. Furthermore, given the shortcomings of the strategic defensive forces at the time, the Soviet offensive forces were compelled to carry the full burden of offsetting the American intercontinental capability. The work to be done centered on development of ICBMs since the Soviet force was oriented toward attacks on relatively soft area targets.

Hard Point Target Assignments

The sudden proliferation of U.S. Minuteman ICBMs (and cancellation of additional deployments of first-generation intercontinental missiles)

6. Desmond Ball, *Politics and Force Levels: The Strategic Missile Programs of the Kennedy Administration* (University of California Press, 1980), pp. 116–17, 137; *Public Papers of the Presidents: John F. Kennedy, January 20 to December 31, 1961* (U.S. Government Printing Office, 1962), pp. 233–34; *Department of Defense Semi-Annual Report and the Semiannual Reports of the Secretary of the Army, Secretary of the Navy, and Secretary of the Air Force for January 1 to June 30, 1960* and the reports for 1961–63. Defense planning in 1962 was based on Kennedy's fiscal 1963 budget request. The *Long Beach* refit would have put eight Polaris SLBMs on a nuclear-powered surface ship.

created a new set of targeting requirements sooner than the USSR was prepared to respond to them. Instead of having only hundreds of area targets to cover, the intercontinental strike forces would be faced by 1967 with the addition of over one thousand Minuteman ICBMs supported by one hundred launch-control centers (see table C-6). The new U.S. missiles, in hardened, underground launchers, would be less vulnerable to Soviet attack, and with their greater accuracy and numbers would increase the threat to the Soviet Union's own ICBM force.

To mount a response to this threat, posed by the Minuteman ICBM, the USSR turned for an interim solution to the development programs for its third-generation ICBMs. The SS-9 Scarp ICBM seems to have been selected as the main instrument for militarily offsetting the Minuteman force. (Fortuitously, the SS-9 was the first of the third-generation ICBMs to become available.) This missile seems to have been intended as a replacement for the SS-7.[7] With its substantial throw weight, the SS-9 was capable of delivering large-yield warheads which would have been quite effective against the area targets that it was probably originally designed to strike. This same capability, coupled with the missile's relatively accurate guidance system, made the SS-9 effective for use against the Minuteman silos and launch-control centers.

The SS-9 was unlikely, however, to be able to close the U.S. lead in ICBM deployments in the short term. The deployment rate for SS-9 launchers averaged less than 30 percent that of its smaller contemporary, the SS-11 Sego (table C-7), and the Soviet Union may not have been able to afford to increase the deployment rate of the large and expensive SS-9.[8]

This apparent inability to produce and deploy the SS-9 rapidly enough to fulfill Soviet political and military requirements may have persuaded the USSR to adopt a more diversified approach to meeting its objectives. As a means of politically and militarily offsetting the U.S. Minuteman ICBM force it may have turned to its smaller, more easily produced ICBMs to match the Minuteman in numbers while relying on its SS-9s to provide a means of neutralizing the one hundred critical command-and-control links of the Minuteman force before the launchers could send up missiles. Both the urgency to begin deploying some type of intercontinental missile and the limited choices available would make

7. It had twice the accuracy and three times the yield of the SS-7.
8. At the rate at which SS-9s were being deployed, it would have taken until the 1980s to match the number of Minutemen in service.

such an approach appealing. Certainly, it was a strategy with a potentially high payoff, although with some uncertainties. Assigning two SS-9 warheads for use against each launch-control center would have given the Strategic Rocket Forces significant strength for attacking the U.S. ICBM force (see table C-8). By 1971, the SS-9 force could have covered all of the centers plus the small number of additional very hard targets in the United States. The crucial year of vulnerability for U.S. ICBMs would have been 1967, when a relatively small number of SS-9s could have neutralized 40–60 percent of the launch-control centers.

The uncertainties of such a scheme lie in just how the Minuteman force would operate in wartime. If each control center were responsible for launching a squadron of Minutemen (50 missiles) rather than a flight (10 missiles) as in peacetime, then a strike that was expected to neutralize whole squadrons by attacking particular control centers might fail to disrupt any of the launchers. After 1967 the uncertainty of disrupting the U.S. control system was compounded by the U.S. introduction of an airborne system of launch control.[9] Yet the command-and-control system remained the critical element in the survival of the U.S. land-based missile force. Redirection of the SS-9 program to cover the Minuteman control centers would have been a logical Soviet response to the rapid change in the U.S. intercontinental strategic threat in 1961. Not only would such a strategy counter the U.S. Minuteman threat, but it would be consistent with the generally high value that the Soviets place on command and control and on disabling the enemy's command system in wartime.[10]

Other variants of the successful SS-9 program help to illuminate the changing nature of the problems that faced Soviet force planners in the 1960s. The third modification of the SS-9, a fractional orbital bombardment system (FOBS), could deliver a high-megaton device either by following a depressed trajectory which would reduce the flight time of the ICBM, or by going around the South Pole and outflanking U.S. ground-based early-warning radars. This system was probably a response to the late 1950s problem of neutralizing the prospective U.S. B-52 intercontinental-range bombers. The third modification of the SS-9 and perhaps the SS-10 missiles were probably an attempt to produce

9. *Fiscal Year 1973 Authorization for Military Procurement, Research and Development, Construction Authorization for the Safeguard ABM, and Active Duty and Selective Reserve Strengths,* Hearings before the Senate Armed Services Committee, 92 Cong. 2 sess. (GPO, 1972), pt. 3, p. 1462.

10. Joseph D. Douglass, Jr., and Amoretta M. Hoeber, *Soviet Strategy for Nuclear War* (Hoover Institution Press, 1979), pp. 49–50, 77–80.

a system that could reduce the American warning time to the point that U.S. strategic bombers on alert (and even the early generation of U.S. ICBMs) would be caught and destroyed at their bases. The liquid-fueled SS-10 Scrag missile could also have been planned as a fractional orbital bombardment system to be used against air bases.

These unusual weapons may also have been planned for use in a precursor strike on U.S. national command facilities in order to deny the United States the option of launching its Minutemen before the SS-9s could strike their control centers. Or they may have been a response to the Soviet search for a global rocket that could cover any target on the earth—like the ability of the U.S. strategic bombers to circle the world.[11]

The Soviet FOBS program seems to have fallen victim to changes in the threat facing the USSR as well as technological advances in the American warning system. With the deployment of U.S. early-warning satellites in 1968, the utility of the FOBS for undertaking a surprise attack was largely obviated;[12] probably as a consequence of this, only eighteen SS-9 FOBS launchers were ever put in operation.[13]

While the SS-9 ICBM may have offered a promising means for neutralizing the Minuteman ICBM force in wartime, it did not help much in ending the image of Soviet military inferiority vis-à-vis the United States. Nor could it increase the overall survivability of the Soviet ICBM force since the American force was growing so much more rapidly than the Soviet and the SS-9's silos were vulnerable to a U.S. missile attack.

Among the missiles in development in the 1960s that the Soviet Union may have been counting on to fulfill the requirements that the SS-9 could not satisfy was the SS-13 Savage. In many respects this ICBM appears to have been originally intended as the Soviet counterpart to the American Minuteman I—it apparently started in development about the same time in the late 1950s and like the American Minuteman was small and propelled by solid fuel. The smaller size of the SS-13 presumably would have allowed it to be produced and deployed at a pace closer to

11. *Development of Strategic Air Command 1946–1976* (Office of the Historian, Headquarters Strategic Air Command, U.S. Air Force, 1976), pp. 13, 62.

12. The initial contract for the ballistic-missile early-warning system was awarded in 1958, with completion of the first site scheduled for 1960. The first system that performed the duties began operating in 1968. See Philip J. Klass, *Secret Sentries in Space* (Random House, 1971), pp. 33–34, 173–84.

13. These were located at Tyuratam; see U.S. Department of State, Bureau of Public Affairs, *SALT II Agreement, Vienna, June 18, 1979*, Selected Document 12A (GPO, 1979), p. 19. These weapons would have had some capability in a hypothetical depressed-trajectory attack against a portion of the SAC alert-bomber force.

that of the American ICBM deployment, enabling the USSR to expeditiously end the U.S. advantage in ICBM numbers.

Certain evidence suggests that the SS-13 may have been intended by the Soviet leadership to serve as a more survivable strategic reserve component of the Soviet land-based ICBM force. The missile's solid-fuel propulsion system gave it the capability to be deployed as a less-vulnerable, land-mobile ICBM[14] (derivatives of the SS-13 were eventually deployed as regional-range, mobile missiles). Soviet plans to make the SS-13 mobile would have paralleled U.S. decisions made during the Eisenhower administration (but canceled by the Kennedy administration)[15] to deploy a certain portion of the Minuteman force as mobile ICBMs. Furthermore, during the mid-1960s Soviet military officials claimed to have developed a mobile ICBM.[16] Thus, the USSR may have intended to complement its larger, silo-based ICBMs (the SS-7s, SS-9s, and SS-XLs) with some number of land-mobile SS-13 ICBMs in order to improve the survivability of its land-based missile force. The SS-13, as a more survivable portion of the force, would serve both as a hedge against a U.S. first strike on the Soviet ICBM forces and a strategic reserve capable of surviving even during a prolonged nuclear conflict.

The SS-13's solid-fuel propellant may have also provided it with the ability to be quickly launched after warning of an incoming enemy missile attack. Whether the Soviet Union was interested in deploying silo-based SS-13 ICBMs to provide a launch-under-attack option is not clear.[17] But in 1967, when the SS-13 Savage was first deployed, Marshal N. I. Krylov, commander of the Strategic Rocket Forces, clearly outlined the feasibility of this type of capability for foiling a preemptive strike by an aggressor.[18]

14. About one-third of the projected SS-13 production (50–60 per year beginning in 1967) was estimated to be for mobile launchers. See Lawrence Freedman, *US Intelligence and the Soviet Strategic Threat* (Westview, 1977), p. 113. "Statement of Secretary of Defense Robert S. McNamara before the Senate Armed Services Committee on the Fiscal Year 1969–73 Defense Program and 1969 Defense Budget," declassified material (U.S. Department of Defense, 1968), p. 58. Derivatives of the SS-13 were eventually deployed as regional-range, mobile missiles.

15. Bill Gunston, *The Illustrated Encyclopaedia of the World's Rockets & Missiles* (Crescent Books, 1979), pp. 66–67.

16. Thomas W. Wolfe, *Soviet Power and Europe, 1945–1970* (Johns Hopkins Press, 1970), p. 434, see nn. 24 and 25.

17. The SS-13 was also conceived of as a mobile missile in that period.

18. "The Nuclear-Missile Shield of the Soviet State," in U.S. Foreign Broadcast Information Service, *Selected Translations: Voyennaya mysl' (Military Thought)*, November 1967, pp. 13–21.

However critical the SS-13's role may have been in Soviet force planning, the missile was never developed, apparently because it suffered from serious technical problems. The failure of the SS-13 ICBM to come through for the USSR during this critical phase may have had a series of important repercussions. It may have altered the Soviet leadership's attitude toward relying on land-mobile ICBMs for a survivable strategic reserve force. It immediately focused their concern on the necessity to find a replacement for the SS-13 to fulfill its still unmet requirements.

The Search for Expedient Solutions: The SS-11's Growing Role

The Soviets turned for help to V. N. Chelomei's design bureau, which until then had only designed naval missiles. It was this bureau's SS-11 Sego ballistic missile that would eventually satisfy the Soviet requirement for an ICBM that could be produced in sufficient numbers to match U.S. Minuteman deployments.

The original intention in the mid-1950s behind development of the long-range SS-11 seems to have been to provide a land-based missile system that could be used to target the enemy's naval task forces at various ranges. At that time, nuclear-armed carrier-based aircraft were a main component of the American strategic strike force, and the Soviet navy was trying to extend its defensive perimeter against these Western attack carriers.[19] But the original design requirements of the SS-11, much like those of the SS-9 ICBM were probably superseded by the rise of new, more important targeting requirements. Compared to the early ICBMs then in development at the other design bureaus, the initial version of the SS-11 was quite distinctive since it was small in size and payload and had a relatively short range. The particular technical characteristics of the SS-11 and its origins from a design bureau long associated with naval missiles suggest that initially it may have been designed as a land-based system for striking U.S. carrier task forces on the open oceans. That possibility is reinforced by the fact that during the same year that the first SS-11 ICBMs were tested, the Soviet ocean reconnaissance satellite system was also first tested.[20] It could have

19. Fleet Adm. S. G. Gorshkov, "The Development of Soviet Naval Science," in Defense Intelligence Agency, trans., *Selected Articles from U.S.S.R. Naval Digest (Morskoy Sbornik)* (DOD, 1967), pp. 18–21.

20. *United States Military Posture for FY 1980* (U.S. Office of the Joint Chiefs of Staff, 1979), p. 57.

detected carrier task forces at sea and provided target information to the land-based missiles. Only a handful of SS-11 missiles would have been required to strike at enemy aircraft carriers (tables C-9 and C-10). Yet from 1966 the USSR deployed enough SS-11s (over 150 launchers a year) to erase the American advantage in terms of overall ICBM launchers by 1969.[21] The USSR was able to do this in part because of the rapid deployment pace of the SS-11 program. By 1971 a total of 970 SS-11s would be deployed including those in the Eurasian-range missile fields.[22]

The shift in development of the SS-11 to afford a means of matching Minuteman deployments in number was probably eased by the fact that the Kennedy administration's plan that had created this requirement had also downgraded the role of the aircraft carrier as American SSBNs became available.[23] Assuming that the combination of the failure of the SS-13 program and the rapid change in the nature of the strategic threat facing the USSR in the early 1960s led the Soviets to redirect the SS-11 program helps explain some of the anomalies of this program. Its sudden appearance in 1965 came as something of a surprise to U.S. intelligence analysts, in part because it was detected in an area normally associated with testing of naval missiles and not ICBMs.[24] Such technical characteristics as the variable range of the SS-11 suggest that a decision to redirect and upgrade this missile system occurred sometime during its later development phase in the early 1960s.[25]

The specific military role of the SS-11 ballistic missiles is a matter of greater debate, since some of them seem to have been dedicated to wartime missions other than striking urban and industrial targets in the U.S. mainland. Clearly an important mission was to provide a survivable and effective means of covering targets in the regional theaters of military operations. Beyond the deployments of 120 SS-11s in western Russia, and 200 in eastern Russia, some of the SS-11s may have been dedicated

21. International Institute for Strategic Studies, *The Military Balance 1972–1973* (London: IISS, 1972), p. 65; Wolfe, *Soviet Power and Europe*, p. 432.

22. IISS, *Military Balance 1972–1973*, p. 65.

23. Norman Polmar, *Aircraft Carriers: A Graphic History of Carrier Aviation and Its Influence on World Events* (Doubleday, 1969), pp. 666–67.

24. Walter Pincus, *Washington Post*, June 26, 1980. V. N. Chelomei, originally a specialist in aviation propulsion, applied this technology to naval cruise missiles. Nikita Khrushchev, *Khrushchev Remembers: The Last Testament*, ed. and trans. Strobe Talbott (Little, Brown, 1974), p. 43. Freedman, *US Intelligence*, p. 107.

25. Thus given its initial test date of 1965, a fundamental decision would have possibly been reached sometime between 1961 and 1963. In 1963 silo construction began for the SS-9 and SS-11.

to fulfilling the original requirement of a land-based missile system for use against naval forces. A radar ocean-reconnaissance satellite (RORS) system and other ocean surveillance systems were available to provide targeting information. And third and fourth modifications of the SS-11 seem suitable for naval tasks. The third modification with its three warheads[26] could strike at surface vessels in transit during a nuclear conflict, and the fourth modification with its slower reentry speeds could rapidly deliver chemical agents[27] against carrier task forces during a nonnuclear conflict. Though a land-based missile may be an unconventional means (by Western standards) for neutralizing naval forces, it is not implausible.

Presumably, the primary mission of the 650 SS-11s deployed outside of Eurasian-range missile fields was intercontinental strikes. Their modest yield and accuracy suggest that these ICBMs were targeted against relatively soft urban and industrial centers.[28] But it is difficult to find more than a couple of hundred of these U.S. targets worth attacking in wartime, and it seems more likely that they would have been the responsibility of the SS-7s and SS-8s, whose numbers and physical characteristics seem more suitable for covering such targets.[29]

The SS-11 Sego may have been expected to match the Minuteman deployment silo-for-silo and to militarily counter the U.S. missiles at a time when China was not an adversary. In a traditional military sense, the SS-11 would offer a counter-battery capability against the Minuteman, to be used to attack Minuteman silos in case attacks on the command-and-control system should fail. Indeed, the SS-19 ICBM, the primary fourth-generation replacement of the SS-11, provides evidence of Soviet interest in a redundant capability.[30]

The SS-11 ICBM fell quite short of attaining either the capability or the numbers necessary for an effective attack on the Minuteman silos.

26. *United States Military Posture for FY 1976*, p. 10.

27. While it is not clear if any of the fourth modification are deployed, it is believed testing occurred in the mid-1970s. This system could eventually have utility against submarines if adequate space or airborne sensors were available. "DIA Official Notes Uncertainty about 'MOD 4' of Soviets' SS-11 ICBM," *Aerospace Daily*, December 18, 1979, p. 239.

28. News release, Office of the Assistant Secretary of Defense (Public Affairs), May 30, 1979, p. 3.

29. We estimate that some 300 major urban industrial centers were targeted in the early 1960s.

30. This missile had the reentry speed, accuracy, and yield to be used in attacks on silos.

To achieve high or even modest levels of damage, the SS-11 would have to fall within one-half a mile of its target (table C-11); its damage-expectancy rating, however, was very low. It is possible that its utility lay in secondary effects from nearby detonations that might disable the Minutemen and their support equipment. These less certain, indirect means of neutralizing the enemy's military system are not customary in the West. Yet, the Soviet Union may have chosen such an approach over the unattractive alternative of leaving this important part of the threat unexposed to attack. Furthermore, contaminating the areas around the missile silos would impede U.S. measures to enter the Minuteman silos and launch their ICBMs after the launch-control centers had been attacked. This seemingly improbable American action could have been a matter of concern to Soviet planners accustomed to predicating a prolonged nuclear conflict and planning for the worst case.

Fourth-Generation Deployments

While third-generation ICBM forces deployed by the Soviet Union in the 1960s left much to be desired, the fourth generation of Soviet ICBMs made impressive gains in effectiveness, flexibility, and survivability. The large SS-18, the first to be deployed, was designed by the Yangel bureau, which was responsible for the SS-7 and SS-9 series. The initial version of the SS-18 had a large, single warhead that could either be used for direct attacks against the U.S. national command authority and associated military commands or for sequential, high-altitude, high-megaton bursts in the patrol areas of U.S. launch-control aircraft and against the entire national communication grid. All of these targets are susceptible, to some degree, to the effects of electromagnetic pulses (EMP) emanating from a nuclear detonation. The second modifications of the SS-17 and the SS-19 also carry large single warheads, suitable for striking tactical and naval command-and-control nodes. These ICBMs are indicative of a continuing Soviet requirement to neutralize the entire range of important U.S. command, control, and communication centers and other very hard targets.

Two of the new ICBMs also were significant improvements in the Soviet Union's ability to counter the Minuteman force. The second modification of Yangel's SS-18 and the first and third modifications of Chelomei's SS-19 missiles with multiple warheads offered a substantial increase over the SS-9 and SS-11 ICBMs in the ability to neutralize the launch-control centers as well as the ICBM silos of the U.S. force. Each

ICBM could be quite effective against both types of targets, especially if more than one of its warheads were directed at each target. Probably the powerful SS-18 was intended as the primary system for countering the Minuteman, while the SS-19 offered an additional hedge. This gave the USSR a redundant capability since either ICBM could be utilized in this mission. The fourth generation satisfied the Soviet need for a direct means of countering the ICBM launchers as well as the U.S. command-and-control system. The ability to destroy the silos with a nuclear blast became increasingly important as the United States in the 1970s strengthened its airborne command posts and protected its silo-based ICBMs against the side effects of nuclear blasts.[31]

The models of the SS-19 and SS-18 that were deployed in the mid-1970s probably have to rely on two warheads directed against each target in order to achieve a high probability of destruction. If the Strategic Rocket Forces are capable of successfully performing the very intricate timing involved in a second-echelon strike against the widely dispersed U.S. Minuteman force, then the overall survivability of the Minuteman force will become open to question by the mid-1980s. The accuracy necessary to annihilate modern Minuteman silos in a single-warhead attack is so great that it seems to be outside the accuracy range of the missiles deployed in the 1970s (see table C-11). This is probably an objective for the fifth generation of ICBMs, or for later models of the SS-18 and SS-19.

On the other end of the Soviet targeting spectrum from the U.S. Minuteman are large, soft targets such as strategic bomber airfields, conventional military bases, and administrative and economic centers. The SS-17, designed by the Yangel bureau, appears aimed at replacing the SS-7 in covering such area targets as bases for strategic, tactical, and airlift aircraft or the division headquarters of U.S. army forces. The SS-17 is probably capable of handling the targeting responsibility that the SS-7 shared with long-range sea-based missiles for covering important area targets in the U.S. mainland.

The Soviet ICBMs that are capable of striking maritime targets at sea include the third and fourth modifications of the SS-11 and the third modification of the SS-18, which has been tested at ranges as great as 8,000 nautical miles.[32] The latter weapon may have been deployed to ensure that the Strategic Rocket Forces maintain a global reach, espe-

---

31. This included the refinement of the airborne network and the hardening of missile components.

32. *United States Military Posture for FY 1978*, p. 10.

cially in light of the SALT II treaty's requirement that the USSR dismantle its SS-9 FOBS test launchers.

The fourth generation of Soviet ICBMs provides missiles for covering a wide range of targets in the intercontinental theater of military operations. The silo-based SS-17, SS-18, and SS-19 missiles with multiple warheads offer increased coverage of targets and a hedge against a possible U.S. ABM deployment.[33] Those with single warheads can be useful in a protracted nuclear exchange when the location of targets is uncertain and their number relatively low.[34] Yet the variations in these ICBMs may be an indication of the diversity of their missions in wartime. As figure C-3 shows, the targeting priorities of the Strategic Rocket Forces, for example, have never been centered solely on silos, nor are they likely to be. Soviet ICBMs, as a force, against a nearly pure set of targets (90 percent hard or 90 percent soft) show a greater potential against soft targets than hard targets. When a balanced and changing set is presented, the force still appears most effective against relatively softer, more numerous aim points. By limiting its targets to missile silos, the ICBM force would fall far short of its maximum value.

The Evolution of Sea-based Missile Targeting

By the late 1960s the USSR began to significantly expand its force of sea-based ballistic missiles. While the addition of the Yankee-class submarine and its SS-N-6 Sawfly missile generally enhanced the Soviet Union's political and military position, this SSBN was actually accorded a limited role in the intercontinental strike mission against the American mainland. Not until it deployed the Delta-class SSBN in the 1970s did the USSR acquire a sea-based missile force truly capable of such a mission. Like the land-based programs, the Soviet sea-based ballistic missile forces also were redirected to meet the Soviet Union's changing strategic requirements. Before that occurred, however, the Soviet Navy began to deploy Golf- and Hotel-class ballistic-missile submarines in forward areas.

The deployment of the Yankee SSBNs signaled the beginning of an important role for the Soviet ballistic-missile submarine force in covering strategic targets both in the regional and in the intercontinental theaters

33. The U.S. ABM system began operation at roughly the same time the fourth generation of Soviet ICBMs began to be deployed.
34. *United States Military Posture for FY 1978*, p. 10.

Figure C-3. Efficiency of SRF Missiles against Soft, Hard, and Mixed Targets, 1965–80

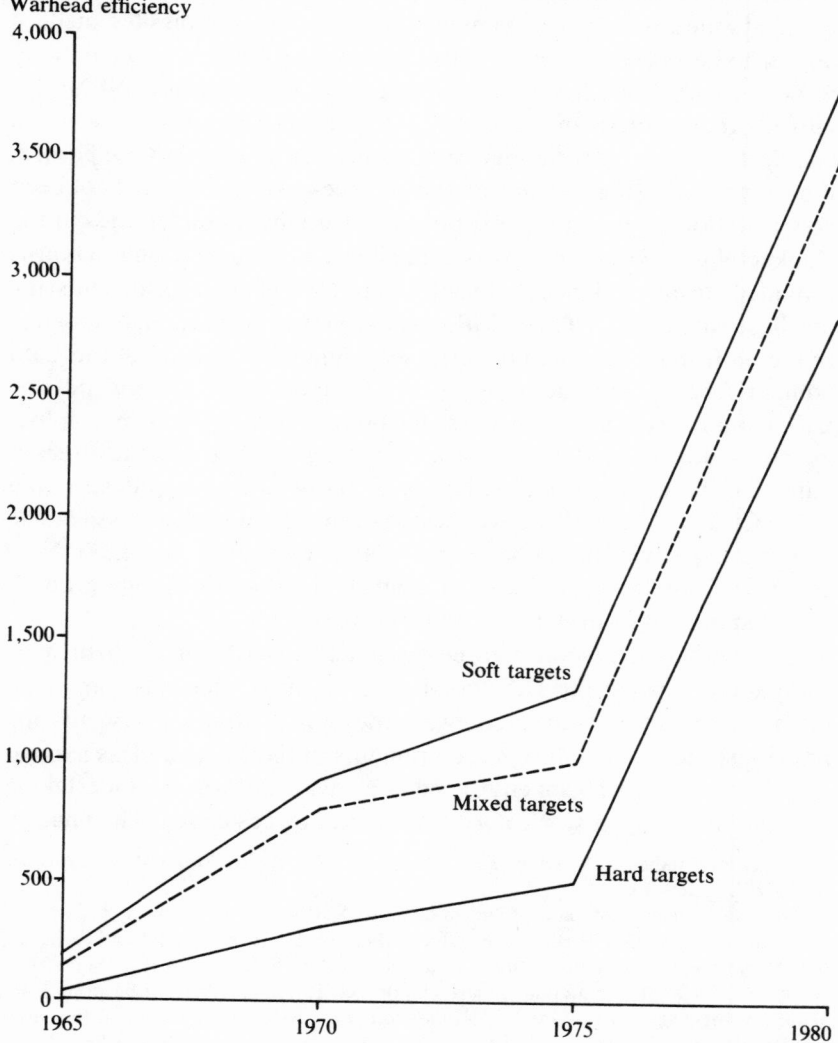

Warhead efficiency

Soft targets

Mixed targets

Hard targets

Notes: Warhead efficiency is an estimated value of the kill probability of the Soviet missile force against targets of a known hardness in a given year. It is based on the single-shot kill probability and number of units of each missile in service in that year. The curve for soft targets assumes that 10 percent are hardened at 2,000 pounds per square inch (psi) and 90 percent at 10 psi, while the curve for hard targets assumes that 10 percent are hardened at 10 psi and 90 percent at 2,000 psi. The curve for mixed targets assumes that for 1965, 5 percent are hardened at 2,000 psi, 20 percent at 100 psi, and 10 percent at 75 psi; for 1970, 5 percent, 25 percent, and 70 percent so hardened; for 1975, 15 percent, 25 percent, and 60 percent; and for 1980, 15 percent, 30 percent, and 55 percent (targeting data from *Fiscal Year 1977 Authorization for Military Procurement, Research and Development, and Active Duty, Selected Reserve and Civilian Personnel Strengths*, Hearings before the Senate Armed Services Committee, 94 Cong. 2 sess. [GPO, 1976], pt. 5, p. 3009).

of operations. Despite the increasing importance of the SSBN within the Soviet Navy, the mission of the Yankee force is not clear. The 1,300-nautical-mile range of the Yankee's SS-N-6 ballistic missiles made it appear to be a new and serious threat to the American strategic bomber force. In particular, it was feared that with Yankee-class SSBNs deployed off the American coasts the USSR could launch a surprise attack and destroy many of the American bombers on alert.[35] As time passed, it became increasingly clear that the Yankee-class SSBNs had not been conceived or deployed for this purpose. Certain characteristics in the Yankee-class SSBN's weapons capability and its operational patterns provided strong evidence that such an attack was not a serious mission for these submarines. The USSR never deployed large enough numbers of them off the U.S. coast to surprise a significant portion of the U.S. bomber force,[36] and additions to normal deployments would put the U.S. command on alert to disperse the bomber force.[37] Only by employing an SLBM with a depressed-trajectory flight path could the attacker minimize the number of U.S. bombers that would escape destruction (table C-12).[38] The USSR never tested or deployed such a missile. The fact that the Soviet threat never materialized was reflected in the U.S. cutback of satellite bases for its bombers and reduction of their ground-alert component from 40 percent to 30 percent.[39]

If the Yankee-class SSBN force was not deployed primarily to provide a capability against the U.S. bomber force, then what mission was it intended to fulfill? Consistent with traditional Soviet Navy mission priorities, the original design requirements of the Yankee-class submarine force may have been envisaged as a naval platform for undertaking nuclear strikes against Western carrier task forces at sea. The engage-

35. Drew Middleton, *New York Times,* March 26, 1972; *United States Military Posture for FY 1972,* pp. 9–10.

36. The standard estimate of the number of SSBNs to constitute a threat is 20 submarines or about 300 SLBMs. See Office of Director, Defense Research and Engineering, Department of Defense, "Joint Strategic Bomber Study," vol. 2: "Supporting Analysis," declassified material (Department of Defense, September 1, 1974), pp. 9, 46, 52, 55, 70. Also see *Fiscal Year 1972 Authorization for Military Procurement, Research and Development, Construction and Real Estate Acquisition for the Safeguard ABM, and Reserve Strengths,* Hearings before the Senate Armed Services Committee, 91 Cong. 1 sess. (GPO, 1971), pt. 4, pp. 2868–69.

37. *Department of Defense Annual Report Fiscal Year 1978,* p. 123.

38. For a detailed analysis of this issue, see Alton H. Quanbeck and Archie L. Wood, *Modernizing the Strategic Bomber Force: Why and How* (Brookings Institution, 1976), pp. 39–62, 108–11.

39. *Baltimore Sun,* February 12, 1975; *Department of Defense Annual Report Fiscal Year 1976 and Fiscal Year 197T,* p. II-35.

ment and destruction of high-value naval units at sea was an important part of the Soviet Navy's traditional requirement to neutralize the enemy's sea-based nuclear systems.[40] Strategic defense was the Navy's main mission when the Yankee-class SSBN and its weaponry were first designed and developed and it continued to be a very high priority into the 1960s. As a result the submarine may have been intended as a platform for launching tactical ballistic missiles.[41] The SS-N-6 is similar to the experimental SS-NX-13 tactical SLBM, which the USSR may have intended to deploy on the Yankee-class submarines.[42] This missile, directed by an ocean reconnaissance satellite, would have presented a severe threat to the survivability of Western aircraft carriers. Other analysts have suggested that other versions of the SS-NX-13 may have been intended for use in antisubmarine warfare.[43]

The SS-NX-13, however, was never deployed—perhaps because of technical difficulties such as creating a feasible system of target acquisition, or because its similarity to the SS-N-6 would cause the missile to be counted against the SALT limits.[44] The need for such a platform diminished during the 1960s as the Soviet Union successfully deployed other weapons and the strategic strike role of U.S. aircraft carriers diminished.

The inherent versatility of the Yankee-class SSBN enabled it to provide an expedient response to the sudden shift in 1961 in Soviet strategic requirements. These new requirements were to improve the overall survivability and target coverage of the Soviet strategic forces as well as to match the growing U.S. Polaris SSBN force. The changes in the Yankee were also motivated by technical failures plaguing the other Soviet missile programs.

---

40. James M. McConnell, "Strategy and Missions of the Soviet Navy in the Year 2000," in James L. George, ed., *Problems of Sea Power As We Approach the Twenty-First Century* (Washington: American Enterprise Institute for Public Policy Research, 1978), pp. 47–49.

41. See K. J. Moore, Mark Flanigan, and Robert D. Helsel, "Developments in Submarine Systems, 1956–76," in Michael MccGwire and John McDonnell, eds., *Soviet Naval Influence: Domestic and Foreign Dimensions* (Praeger for the Centre for Foreign Policy Studies, Department of Political Science, Dalhousie University, 1977), p. 170; Richard T. Ackley, "The Wartime Role of Soviet SSBNs," *United States Naval Institute Proceedings*, vol. 104 (June 1978), p. 39.

42. *United States Military Posture for FY 1978*, p. 16; and Moore, Flanigan, and Helsel, "Development in Submarine Systems," p. 172.

43. Moore, Flanigan, and Helsel, "Developments in Submarine Systems," p. 172; Ackley, "Wartime Role of Soviet SSBNs," pp. 38–39.

44. Michael Getler, *Washington Post*, November 14, 1974.

Probably drawing on components from its SS-11 missile program, the Chelomei design bureau expeditiously produced a medium-range SLBM, the SS-N-6 Sawfly, to fit the Yankee's launch tubes. Though the missile could strike almost the full range of U.S. mainland targets from forward patrol areas, institutional resistance to the growing strategic role of the Navy appears to have limited its coverage to coastal areas. From there it could strike U.S. SSBN support and communication facilities; major U.S. home fleet centers such as New London, Mayport, Norfolk, and San Diego; and most important, the U.S. SSBN base at Charleston. Such strikes would be an extension of the Navy's traditional priority of combating the enemy's fleet, and attacks on major American ports would be a direct means of disrupting the enemy's sea lines of communication. The Yankees could also be used as a supplement to land-based missiles in covering the expanding regional targets of the 1960s.

Another possibility is that while the forward deployed Yankee SSBNs were primarily dedicated to striking coastal targets in wartime, the Soviets may not have ignored the SSBN's relative advantage in rapidly striking various American command-and-control centers. One important target set within the American command-and-control system is the Strategic Air Command's airborne command aircraft. With their short flight time, the SS-N-6 SLBMs on the forward-deployed Y-class SSBNs could pose a significant threat to the small number of SAC bases housing the airborne command network (table C-12), particularly those capable of launching and retargeting the Minuteman ICBMs. This airborne command system became operational only one year before the first Yankee SSBN was deployed; an attack on the U.S. aircraft while they were still on the ground might have been seen as a way of regaining the denial capability lost when the U.S. airborne system became operational. Many of the limitations that prevented the Yankee-class SSBN from staging a preemptive strike against the U.S. bomber force, such as the lack of a missile with a depressed trajectory, would also be relevant in this case.

The Strategic Reserve Assignment

At some point in the mid to late 1960s, Soviet leaders apparently decided to enhance the survivability of Soviet intercontinental strategic strike forces by deploying extremely long-range sea-based missiles. This national decision to back up the silo-based ICBM force with a substantial strategic reserve capability at sea eventually would have a profound impact on the role and character of both the SSBN force and the Soviet Navy as a whole.

With the deployment of the Delta-class SSBNs the long-range SLBMs were allowed to share with the Strategic Rocket Forces in the deep-strike mission against a wide range of U.S. mainland targets. To ensure the survivability of this SSBN force, the Soviet Navy adopted a strategic-support mission in which its surface ships and other forces would be used to actively defend the Soviet SSBN force in wartime. These two new roles, plus the Navy's traditional strategic defense mission against enemy sea-based nuclear forces, transformed it in many respects into a strategic-mission navy.

The Soviet decision to acquire this new sea-based force may have been partly a result of the failure of the SS-13 program to furnish the USSR with a land-mobile ICBM. The timing of the SS-N-8 SLBM's development program suggests this,[45] as does the nature of its platform, the Delta-class SSBN, which is more a modification of the Yankee-class hull than a new design.[46] Concurrently the Soviet Navy was probably just realizing how ineffective its anti-SSBN efforts were and how potentially vulnerable its own SSBNs were.

The deployment of longer range SLBMs on Delta-class SSBNs beginning in 1973 also reflected a fundamental evolution in the mission priorities of the Soviet Navy as well as the Soviet Union's willingness to move away from total dependence on fixed-site ICBMs and their uncertain future to a generally more survivable force based at sea. Soviet SSBNs had earlier been restricted to striking coastal targets in the United States as an extension of their traditional naval missions, while strikes on military and economic targets deep within the United States were mainly the responsibility of the Strategic Rocket Forces, which also were credited with a capability to strike naval targets at sea and on the coasts.[47] In the early 1970s, Soviet writers began to discuss the Soviet

45. Of particular interest was the progressive increase in the SS-N-8's range during a lengthy series of tests. See *New York Times,* February 27, 1972; Michael Getler, *Washington Post,* March 22, 1972; Edgar Ulsamer, "A Searching Look at 'The ICBM Challenge,' " *Air Force Magazine,* July 1973, p. 70.

46. *Hearings on Military Posture: Department of Defense Authorization for Appropriations for Fiscal Year 1974,* Hearings before the House Armed Services Committee, 93 Cong. 1 sess. (GPO, 1973), pt. 1, p. 384.

47. Marshal of the Soviet Union V. D. Sokolovskiy, *Soviet Military Strategy,* 3d ed., ed. Harriet Fast Scott (Crane, Russak, 1975), pp. 203, 246, 290, 302.

SLBM force's ability to destroy land targets not only on the enemy's seaboard but also deep in his rear.[48] Consequently, it probably was not until the early 1970s that the Soviet SLBM force began to acquire the fuller role in the strategic strike mission that had been a mission of the American SSBN force from its inception. The recent Soviet assignment of the deep-strike mission to the SSBNs is reflected in the fact that the Delta-class submarines have essentially the same hull and propulsion system as the Yankee class and had to be enlarged in order to carry larger SS-N-8 and SS-N-18 SLBMs.

The large number of SS-N-8 and SS-N-18 SLBMs on Delta-class SSBNs deployed by the USSR over the past few years has substantially increased its strategic capability at sea and enhanced the overall survivability and endurance of the Soviet strategic forces. The long range of the SS-N-8 and SS-N-18 missiles improves the responsiveness of the sea-based missile force by enabling the USSR to more rapidly augment the number of SLBMs within range of their targets in the U.S. mainland while still remaining safely deployed in home waters, and the multiple warheads of the SS-N-18 provide additionally greater target coverage.

As noted earlier, the USSR may have been seriously counting on the successful development of the SS-13 Savage missile to provide it with a land-mobile ICBM capable of fulfilling its requirement for a survivable, strategic reserve force. The failure of the mobile SS-13 ICBM to materialize during this critical period may have been instrumental in persuading Soviet leaders to develop a strategic reserve capability in the form of sea-based ballistic missiles. Nevertheless, land-mobile ICBM development has continued. The combination of the possibility of a continuing threat to the Soviet land-based missile probably accounted for the SS-X-16 mobile ICBM program that was a part of the fourth generation of Soviet ICBM developments.[49] This ICBM was a lighter missile than its contemporaries and capable of delivering only a relatively small payload. The Soviets may have envisaged it as a hedge against a new U.S. ICBM capable of threatening even the very hard silos of the Soviet fourth-generation ICBMs. That threat did not materialize, which probably made the USSR willing to accept limits prohibiting SS-X-16 deployment as part of the proposed SALT II treaty.

48. For instance, see Marshal of the Soviet Union A. A. Grechko, *On Guard for Peace and the Building of Communism*, JPRS 54602 (National Technical Information Service, U.S. Department of Commerce, 1971), p. 37.

49. *United States Military Posture for FY 1979*, pp. 24–25.

Table C-1. Tactical Nuclear Strike Systems in Western Europe, 1953–80

Controlling authority and weapon system	Year introduced	Range (nautical miles)	Number in service
Introduced 1953–60			
United States			
Nuclear cannon, 280mm	1953–56	12	20–24
Honest John SSM	1956–58	20	14–24
Corporal SSM	1956–58	75	18–24
Redstone SSM	1958	216	16
Nuclear cannon, 203mm	1958	10	84
Lacrosse SSM	1959	16	8
Great Britain			
Corporal SSM	1958	75	24
NATO			
Honest John SSM	1958	20	128
Introduced 1961–70			
United States			
Davy Crockett, small cannon	1962	2.5	20
Nuclear cannon, 203mm, self-propelled	1962	10	44
Nuclear cannon, 155mm, self-propelled	1964	10	360
Sergeant SSM	1964	75	6
Pershing SSM	1964	400	108
Nuclear mines	1964	a	500+
NATO			
Nuclear cannon, 203mm, self-propelled	1962	10	282
Nuclear cannon, 155mm, self-propelled	1964	10	324
West Germany			
Sergeant SSM	1964	75	20
Pershing SSM	1964	400	72
Introduced 1971–80			
United States			
Lance SSM	1973	65	24
France			
Pluton SSM	1973	75	32
NATO			
Lance SSM	1975	65	44

Sources: Stockholm International Peace Research Institute (SIPRI), *Tactical Nuclear Weapons: European Perspectives* (London: Taylor and Francis, 1978), pp. 16, 109–16, 124–34, 130–36; Bill Gunston, *The Illustrated Encyclopaedia of the World's Rockets & Missiles* (Crescent Books, 1979), pp. 34–41; George H. Quester, *Nuclear Diplomacy: The First Twenty-five Years* (Dunellen, 1970), p. 111; *Department of Defense Semiannual Report and the Semiannual Reports of the Secretary of the Army, Secretary of the Navy, Secretary of the Air Force, January 1 to June 30, 1956* and the reports for 1957–61; *Aviation Week and Space Technology*, February 25, 1963, p. 105; International Institute for Strategic Studies, *The Military Balance* (London: IISS), selected years.

SSM. Surface-to-surface missile.

a. Deployed with engineer units to create crater ranging up to 1,000 feet wide.

Table C-2. U.S. and NATO Regional Nuclear Weapon Systems Capable of Striking the Soviet Union, 1953–80

Operating authority and weapon system	Year introduced	Combat radius (nautical miles)	Number in service
Introduced 1953–60			
United States			
F-84 Thunderjet	1953	870	72
B-47	1953 ·	1,300	135[a]
Matador cruise missile	1954	500	72
F-100 Super Sabre	1956	500	216
A-3 Skywarrior	1956	900	32[b]
B-66 Destroyer	1956	900	72
Mace cruise missile	1957	1,000	144
F-101 Voodoo	1958	525	72
Regulus I cruise missile	1958	500	157[c]
Great Britain			
Valiant, Victor, and Vulcan	1955–58	1,700	303
Canberra	1955	400	48
Thor IRBM	1959	1,700	60
NATO			
F-84 Thunderjet	1955–56	870	696
France			
F-100 Super Sabre	1956	500	68
West Germany			
Matador cruise missile	1957	600	72
Italy and Turkey			
Jupiter IRBM	1960	1,700	45
Introduced 1961–70			
United States			
F-105D Thunderchief	1961	400	144
A-6A Intruder	1963	750	60[d]
F-4 Phantom II	1966	400	336
Great Britain			
Buccaneer	1962	800	150
NATO			
F-104G Starfighter	1963–64	500	552
France			
Mirage IV A	1964	600	62
Introduced 1971–80			
United States			
F-111E	1971	800	72
F-111F	1977	800	84
Great Britain			
Buccaneer	1972	800	24
France			
Mirage IIIE and Jaguar	1973	400	75

Sources: See table C-1. Table does not include U.S. systems in the Far East or Polaris missile submarines. Numbers in the table are not additive.

IRBM. Intermediate-range ballistic missile.

a. Stationed at eight air bases in Britain, North Africa, and Spain.

b. Stationed on five aircraft carriers in the Mediterranean Sea and the Western Pacific. Does not include 26 aircraft on carriers in the Atlantic and Pacific oceans.

c. At various times deployed on five submarines, four cruisers, and ten aircraft carriers.

d. Stationed on five aircraft carriers in the Mediterranean Sea and in the Western Pacific.

Table C-3. Targets of Soviet Regional Forces, Early 1960s and Late 1970s

	Number of targets	
Target area and objective	*Early 1960s*	*Late 1970s*
NATO	1,025–1,225	1,400–1,525
Nuclear threat	550–650	650–675
Conventional military threat	325–375	600–650
Administrative and economic centers	150–200	150–200
Middle East and Far East	120–185	75–115
Nuclear threat	5–10	10–15
Conventional military threat	100–150	50–75
Administrative and economic centers	15–25	15–25
China	0	1,390–1,650
Nuclear threat	0	90–100
Conventional military threat	0	400–450
Administrative and economic centers	0	900–1,100
All targets	1,145–1,410	2,865–3,290

Sources: IISS, *The Military Balance*, selected years; SIPRI, *Tactical Nuclear Weapons: European Perspectives*, pp. 15–22, 26–29, 110–14, 179–97; V. D. Sokolovskiy, *Soviet Military Strategy*, 3d ed., ed. Harriet Fast Scott (Crane Russak, 1968), pp. 93–101.

Table C-4. Number of Soviet Regional-range Weapons and Warheads, 1955–80

Instrument	1955	1960	1965	1970	1975	1980
Weapons	1,320	1,580	1,718	2,060	2,219	2,132
Land-based missiles	24	248	733	971	990	1,032
SS-3	24	48	28	0	0	0
SS-12	0	0	0	54	72	72
SS-4	0	200	608	508	508	360
SS-5	0	0	97	90	90	40
SS-14	0	0	0	29	0	0
SS-20	0	0	0	0	0	180
SS-11[a]	0	0	0	290	320	260
SS-19[a]	0	0	0	0	0	120
Sea-based missiles[b]	0	36	105	365	569	445
SS-N-4, SS-N-5	0	36	105	93	89	57
SS-N-6	0	0	0	272	480	388
Bombers[c]	1,296	1,296	880	724	660	655
TU-4	996[d]	296	0	0	0	0
TU-16	300	1,000	775	550	475	445
TU-22	0	0	105	174	170	140
TU-22M	0	0	0	0	15	70
Warheads	324	1,034	2,085	2,301	2,467	3,497
Land-based missiles	24	248[e]	733[f]	969[g]	990[g]	1,992[h]
Sea-based missiles	0	36	105	365	569	445
Bombers	300	750	1,247	965	908	1,060

Sources: IISS, *The Military Balance*, selected years; Edward L. Warner III, *The Military in Contemporary Soviet Politics: An Institutional Analysis* (Praeger, 1977), pp. 187–200; "Statement of Secretary of Defense Robert S. McNamara before a Joint Session of the Senate Armed Services Committee and the Senate Subcommittee on Department of Defense Appropriations on the Fiscal Year 1966–70 Defense Program and 1966 Defense Budget," declassified (U.S. Department of Defense, January–February 1965) and declassified statements for the budgets of 1967 and 1970; Robert P. Berman, *Soviet Air Power in Transition* (Brookings Institution, 1978), p. 25; *Department of Defense Annual Report Fiscal Year 1982*, pp. 66.

a. Includes only those missiles facing Western Europe and China.
b. Those with less than an intercontinental range; does not include forward-deployed units.
c. Roughly 75–80 percent are strike aircraft.
d. Conventional capability only.
e. Plus a reload capability of about 200 SS-4s.
f. Plus a reload capability at soft sites of about 514 SS-4s and SS-5s.
g. Plus a reload capability at soft sites of about 466 SS-4s and SS-5s.
h. Plus 180 SS-20s and a reload capability at soft sites of about 265 SS-4s and SS-5s.

Table C-5. Targets of Soviet Intercontinental Forces, Early 1950s and Early 1960s

Category	Number of targets	
	Early 1950s	Early 1960s
Nuclear threats	19	342
Strategic Air Command bases	19	46
ICBM launch control centers	. . .	28
ICBM launchers	. . .	268
Conventional threats: Active army divisions, tactical fighter air bases, and navy ports	114	114
Administrative and economic centers[a]	233	333
All categories	366	789

Source: *Development of Strategic Air Command 1946–1976* (Office of the Historian, Headquarters Strategic Air Command, U.S. Air Force, 1976), pp. 20, 76; U.S. Bureau of the Census, *Statistical Abstract of the United States, 1978* (GPO, 1978), pp. 18–26.

ICBM Intercontinental ballistic missile.

a. Places with 50,000 or more inhabitants; the total urban area of these centers was 28,000 square miles in the early 1950s and 40,000 square miles in the early 1960s.

Table C-6. Targets of Soviet Intercontinental Forces, 1970s

Category	Type	Number
Nuclear threats	. . .	1,534
National Command Authority centers	Hard and soft	60
Airborne command network air bases	Soft	5
ICBM launch control centers	Hard	114
ICBM silos (operational and test)	Hard	1,068
SSBN transmitters	Soft	60
Bomber bases	Soft	29
Bomber dispersal bases	Soft	27
Submarine bases and underwater monitoring centers	Soft	10
Radars	Soft	132
Fighter-interceptor sites	Soft	28
ABM test site	Soft	1
Conventional threats	. . .	258
Active army divisions, tactical fighter bases, and military airlift bases	Soft	52
Reserve army division and tactical fighter air bases	Soft	58
Aircraft carrier bases	Soft	4
Army, navy, and air force ammunition sites	Hard	144
Administrative and economic centers	. . .	373
Urban industrial areas (50,000 or more inhabitants)	Soft	333
Major ports	Soft	40
All categories	. . .	2,165

Sources: Estimated from a wide variety of sources, including IISS, *The Military Balance 1980–1981;* Donald B. Vought and J. R. Angolia, "The United States Army," and Robert N. Ginsburgh, "The United States Air Force," in Ray Bonds, ed., *The US War Machine: An Illustrated Encyclopaedia of American Military Equipment and Strategy* (Crown, 1978).

ICBM Intercontinental ballistic missile.

SSBN Nuclear-powered ballistic-missile submarine.

ABM Antiballistic missile.

Table C-7. Number of Soviet Intercontinental-range Weapons and Warheads, 1960–80

Instrument	1960	1965	1970	1975	1980
Weapons	149	434	1,456	1,652	1,696
Land-based missiles	4	224	1,220	1,267	1,018
SS-6	4	4	0	0	0
SS-7	0	197	197	190	0
SS-8	0	23	23	19	0
SS-9	0	0	240	278	0
SS-11[a]	0	0	720	650	320
SS-13	0	0	40	60	60
SS-17	0	0	0	10	150
SS-18	0	0	0	10	308
SS-19[a]	0	0	0	50	180
Sea-based missiles	0	15	41	196	522
SS-N-4, SS-N-5	0	15[b]	9[b]	0	0
SS-N-6	0	0	32[b]	64[b]	64[b]
SS-N-8	0	0	0	132[c]	282[c]
SS-N-18	0	0	0	0	176
Bombers[d]	145	195	195	189	156
MYA-4	35	85	85	85	56
TU-20	110	110	110	104	100
Warheads	294	381	1,403	1,875	6,156
Land-based missiles	4	224[e]	1,220[f]	1,537[g]	5,140
Sea-based missiles	0	15	41	196	874
Bombers	290	142	142	142	142

Sources: IISS, *The Military Balance,* selected years; statement of secretary of defense on the budgets of 1963–73; *United States Military Posture for 1982* (U.S. Office of the Joint Chiefs of Staff, 1981), pp. 99, 100.
  a. Includes only those believed to be primarily dedicated to covering intercontinental-range targets.
  b. Forward-deployed missiles.
  c. Including 6 missiles in testbed launchers.
  d. Includes tankers.
  e. Plus a reload capability of 142 SS-7s and SS-8s.
  f. Plus a reload capability of 142 SS-7s and SS-8s.
  g. Plus a reload capability of 131 SS-7s and SS-8s.

Table C-8. Effectiveness of an SS-9 Attack on Minuteman Launch-Control Centers

Number of centers[a]	Year	Number of SS-9s	Damage expectancy (percent)[b] First strike	Damage expectancy (percent)[b] Second strike	Number of centers destroyed
95	1966	72	39.6–23.8	. . .	28–23
100	1967	114	55.0–33.0	7.7–4.6	63–38
100	1968	156	55.0–33.0	30.8–18.5	86–52
100	1969	198	55.0–33.0	53.9–32.3	100–65
100	1970	240	66.0–39.6	66.0–39.6	100–79
100	1971	288	79.2–47.5	79.2–47.5	100–95

Source: Ernest G. Schwiebert, *A History of the U.S. Air Force Ballistic Missiles* (Praeger, 1965), p. 227.
  a. Assumes hardness of 1,000 psi. Each center controls 10 Minuteman missiles.
  b. Each SS-9 is assumed to have a yield of 20 megatons, a reliability of 75 percent, and variations in accuracy of 0.50–0.75 nautical mile.

Table C-9. Number of Ballistic Missiles Required to Destroy an Aircraft Carrier, by Range[a]

	Range of target[c]		
Warhead and yield[b]	3,500 nautical miles	1,600 nautical miles	400 nautical miles
Single 950-kiloton	10	8	5
Three 350-kiloton	. . .	11	6
Single 250-kiloton	. . .	. . .	5
Single 700-kiloton	. . .	. . .	5

a. Assumes a carrier speed of 30 knots and lethal overpressures of 15 psi. It is assumed that all intelligence-collection systems are attempting to build up a real time plot of carrier deployments and that each carrier's future position will remain within a 90° sector of a circle.

b. These combinations are similar to those of the land-based SS-11 and the sea-based SS-N-6 and SS-NX-13.

c. The SS-11 has a range of 3,500 nautical miles, the SS-N-6 a range of 1,600 nautical miles, and the SS-NX-13 a range of 400 miles.

Table C-10. Number of Ballistic Missiles Required to Destroy Five, Ten, and Fifteen Aircraft Carriers[a]

	Number of missiles[b]		
Number of carriers	SS-11	SS-N-6	SS-NX-13
5	72–50	79–43	8–36
10	143–100	158–86	15–72
15	215–150	237–129	22–108

a. Reliability of 70 percent is assumed.

b. Missiles are assumed to have effects outlined in table C-7. Numbers required range from least-effective single-warhead missiles to most effective multiple-warhead missiles. For the SS-NX-13 the lower figures assume terminal guidance of the warhead.

Table C-11. Accuracy Required to Achieve Various Damage Levels with SS-11, SS-18, and SS-19 Warheads[a]

Warhead and reliability level	Warhead accuracy (nautical miles) to achieve		
	Annihilation[b]	Neutralization[c]	Harassment[d]
SS-11			
70 percent	0.23	0.44	0.85
75 percent	0.26	0.45	0.86
80 percent	0.28	0.48	0.90
SS-18, 550-kiloton			
70 percent	0.11	0.19	0.36
75 percent	0.11	0.20	0.38
80 percent	0.12	0.21	0.40
SS-18, 900-kiloton			
70 percent	0.12	0.23	0.44
75 percent	0.13	0.23	0.46
80 percent	0.14	0.25	0.48
SS-19			
70 percent	0.11	0.19	0.36
75 percent	0.11	0.20	0.38
80 percent	0.12	0.21	0.40

a. The target is assumed to be a 300 psi silo for intercontinental ballistic missiles in the case of the SS-11 attack and a 2,000 psi silo in the case of the SS-18 and SS-19.

b. Assumes target's effectiveness is reduced 60 percent.

c. Assumes target's effectiveness is reduced 30 percent.

d. Assumes target's effectiveness is reduced 10 percent.

Table C-12. Vulnerability of U.S. Strategic Air Command Bases to a Soviet Submarine Attack

Number of submarines and warheads in attack[a]	Percent of force destroyed	Number of aircraft surviving[b]
SAC main operating bases[c]		
5 Yankees		
SS-N-6 mod. 2[d]	1	124(186)
SS-N-6 mod. 3[e]	3	121(182)
SS-N-6 mod. X[f]	8	115(173)
10 Yankees		
SS-N-6 mod. 2[d]	3	121(182)
SS-N-6 mod. 3[e]	5	119(179)
SS-N-6 mod. X[f]	15	106(160)
20 Yankees		
SS-N-6 mod. 2[d]	5	119(179)
SS-N-6 mod. 3[e]	10	113(207)
SS-N-6 mod. X[f]	31	86(130)
30 Yankees		
SS-N-6 mod. 2[d]	8	115(173)
SS-N-6 mod. 3[e]	15	106(160)
SS-N-6 mod. X[f]	46	68(102)
SAC airborne command bases[g]		
3 Yankees		
SS-N-6 mod. 2[d]	22	18
SS-N-6 mod. 3[e]	33	15
SS-N-6 mod. X[f]	100	0
5 Yankees		
SS-N-6 mod. 2[d]	41	14
SS-N-6 mod. 3[e]	61	9
SS-N-6 mod. X[f]	100	0

Sources: Alton H. Quanbeck and Archie L. Wood, *Modernizing the Strategic Bomber Force: Why and How* (Brookings Institution, 1976), p. 48; *Hearings on Military Posture: Department of Defense Authorization for Appropriations for Fiscal Year 1976*, Hearings before the Senate Armed Services Committee, 94 Cong. 1 sess. (GPO, 1975), pt. 10, pp. 5522–23; Office of Director of Defense, Defense Research Engineering, Department of Defense, "Joint Strategic Bomber Study," vol. 2: "Supporting Analysis," declassified version (Department of Defense, September 1974), pp. 46–58.

a. Each submarine has 16 launcher tubes with 75 percent reliability. Three submarines are considered to be a normal patrol practice, five a high but normal practice.

b. Numbers in parentheses are of bombers surviving a crisis alert.

c. Assumed to be 2 bases housing 60 FB-111s and 26 bases housing 316 B-52s. In a normal alert, 30 percent (or 125) of the bombers are assumed to be on alert, in a crisis 50 percent (or 188) of the bombers.

d. This 650-kiloton missile has a minimum-energy-trajectory flight time of 800 seconds.

e. This 350-kiloton missile, with three warheads, has a minimum-energy-trajectory flight time of 800 seconds.

f. This hypothetical 350-kiloton missile, with three warheads, has a depressed trajectory flight time of 525 seconds.

g. This is the U.S. post-attack command-and-control system, made up of 23 aircraft located at five bases on fifteen-minute ground alert. Once airborne, this force hypothetically would have to maintain eight orbits to launch retaliatory missile strikes.

Strategic Defensive Forces

ONE OF THE greatest distinctions between U.S. and Soviet strategic forces is in the priority they accord to defensive forces. The Soviet Union maintains a large and expensive air defense system despite the fact that defenses against ballistic missiles are prohibited by the Antiballistic Missile (ABM) Treaty. It also continues to spend large sums on other defensive programs, including ABM research and development as well as civilian defense measures. By contrast, the United States allowed its strategic air defenses to decline after the mid-1960s, when ballistic missiles replaced long-range bombers as the major strategic offensive weapon. The United States has also increasingly favored an offense-dominated strategic force posture as the best means of deterrence.

The Soviet Union, by comparison, has generally maintained and expanded its strategic defenses since the mid-1960s. Its greater commitment to strategic defenses arises in part from the fact that strategic bombers continue to be a significant portion of the American strategic force and bombers and fighter-bombers are the primary attack instruments of its regional nuclear foes. Moreover, the character of Soviet doctrine compels the use of defensive as well as offensive forces to prohibit nuclear attack on the USSR.

Strategic defensive forces would attempt to prevent Western retaliatory forces from attacking Soviet political and military command posts, industrial centers, military complexes, and a variety of other targets. The high costs that will result from even a small number of nuclear-armed enemy forces reaching their targets make this an almost impossible mission. Yet, given the Soviet Union's conception of the likely duration of a modern war, even a marginal defensive capability against the enemy's offensive forces is worthwhile. Furthermore, military establishments often attempt to do the best they can in solving any particular problem while hoping for some further breakthrough in military technology to improve the situation.

All of the Soviet strategic defensive forces were under the command of the National Air Defense Force of the Homeland (PVO Strany) from 1954 to 1980. Within PVO Strany's domain were early-warning radars and satellites, aviation units (APVO), surface-to-air missiles (Zenith Missile Troops—ZMT), antiballistic missiles (PRO Strany), and anti-satellite systems (PKO Strany). Antiaircraft forces would counter the manned aircraft that both the United States and China rely on to deliver nuclear weapons; antimissile forces, relegated to one site by the ABM treaty, shield the national command in Moscow from ballistic missile attacks; anti-space forces can reduce the effectiveness of supporting elements of the West's strategic forces, and civil defense forces can protect key elements of the Soviet population.

Air Defense Deployment

In a major national effort to modernize its air defense force—about 1,000 fighters of World War II vintage supported by a visual reporting system—the Soviet Union had by 1953 doubled the number of its fighters, and all were of modern jet design.[1] Large numbers of antiaircraft artillery supplemented the fighter force, and electronic early-warning systems allowed detection of U.S. and British bombers before they reached the Soviet homeland. Two special National Air Defense districts were created with headquarters in Moscow and Baku[2] to cover what has been traditionally considered the political and economic heartland of the USSR, and the Warsaw Pact countries were brought into the Soviet strategic air defense system.[3] Relying primarily on the MIG-15 and MIG-17 interceptors, the USSR was equipped to counter the kind of high-altitude, clear-weather bombing raids in daylight that the U.S. B-29s had carried out over Korea. Yet by this time the West had shifted its planning to an air offensive employing the more advanced B-36 and B-47 strategic

1. Lt. Gen. M. Gareyev, "Ever Guarding the Achievements of October," U.S. Air Force, Directorate of Soviet Affairs, Air Force Intelligence Service, *Soviet Press Selected Translations,* no. 78-4 (April 1978), p. 105; Thomas W. Wolfe, *Soviet Power and Europe, 1945–1970* (Johns Hopkins Press, 1970), p. 48.

2. Other air defense districts were located in other military districts in the USSR.

3. U.S. Defense Intelligence Agency, *Handbook on the Soviet Armed Forces* (DIA, 1978), p. 11-1.

bombers whose operations were limited neither by weather nor by altitude. Setting a pattern that would be replayed time and again, the large Soviet air defense system seemed to trail one step behind the strategic bomber threat it was to counter.

During the mid-1950s concentric circles of early SA-1 launchers were deployed around Moscow for the protection of the top Soviet leadership.[4] Shortly afterwards, the SA-2, a missile dedicated to the high-altitude, area defense of vital targets, entered large-scale production and deployment, and surface-to-air missiles (SAMs) were deployed for the first time. These weapons were assigned to the Zenith Missile Troops, the most important element of the air defense forces, who were to defend Soviet command, industrial, and military targets against an enemy air attack. Fighter planes were assigned the lesser duty of intercepting attacking aircraft on the distant approaches to the defended areas.

Air Defense in the 1960s and 1970s

During the 1960s the Soviet defense system relied on the YAK-28 interceptor and the SA-5 missile, which provided a good high-altitude defense against enemy bomber attack, and the MIG-25 Foxbat, which could operate at high speeds and high altitudes. The system had been designed to counter the threat posed by the American B-70 and the Skybolt missile, both canceled years earlier. While it may have been a useful instrument to counter the U.S. SR-71 reconnaissance aircraft, the Soviet defense system was not adequate as a counter to low-altitude-penetration tactics the United States had begun to emphasize.[5]

This recurring shortfall of the air defense forces is symptomatic of the problems of the Soviet air defense system.

Qualitatively, the lagging effectiveness of the APVO and the ZMT is an excellent illustration of how shortcomings in the basic technological capacity of a country can limit the range of military options it has

4. Ibid.

5. Robert P. Berman, *Soviet Air Power in Transition* (Brookings Institution, 1978), pp. 17–18; Strategic Air Command, Office of the Historian, *Development of Strategic Air Command 1946–1976* (U.S. Air Force, 1976), p. 77. Throughout the 1950s, high-altitude penetration of Soviet air space by U.S. reconnaissance aircraft proved successful—in the early 1950s by the RB-36, from 1956 to 1960 by some thirty U-2s which may have photographed as much as one-third of the USSR. See *Bulletin of Atomic Scientists*, April 1977, p. 27; Lawrence Freedman, *US Intelligence and the Soviet Strategic Threat* (Westview, 1977), p. 69.

available, possibly at the expense of its military effectiveness. The Soviet lag in certain advanced data-processing and sensor technologies, which prevented it from fielding promptly the interceptors and airborne warning-and-control aircraft (AWACs) that are necessary to find and kill bombers flying at low altitudes,[6] was a major factor in limiting Soviet effectiveness against the American bomber force through the 1970s. The sheer size of the Soviet Union is also a severely limiting factor. Many thousands of radars, interceptors, and surface-to-air missiles must be deployed for long lengths of time to adequately cover the important areas in the USSR. Such a vast defense network requires years to complete, and the United States meantime can devise new tactics or penetration aids to offset new Soviet developments.[7] To aggravate all the other problems, the advent of nuclear weapons drastically reduced the number of penetrations that the defender can withstand. The air defense forces have depended on a very restrictive, ground-based control system that detects enemy bombers and directs the interceptors to their targets.[8] Precursor strikes by either ballistic missiles or bomber-launched missiles could seriously degrade the Soviet air defense network by destroying these ground-based control centers or interrupting their communications. Recently Soviet pilots have been allowed greater initiative.

Although the Soviet air defense system is not well prepared to counter the U.S. bomber force, it probably has a formidable capability against the strategic bombers of such regional foes as Great Britain, France, and China. And in the late 1970s the USSR was finally able to deploy new radars and low-altitude interceptors such as the late-model MIG-23 Flogger and the SU-15 Flagon E and F that would be effective against low-level penetration attacks. The SA-10 missile, which was probably designed to intercept high-speed attack missiles carried by the U.S. B-52 and FB-111 and the bombers themselves, is soon to be deployed, as is the SA-N-6 missile that will attempt to provide a counter for the U.S. Harpoon missile.

6. The United States was able some years ago to deploy an AWAC aircraft and fighters whose radar is capable of discriminating and tracking aircraft flying near the surface without losing them in the ground clutter that would be picked up on a regular radar.

7. The United States has developed decoys and a standoff missile and has improved electronic countermeasures of bomber aircraft at regular intervals.

8. International Institute for Strategic Studies, *The Military Balance 1980–1981* (London: IISS, 1980). The aircraft are located at some 80 bases. See *Aviation Week and Space Technology*, June 16, 1980.

Air Defense Today

A major reorganization has been taking place in the Soviet Air Defense Forces[9] that seems to be aimed at making more flexible responses to air and missile threats. The Strategic Rocket Forces (SRF) will play the central role in denying the United States the use of its intercontinental ballistic missiles (ICBMs) and their command-and-control centers. The Air Defense Forces have an equally important role in denying the United States the use of its bomber force. About one-third of the U.S. bomber force (100 aircraft) can be expected to escape even a devastating ballistic-missile attack and they carry some 1,000 nuclear weapons. The bombers will be assisted by U.S. ICBMs aimed at suppressing and cutting corridors through the Soviet defenses.[10] The Air Defense Forces will thus have an enormous task in defending the Soviet Union. Their tactics are both active and fluid. Rather than providing uniform coverage over the USSR, both aircraft and SAMs are concentrated on protecting the most vital and important targets. Interceptor aircraft are used at extreme ranges and before bombers have penetrated Soviet airspace. They, along with some SAMs, would also harass the attacking aircraft enroute to the target. At the target itself clusters of surface-to-air missiles would be used for point defense.

Future Developments

In the 1980s and 1990s the airborne threat to the USSR could increase in complexity as well as in demand on the Soviet strategic defense. Rather than only having to defend against penetrating bombers, the USSR will be faced in the 1980s with the prospect of several thousands of small, low-flying cruise missiles that can be released at long distances from outside existing Soviet air defenses. For the 1990s the United States is considering deployment of penetrating bombers that will be invisible to Soviet air defense sensors. These developments would pose a serious challenge to the Soviet air defense system that would be compounded if advanced, long-range cruise missiles were also available to nuclear powers in the regions surrounding the Soviet Union.

9. *Washington Star,* July 16, 1981.
10. DIA, *Handbook,* p. 11-1.

The USSR, in order to upgrade its low-altitude detection, must improve its command and data-processing capability and possibly over haul its command structure. By deploying a true airborne warning and control system (AWACS) aircraft—which is reportedly under development—and developing a capacity to look down and shoot down in its Foxbat and a new generation of interceptors, it could present a severe threat to low-altitude bombers and offer some capability against the early model cruise missile.[11] Yet even these forces, supported by improved radar and surface-to-air missiles, would not be sufficient to deal with large numbers of improved cruise missiles.

The air defense force will be compelled to examine more innovative methods if it is to offset the U.S. threat. With current resources it could establish stand-off air defense barriers at a point before U.S. bombers can launch their cruise missiles. This would require an aircraft with a long range that can be refueled in the air, plus a large force of refueling tankers and detection devices.[12] The change would be expensive and would probably require significant change in the traditional Soviet operational approach that relies on ground-directed interceptions. A low-technology option would feature the deployment of acoustic sensors and thousands of mobile, multibarrel guns or infrared platforms for point defense of critical targets. The most innovative would use high-energy lasers as a target acquisition system or as weapons against cruise missiles or bombers. This would be a high-risk option requiring large-scale investment.

Ballistic Missile Defenses

Soviet interest in ballistic missile defenses, which dates back to the 1950s, is a logical extension of the Soviet adherence to an active doctrine. Soviet ABM deployments preceded those of the United States and have been oriented toward defending administrative and economic centers rather than protecting land-based strategic forces as the U.S. program has been. Because they were originally designed to protect political centers and population and industrial areas Soviet ABMs may have had

11. Clarence A. Robinson, Jr., "Soviets to Field 3 New Fighters in Aviation Modernization Drive," *Aviation Week and Space Technology,* March 26, 1979, pp. 14–16.

12. Clarence A. Robinson, Jr., "Carter Warned on Soviet Nuclear Advantage," *Aviation Week and Space Technology,* November 7, 1977, pp. 18–21.

different technical requirements than if they had been built for protecting ICBM sites. The most obvious difference would be the long range needed to intercept incoming missiles before they detonated near the area that was being protected. The major adversary for a Soviet ABM would have probably been submarine-launched missiles whose closer range would allow a steeper reentry angle and slower reentry speed than those of most ICBMs. Regardless of what their target was, the Soviets still had difficulty in developing an ABM system that would work.

Soviet ABM testing began in 1962 with the eight-ton Griffon. Although deployment of the system began around Leningrad, in the next year it was stopped and the system was dismantled by 1964, possibly because of the lack of adequate data processing and poor missile performance. It was undoubtedly deployed as a defense against the U.S. Atlas and Titan missiles, which entered service in 1958, as well as the Thor and Jupiter missiles based in Europe. The Galosh system began to be built around Moscow in 1964 in locations similar to those of the first SA-1 SAM sites eight years earlier. Four complexes each with target acquisition radars, tracking radars, and sixteen ABM launchers on soft sites were installed by 1968.[13] They would have been in response to the U.S. Polaris A-1 and Minuteman I deployments in 1960 and 1962. The Galosh is a slow-reacting, thirty-six-ton, exoatmospheric missile. The improved version reportedly can loiter in space by stopping and restarting its engines, thus giving its land-based radars time to discriminate between live warheads and chaff or decoys. This system would be an appropriate response to attacks by U.S. Polaris A-3 and Minuteman II missiles equipped with multiple warheads and penetration aids.

The weak link in the Soviet ABM system has clearly been the radars. The missile defense forces have relied on Hen House phased radars for the initial detection of a missile attack, and a combination of Dog and Cat House phased-array battle-management radars, along with the mechanically scanning Try Add engagement radars to perform the actual task of missile interception. The slowness of the Try Add radars and low speeds of the data-processing computers that support the Dog and Cat House radars leave the entire ABM system inadequate against a high-intensity attack in a cluttered environment.[14] All of them are vulnerable

13. Michael Getler, *Washington Post,* April 28, 1971.
14. Johan J. Holst, "Missile Defense, the Soviet Union, and the Arms Race," in Johan J. Holst and William Schneider, Jr., *Why ABM? Policy Issues in the Missile Defense Controversy* (Pergamon, 1969), pp. 145–86.

to the electromagnetic and blast effects of nuclear weapons.[15] In the 1970s the Soviet Union began deploying large phased-array radars on the periphery of the country and expanded the use of early-warning satellites for earlier missile detection.

The 1972 ABM treaty, as amended in 1974, limits the Soviet Union to one ABM site with 100 launchers. The USSR chose to retain its 64 Galosh launchers around Moscow. Recently it removed 32 of them, perhaps in anticipation of a new ABM system in testing since the 1970s. The remaining launchers provide an adequate defense only against a small, unsophisticated missile attack. The Soviet Union's motive in signing the ABM treaty has been a matter of debate since the USSR initially showed great reluctance to consider limits on ABMs. A number of explanations exist concerning Soviet agreement to the treaty. The Soviet agreement not to deploy any new strategic antiballistic missile defense systems was probably prompted by the continuing shortcomings of the Soviet strategic defensive force in general. Research and development on ABM systems have continued at a vigorous pace.[16] Yet in none of the defensive programs was there significant enough progress during the 1970s to meet defense requirements. Technological limitations, American actions, and the inherent difficulties of the problem continued to obstruct the strategic defense program.

In signing the ABM treaty, Soviet political leaders—if not military leaders—may have been accepting the Western concept of deterrence based on "mutual assured destruction." Or they may simply have been recognizing the inferiority of their ABM technology to that of the United States. But Soviet leaders may have concluded that they could best ensure the USSR's future ability to strike the U.S. Minuteman force by preventing U.S. deployment of an effective ballistic-missile defense system. The uncertainty of providing an effective ABM defense of its own urban centers, and the increasing capability of the Strategic Rocket Forces for performing its strike mission against U.S. land-based strategic

15. *Aviation Week and Space Technology,* July 20, 1970, p. 20; Johan Jorgen Holst, "Comparative U.S. and Soviet Deployments, Doctrines, and Arms Limitations," in Morton A. Kaplan, ed., *SALT: Problems & Prospects* (Morristown, N.J.: General Learning Press, 1973), p. 64.

16. Clarence A. Robinson, Jr., "Soviets Push ABM Development," *Aviation Week and Space Technology,* April 7, 1975, p. 12; *Aviation Week and Space Technology,* May 24, 1976, pp. 20–21, April 28, 1980, p. 20, February 9, 1981, pp. 28–29, March 23, 1981, pp. 22–23. Between 1972 and 1976, there were 55 ABM test launches, including tests of high-acceleration missiles using both conventional and infrared guidance systems.

forces, may have led the USSR to conclude that the ABM treaty was a net advantage in terms of Soviet strategic doctrine.

One of the most crucial elements in the strategic balance is defense. It is also the area of greatest uncertainty because of the high technological risk and investment in resources that it requires. To meet its defensive requirements—the one element of its operational doctrine that has yet to be adequately fulfilled—the Soviet Union may look to technical solutions, including site defense of silo-based ICBMs to ensure the survivability of its ICBMs and directed-energy weapons such as laser systems of charged particle beams (CPBs) for areawide defense. Of course, a decision to deploy such weapons would require a complete reassessment of the strategic relationship with the United States recognizing that the United States would deploy similar systems.

Anti-Space Defense

The Soviet Union's antisatellite (ASAT) program was one of the most actively developed in the 1970s. Its main objective was to develop satellites that could be used to destroy U.S. support systems based in space. The ability to destroy U.S. reconnaissance, navigation, and electronic intelligence (Elint) satellites located in orbits near the earth by nonnuclear means would be important during either nuclear or nonnuclear conflict. And the ability to counter the fledgling Chinese space program would be politically as well as militarily valuable to the USSR.[17]

Between 1968 and 1981 the Soviets tested nineteen interceptor and inspector satellites (see table D-1). In the tests between 1968 and 1971, 70 percent of the flights appear to have been successful; in those between 1976 and 1981 the success rate was 72 percent for two-orbit attacks but only 40 percent for one-orbit sorties.[18]

Interceptor satellites are launched by SS-9 missiles similar to the SS-9 modification that used a fractional orbital bombardment system (FOBS). The attack satellite weighs 2.5 tons and is equipped with five main rocket

17. Lawrence Freedman, "The Soviet Union and 'Anti-Space Defense,' " *Survival*, vol. 19 (January–February 1977), pp. 22–23.

18. *Washington Post*, July 27, 1976; *Aviation Week and Space Technology*, April 28, 1980, p. 20, February 9, 1981, p. 28, March 23, 1981, pp. 22–23.

engines for maneuverability. It can close on its target at nearly thirteen miles a minute and when less than 100 feet from the target can explode on ground command, destroying the target with its debris.[19] Satellites with external solar panels would be particularly vulnerable to this type of attack.

All of the ASAT tests took place at altitudes of 600 miles or less. They followed several experimental means of attack, which may account for the overall variation in the reliability of the antisatellite system. Some of the attack profiles involved eccentric orbits (six in 1968–71, three in 1976–81) where high speed and an eventual explosion were characteristic; some had circular orbits (one in 1968–71, three in 1976–81) where slow speed and inspection seemed to be key; and some used a pop-up technique (five from 1976 to 1981) that requires only one orbit before the satellite leaves to attack a target at a higher orbit.[20] Soviet space vehicles were used in the tests to represent different types of targets. Two satellites in the series (Kosmos 185 and 271) appear to have been either engineering tests or targets that never achieved proper orbit. Fifteen were successfully launched (table D-2), all but two of them for tests at altitudes at which U.S. electronic intelligence gathering and navigation satellites orbit.[21] In every instance it was the interceptor satellite that exploded rather than the target vehicle.

The Soviet ASAT program has not demonstrated any utility against early-warning satellites, which orbit at 23,000 miles and cannot be reached in less than six hours even in a direct ascent. Soviet antisatellite forces are capable of neutralizing U.S. reconnaissance and Elint satellite systems and early navigation satellites, which many services continue to utilize; they thus could affect decisionmaking by high-level U.S. groups. Indeed, through the late 1960s and into the 1970s the Soviet Union's pursuit of the capability to destroy U.S. navigation satellites and thereby degrade the effectiveness of the U.S. SSBNs on patrol may have been its most productive program.

19. *Washington Post,* July 27, 1976; *Aviation Week and Space Technology,* February 5, 1978, p. 19. This issue is still a matter of controversy.

20. *Aviation Week and Space Technology,* February 5, 1978, p. 19.

21. William Beecher, *New York Times,* May 20, 1972; Deborah Shapley, "Soviet Killer Satellites: U.S. Ponders a Response," *Science,* September 3, 1976, p. 865; *Aviation Week and Space Technology,* April 28, 1980, p. 20, February 9, 1981, p. 28, March 23, 1981, pp. 22–23.

Table D-1. Launchings of Soviet Interceptor and Inspector Satellites, 1968–81

Kosmos number[a]	Year launched	Status[b]	Time to intercept (hours)[c]	Result
249	1968	Exploded	3.0	Failure
252	1968	Exploded	3.0	Success
374	1970	Exploded	3.0	Failure
375	1970	Exploded	3.0	Success
397	1971	Exploded	3.0	Success
404	1971	Returned	3.0	Success
462	1971	Exploded	3.0	Success
804	1976	Returned	11.0	Failure
814	1976	Returned	1.5	Success
843	1976	Returned	1.5	Failure
886	1976	Exploded	3.0	Success
910	1977	Returned	1.5	Failure
918	1977	Returned	1.5	Success
961	1977	Returned	3.0	Success
970	1977	Exploded	3.0	Failure
1009	1978	Returned	3.0	Success
1174	1980	Exploded	1.5	Failure
1234	1981	Returned	3.0	Success
1258	1981	Exploded	3.0	Success

Sources: Lawrence Freedman, "The Soviet Union and 'Anti-Space Defense,' " *Survival,* vol. 19 (January–February 1977), p. 19; David Baker, "Killer Satellites," *Flight International,* October 15, 1977, pp. 1129, 1130; "Soviet Space Programs, 1971–75," Senate Aeronautical and Space Sciences Committee, vol. 1, August 30, 1976, p. 425; Stockholm International Peace Research Institute, *World Armaments and Disarmament: SIPRI Yearbook 1978* (London: Taylor and Francis, 1978), p. 110; *Aviation Week and Space Technology,* April 28, 1980, p. 20.

a. Radar sensors were used by Kosmos 249–918; optical sensors were used on Kosmos 961–1258.

b. Satellites exploded in space are possible interceptors; those returned to earth are possible inspectors.

c. Antisatellite missiles are believed, like reconnaissance satellite missiles, to be capable of a quick enough launching to be in orbit in 90 minutes.

Table D-2. Soviet Target Satellites for Interceptor and Inspector Satellite Launches, 1968–81

	Target satellite	
Target type and altitude	*Kosmos number*	*Year launched*
Reconnaissance, 150 nautical miles	291	1969
	450	1971
Elint,[a] 350 nautical miles	248	1968
	373	1970
	394	1971
	752	1975
	803	1976
	959	1977
Navigation, 600 nautical miles	400	1971
	421	1972
	839	1976
	909	1977
	967	1977
	1171	1980
	1241	1981

Sources: Same as table D-1.
a. Electronic intelligence.

The Use of Military Reconnaissance Satellites

A COHERENT space program with direct military applications for the USSR began in late 1962. The Soviets launched five photoreconnaissance satellites that were recoverable. The satellites, which allowed Soviet planners to analyze Western military affairs with greater timeliness than before, provided coverage of the earth for 5.5 percent of each year.[1] By 1965 seventeen reconnaissance satellites were launched annually, with coverage 40 percent of the year.[2] In the early 1970s nearly thirty satellites were being launched each year, allowing annual global photoreconnaissance nearly 75 percent of the time. By the mid-1970s over thirty satellites were being launched annually, providing more than 100 percent annual coverage.[3] Even so, overlapping in launches and failures cause gaps in coverage. The Russian winter presents problems in recovering satellites, and launches in winter months are few. This may have been one of the reasons, for example, that there were no launches during November 1977.[4] The short life of Soviet satellites also contributes to the gaps. Whereas U.S. satellites since the early 1970s have had a life on the order of months and have been able to eject film cartridges and to transmit low-resolution pictures through ground-relay stations, Soviet satellites until recently had a lifetime of only 12–14 days (up from 8 days in late 1962). The early Soviet satellites, with low-resolution cameras, were only able to transmit their data; satellites now have high-resolution cameras, can transmit data and eject film cartridges, and are maneuverable.[5]

1. Philip J. Klass, *Secret Sentries in Space* (Random House, 1971), pp. 124–25.

2. *TRW Space Log 1975* (Redondo Beach, Calif.: TRW Systems Group, TRW Inc., 1976), pp. 42–44.

3. Ibid., pp. 51–55.

4. *Aerospace Daily,* January 5, 1978, p. 15.

5. Through 1976, Soviet space planners were having a difficult time developing a reliable system for ejecting multiple cartridges. See *Newsweek,* August 30, 1976.

The flexibility the Soviets have sought in their spaceborne reconnaissance program is no doubt one of the reasons for the construction of the launch center at Plesetsk. Its high latitude eliminated the penalty in payload for satellites launched from Tyuratam, farther to the south. Reconnaissance launches from Plesetsk for the first time in early 1966 allowed the viewing of early-warning radars in northern Canada.

After the launching of the first weather satellite in 1966, Kosmos reconnaissance satellites could be used more efficiently since their cameras could be shut down when there was cloud cover. In 1968 the first maneuvering satellite was launched for a twelve-day mission;[6] ground controllers could alter the satellite's orbit to examine particular areas. In 1977, some reconnaissance satellites began to fly at a higher orbit, indicating that Soviet planners wanted a wider view of things or that better cameras were being used to obtain similar resolution but for longer periods. Beginning in 1978, the Soviets began to operate thirty-day reconnaissance, solar-panel-equipped satellites that ejected recoverable film pods. One was launched that year, five in 1979, and four in 1980.

Military Applications

Soviet spaceborne reconnaissance systems featuring recoverable photographic satellites, and to a lesser extent ocean reconnaissance satellites, have been used frequently for normal military purposes and during political crises. During a normal preplanned mission, Soviet reconnaissance satellites pass over most points on the earth's surface in eight days or so,[7] photographing 100-square-mile swaths. The extra life of the satellite can be used to obtain clear pictures or to reexamine special areas (the earth's surface is covered by clouds about one-third of the time). To insure full coverage, more than one satellite may also be put into orbit at a time.

During normal operations, Soviet Elint and reconnaissance satellites have been able to record U.S. Strategic Air Command (SAC) and NATO exercises, and Chinese, French, and Indian nuclear tests. The Soviets seem to have had some forewarning of the first Chinese nuclear test.

6. Stockholm International Peace Research Institute (SIPRI), *Outer Space—Battlefield of the Future?* (London: Taylor and Francis, 1978).

7. Klass, *Secret Sentries*, pp. 80–81; SIPRI, *Outer Space*, pp. 4–13.

They had launched two recoverable satellites in August and two in September 1964, including one whose orbital parameters would have taken it over China.[8] Two days before the Chinese nuclear detonation, in October, the USSR launched a satellite that was recovered after only a six-day flight (a normal mission was eight days).[9] Again, in 1980, the Soviets seem to have covered the preparations for China's first full-range ICBM tests, which occurred on May 18 and 21, with three satellites (Kosmos 1177, 1178, and 1180) launched in less than twenty days.[10]

Emerging problems of nuclear proliferation no doubt led to careful examination of film that had been exposed over India when it detonated a nuclear device in 1974 and of film exposed over South Africa in the summer of 1977.[11] Something photographed by the Soviets convinced them that South Africa would soon detonate a nuclear explosive.[12] The United States and other nations, once informed, protested to the South African government. No test ever took place and the facilities that triggered Soviet concern were dismantled.

Regular satellite missions can also be used to monitor open conflicts such as the internecine struggles in Cyprus in 1974 and in Angola in late 1975 and early 1976, the war on the Horn of Africa between Somalia and Ethiopia in 1977 and early 1978, the Vietnamese invasion of Cambodia in 1979,[13] the deployment of the U.S. rapid-deployment force to Egypt in 1980, and the Iran-Iraq war of 1980–81. During the war on the Horn in the summer of 1977, the failure of a Soviet satellite launching may have kept the USSR from passing tactical information to Ethiopia for a couple of weeks.[14]

Table E-1 shows the number of Soviet satellites launched during other selected periods of military importance or crisis. In 1962, while the Soviet spaceborne reconnaissance program was still in its infancy, satellites may have been used to detect changes in the U.S. military posture in order to find out the level of U.S. awareness on the Soviet introduction of weapons into Cuba. On August 29, U.S. Air Force U-2 aircraft flew their first missions over Cuba, followed by missions on

8. *TRW Space Log 1975*, p. 49.

9. Ibid., p. 50.

10. *TRW Space Log 1980*, p. 92.

11. SIPRI, *Outer Space*, pp. 14, 16; *Washington Post*, August 28, 1977.

12. *Washington Post*, August 28, 1977; *SIPRI Yearbook 1978: World Armaments and Disarmament* (London: Taylor and Francis, 1980), pp. 70–79.

13. *Washington Post*, August 13, 1974.

14. *Aerospace Daily*, August 29, 1977, p. 318.

September 5, 17, 26, and 29.[15] A Soviet reconnaissance satellite was launched on September 27 and was recovered on October 1.[16] Recovered photos probably showed no unusual movements of troops to the southern United States that would indicate the United States had discovered any Soviet activity in Cuba. Another satellite (Kosmos 10) launched on October 17[17] possibly did have pictures of a buildup beginning to take place in Florida. Not until the October 14 mission had a U-2 discovered the first hard evidence of offensive missiles in Cuba,[18] and soon afterwards U.S. military forces had begun assembling. Soviet concern about what the United States did know may have been one reason that Kosmos 10 was brought down only four days (October 21) after it had been launched. This satellite reconnaissance—probably very crude—was the Soviets' first made to help forecast its adversary's behavior and assess its strategic capability.

By 1967 the spaceborne reconnaissance program had fully matured and in that year events in the Far and Middle East were recorded by its cameras. During February the first clashes between Chinese and Soviet security forces took place. Kosmos 141, launched February 8, came down after a normal eight-day flight,[19] only two days after fighting had erupted. Information from this and another satellite launched in late February allowed Soviet planners to measure Chinese military posture in previously unknown detail. In June 1967, Kosmos 162, which had been launched June 1, was able to return film footage of the Six Day War between Israel and the Arabs. It came down on June 9, but one day earlier had been joined by Kosmos 164 to permit continuous coverage. Interestingly, Kosmos 164 returned to earth in about six days, two less than normal for the period.[20] Again, Soviet planners were able to monitor and pinpoint Israeli troop positions in the Sinai, West Bank, and Golan Heights quite closely.

The crisis in Czechoslovakia in 1968 prompted the first extensive use of the Kosmos series for reconnaissance. Through the winter and early spring of 1968 the Soviets had been showing concern over the liberalizing trends in Prague. In March they began a military exercise with little

15. Graham T. Allison, *Essence of Decision: Explaining the Cuban Missile Crisis* (Little, Brown, 1971), p. 119.

16. *TRW Space Log 1975*, p. 44.

17. Ibid., p. 44.

18. Allison, *Essence of Decision*, p. 119.

19. *TRW Space Log 1975*, p. 60.

20. Ibid., p. 62.

warning in the area. During March also the Soviets launched four recoverable reconnaissance satellites, probably for both catching up on strategic reconnaissance chores (one had been launched in January but was not recovered and only one other was sent up in February) and measuring NATO dispositions in response to Soviet ground force maneuvers.[21] Another surprise exercise was held in May but this time there were no satellite launches. By the end of May, Soviet and East European troops began to enter Czechoslovakia for an exercise scheduled for mid-June. In June six recoverable satellites were launched providing information on adversary behavior, especially troop dispositions in Western Europe and in China.[22] Once the exercise was held, however, both Soviet and East European forces lingered in Czechoslovakia as a means of exerting pressure and forcing political compromise on the Dubček government. When forces finally did leave in early August, it was only a matter of days before they began reassembling outside Czechoslovakia. The most interesting satellite photography mission during this period may have been that of Kosmos 234. It was launched in late July, only fourteen days after Kosmos 232, which seemed to be a regularly scheduled eight-day mission to cover targets as far north as Iceland.[23] Kosmos 234 was launched at a low orbital inclination that limited its most northern track to upper Poland,[24] and it remained in orbit only six days. Again photo interpreters may have been looking for reactions by NATO forces to Soviet troop movements. The last satellite before the August 20 invasion was launched on August 9 and recovered August 17.[25] It too had a lower orbital inclination than normal and may have performed one final photographic sweep for any hint of Western reaction before Warsaw Pact forces entered Czechoslovakia in force.[26]

In 1969, even more use was made of reconnaissance satellites. The area of concern was China, and the potential for war very real. On the average in early 1969, the Soviets were launching a recoverable satellite every two weeks or so. But when fighting broke out between Chinese

21. Ibid., p. 65.
22. Ibid., pp. 66–67.
23. Ibid., p. 67.
24. Ibid.
25. Ibid., p. 68.
26. For a complete discussion of this affair see Michel Tatu, "Intervention in Eastern Europe," in Stephen S. Kaplan, ed., *Diplomacy of Power: Soviet Armed Forces as a Political Instrument* (Brookings Institution, 1981), pp. 205–64.

and Soviet security forces over Damansky Island, on the Ussuri River, the rate doubled. Kosmos 266 was launched on February 25 from Plesetsk and Kosmos 267 from Tyuratam on February 26.[27] Up through the end of April eight more reconnaissance satellites were orbited providing details on Chinese troop strengths and locations. In May the pace dropped. By June new clashes occurred, near western Mongolia, and tension continued to build until fighting broke out in mid-August. Again the reconnaissance program picked up tempo, with seven satellite launchings in the second half of August and September, some only three days apart. Overall, the Soviets must have had very good data on the location of Chinese troops, which would have allowed them to make best use of their forces available for both defensive and offensive operations. The Chinese, without a similar capability, probably would have been unable to exploit their advantage in numbers had the conflict grown larger.

During 1970 the United States began deploying Minuteman III intercontinental ballistic missiles (ICBMs) equipped with multiple warheads. The Soviet reconnaissance program was thorough enough that no extra satellites were needed to monitor the installation, but the orbital patterns of some satellites launched in this period were more in line with silo observation than others. The extra launchings of reconnaissance satellites in 1970 were concurrent with a minor crisis in the Middle East. Beginning in late August fighting broke out between Palestinian guerrillas and the Jordanian army in Amman; in early September, members of the Popular Front for the Liberation of Palestine (PFLP) hijacked three Western airliners and landed them in Jordan; and by September 15 the guerrillas had taken control of four Jordanian towns. On September 17, civil war broke out between guerrilla and government forces. On September 19, Syrian armored forces entered Jordan but had withdrawn by the 23d. On September 25 with the Jordanian army in control a cease fire was arranged between opposing sides.[28] During this period the Soviets launched three satellites, two of which were probably scheduled (Kosmos 361 launched September 8 and recovered September 21 and Kosmos 364 launched September 22 and recovered October 2) but also one that was not scheduled—Kosmos 363 launched on September 17

27. Klass, *Secret Sentries,* pp. 160–61; *TRW Space Log 1975,* p. 71 (typographical error for Kosmos 267).

28. International Institute for Strategic Studies, *Strategic Survey 1970* (London: IISS, 1971), pp. 90–91.

while Kosmos 361 still had one-third of its life left.[29] Even a low-level conflict in the Middle East seems to have been of enough significance for the Soviet Union to want to keep well informed. Indeed, interest in the overall tactical situation after the Jordanian crisis and President Nasser's death at the end of September may have been part of the reason for increased satellite activity in October.

A spillover from Bangladesh's war of independence was the start of a war on December 3, 1971, between Pakistan and India.[30] It also led eventually to naval deployments to the Indian Ocean.[31] To provide up-to-date information on the tactical situation on the ground, in a normally slow time of year for Soviet space launchings, the Soviet Union had to reshuffle its satellite schedule. It launched Kosmos 463 on December 6, maneuvered it into optimal viewing position, and five days later brought it back to earth. During that time it was able to observe Indian forces crossing the Meghna River. Kosmos 464, launched on December 10, stayed in orbit for six days. It was able to observe the attack on Dacca and the final collapse of Pakistan's army in Bangladesh.[32] The launching of these satellites was not unusual, but their focus on the India-Pakistan conflict and the quickness of their recovery (five and six days compared to a normal twelve days) highlight the interest the Soviet Union had in both India's and Bangladesh's fortunes. The third satellite, launched on December 16 (Kosmos 466), monitored the cease fire in South Asia but also carried on other surveillance activities and was brought down eleven days later.

Reconnaissance satellites were used on two other occasions during 1972 to provide special information for Soviet planners. The first, of course, was the Strategic Arms Limitation Talks (SALT). No doubt up through late May of that year, when agreements and treaties were signed, Soviet reconnaissance satellites were paying special attention to all aspects of U.S. strategic force inventories. Soviet satellites also were busy during the North Vietnamese spring offensive in 1972. On March 30 three North Vietnamese divisions crossed the DMZ in a conventional assault.[33] Over the next sixty days the United States reintroduced

29. *TRW Space Log 1975*, p. 78.

30. IISS, *Strategic Survey 1971*, pp. 46–53.

31. See James M. McConnell and Anne M. Kelly, "Superpower Naval Diplomacy in the Indo-Pakistani Crisis," in Michael MccGwire, ed., *Soviet Naval Developments: Capability and Context* (Praeger for the Centre for Foreign Policy Studies, Department of Political Science, Dalhousie University, 1973), pp. 442–55.

32. *TRW Space Log 1975*, p. 84.

33. IISS, *Strategic Survey 1972*, p. 87.

combat units into the area and mined harbors in an effort to halt the offensive.[34] One more satellite than normal (Kosmos 484) was launched during April—only three days after and eight days before other regularly scheduled reconnaissance flights.[35] In this way the Soviets probably had more reliable information on the situation on the ground than North Vietnam's other ally, China.

The greatest single use of the satellite reconnaissance system is believed to have occurred in 1973 during the October War in the Middle East. During October alone seven recoverable satellites, or five more than usual, were launched.[36] When war broke out on October 6, the Soviets already had one nonmaneuvering satellite in orbit. It had been launched on October 3 and three days after the war's start it was brought back down. About one hour after the war's beginning, Kosmos 597—a high-resolution, maneuvering satellite—was launched;[37] it was brought down, like 596, only six days later. On the first day of its life (October 12) 597 no doubt began to observe the Israeli counteroffensive in the Golan Heights. Kosmos 598 was launched October 10, the day the Soviet airlift began, and again came down six days later. It would have also been able to record the start of the American airlift (October 13) and the Israeli bridgehead on the Egyptian side of the Suez Canal (October 15). Kosmos 598 was a Morse code satellite, allowing nearly simultaneous transmission of data to a ground station in the Crimea. It probably was a regularly scheduled reconnaissance mission and stayed in orbit a normal 13 days. Kosmos 600, launched October 16 and recovered on the 23d, no doubt was the satellite that provided the detailed information on Israeli successes in the Sinai and Egypt. Kosmos 602 and 603, launched October 20 and 27, stayed up nine and thirteen days.[38] Kosmos 602 photos viewed final Israeli positions and the encircled Egyptian Third Army.[39] Kosmos 603 was launched probably as part of the regular surveillance program.[40]

In 1975 the Soviet reconnaissance satellites were used to photograph the tactical situation in South Vietnam soon after the North Vietnamese began their March offensive. Kosmos 719, launched on March 12,

34. Ibid.

35. *TRW Space Log 1975*, p. 85.

36. Ibid., pp. 90–91.

37. G. E. Perry, "Looking Down on the Middle East War," *Flight International*, February 21, 1974, pp. 240, 245.

38. Ibid.

39. Ibid.

40. See IISS, *Strategic Survey 1973*, pp. 13–30.

remained in orbit for thirteen days. Kosmos 720, 721, and 722, launched on March 21, 26, and 27, were brought down on April 1, 7, and 9. By mid and late March, North Vietnamese forces had overrun north and central South Vietnam and captured the cities of Hue and DaNang.[41] Throughout this period these satellites were being maneuvered regularly to provide optimal positioning for observing the progress of the war and South Vietnam's defeat.

In late February 1979 there again was conflict in Southeast Asia but between China and Vietnam, a Soviet ally. Tension and the possibility of conflict had been building along their border since late 1978. Soviet interest in those developments is reflected in the launching of seven satellites (as opposed to a normal two to four) in November and December. In January and February five more satellites were launched providing detailed coverage of the Chinese buildup on the Vietnamese border. Not incidentally the last Kosmos launched in late February (Kosmos 1078) registered a relatively short mission and may have included telemetric transmissions of Chinese troop movements during the Chinese premier's visit to the United States as well as the actual Chinese assault begun on February 24. Normal reconnaissance activity resumed after the conflict had started.[42]

The Soviet satellite reconnaissance program has become an asset in Soviet crisis management and decisionmaking. Its increased use over different geographical regions in a crisis signals an interest in the outcome of those crises, whether national liberation movements or events directly related to the security of the Soviet Union.

Ocean Reconnaissance

Soviet ocean reconnaissance satellites are one part of a layered ocean surveillance system operated by PVO Strany, which is responsible for strategic defense in the USSR. Soviet ocean reconnaissance satellite missions began testing in 1965.[43] The first operational flight was two years later (table E-2). But the first flight that lasted more than ten days was not until 1972, leaving the impression that at least through the early

---

41. *Christian Science Monitor,* April 23, 1975; *TRW Space Log 1975,* p. 96.

42. *TRW Space Log 1980,* p. 88.

43. Robert P. Berman, *Soviet Air Power in Transition* (Brookings Institution, 1978), p. 12.

1970s the program was still in an experimental phase. During 1974 and 1975 the length of the satellites' coverage of oceans increased to about one-third of the year. In 1978, after the failure of Kosmos 954, no ocean reconnaissance satellites were launched.

The earlier satellites had an active radar system powered by a nuclear reactor that could isolate task forces of surface ships,[44] a mission of high priority in the 1950s when locating an aircraft carrier's precise position was important. Later models have a passive signal-gathering system designed to cover wide areas of the ocean in each orbit and isolate emitting Western naval radars, high-frequency communications, and other electronic phenomena.[45] This system, which is not nuclear powered, may be designed to deal with surface forces and possibly submarines. Both systems may be supported by special satellites that relay information to PVO Strany from all of its reconnaissance satellites.

In wartime, ocean reconnaissance satellites could play a key role in denying the use of the seas to the West. Soviet naval vessels with long-range guided missiles and submarines are believed to have links with ocean reconnaissance satellites. Within ninety minutes of detection, enemy combat vessels or high-value convoys on the open seas could be struck by ballistic missiles fired from either the sea or land.

Ocean reconnaissance satellites have been used, although not effectively, to monitor U.S. naval forces in various international events. After the Jordanian crisis of 1970 an ocean reconnaissance satellite was launched but did not even complete one day in orbit, and during the Angolan war in December 1975 a satellite was launched that lasted only one day. In December 1973 after U.S. naval forces had entered the Indian Ocean in response to Soviet forces operating there, an ocean reconnaissance satellite was orbited that lasted some forty-four days and was probably able to report on the disposition of U.S. naval forces in that region. In 1975 both passive and active ocean reconnaissance satellites that were launched (April 2 and 7) to support the USSR's worldwide naval exercise VESNA (April 15–27) could also observe the naval situation in Southeast Asia.

In 1979 and into early 1980 the Soviets launched three nonnuclear

44. *Aerospace Daily,* May 26, 1976, pp. 137–38.

45. K. J. Moore, "Antisubmarine Warfare," in Michael MccGwire and John Mc-Donnell, eds., *Soviet Naval Influence: Domestic and Foreign Dimensions* (Praeger for the Centre for Foreign Policy Studies, Department of Political Science, Dalhousie University, 1977), pp. 194–98.

passive, interferometric sensor satellites to survey the ocean. The latter satellite (Kosmos 1167) may have helped gather data on U.S. naval movement into the Indian Ocean after the Iranian and Afghan crises of 1979 and 1980.[46] In mid-spring of 1980, however, the Soviets launched a nuclear-powered, active-radar satellite, possibly because results of the passive models were unsatisfactory. That launching may have also coincided with annual spring naval exercises carried out by the Soviet fleet.

Further developments in ocean surveillance are likely to focus on reliability and sensor technology to give the Soviet military as much continuous, detailed coverage of the ocean accesses to the USSR as possible.

46. *TRW Space Log 1980*, p. 92.

Table E-1. Number of Soviet Reconnaissance Satellites Launched during Selected Periods of Military or Political Importance, 1962–79

Year	Number of launchings in critical months
1962	1 in Apr.; 1 in July; 1 in Sept.; 1 in Oct.; 1 in Dec.
1967	1 in Jan.; 2 in Feb.; 2 in Mar.; 2 in Apr.; 2 in May; 3 in June
1968	1 in Feb.; 4 in Mar.; 3 in Apr.; 6 in June; 3 in July; 2 in Aug.; 3 in Sept.
1969	2 in Jan.; 2 in Feb.; 4 in Mar.; 4 in Apr.; 3 in May; 3 in June; 2 in July; 4 in Aug.; 4 in Sept.
1970	3 in June; 2 in July; 2 in Aug.; 3 in Sept.; 4 in Oct.
1971	2 in Nov.; 3 in Dec.
1972	2 in Mar.; 3 in Apr.; 3 in May; 4 in June; 4 in July
1973	2 in Sept.; 7 in Oct.; 3 in Nov.; 2 in Dec.
1975	2 in Feb.; 4 in Mar.; 3 in Apr.; 3 in May
1978–79	4 in Nov.; 5 in Dec.; 3 in Jan.; 2 in Feb.; 2 in Mar.

Sources: *TRW Space Log 1975* (Redondo Beach, Calif.: TRW Systems Group, TRW, Inc., 1976); *TRW Space Log 1976; TRW Space Log 1980*.

Index

ABMs. *See* Antiballistic missiles
Ackley, Richard T., 129n
Afanasev, S. A., 76
Aircraft. *See* Bombers; Design bureaus
Air defense system: antiballistic missiles, 71, 147–50; anti-space, 150–51; deployment, 143–44; development, 39–40, 44–45, 144–45; operating level, 11, 12; role, 142–43; trends, 146–47
Alert level, 11–12, 15, 36–37
Alexander, Arthur J., 7n, 23n, 74n
Allison, Graham T., 41n, 52n, 90n, 157n
Andreyev, V., 32n
Antiballistic missiles (ABMs), 71, 147–50
Antiballistic Missile (ABM) Treaty, 61, 62, 149
Antisatellite (ASAT) systems, 57, 150–51
Antisubmarine warfare (ASW), 56–57, 64
Archer, Robert D., 75n
ASAT. *See* Antisatellite systems
ASW. *See* Antisubmarine warfare
Autopilot guidance systems, 87

Bagramyan, I., 10n
Baird, Gregory C., 9n, 10n
Baldwin, Hanson W., 91n
Ball, Desmond, 50n, 51n, 115n
Barron, John, 18n
Basing systems: land, 90–93; sea, 93–96
Batitskiy, P., 40n
Beecher, William, 12n, 13n, 18n, 55n, 59n, 61n, 64n, 92n, 93n, 96n, 151n
Berman, Robert P., 40n, 45n, 144n, 162n
Bombers, 15; development, 45, 46, 66; operating level, 36
Bondarenko, V. M., 92n
Bonds, Ray, 96n
Bradsher, Henry S., 92n
Breyer, Siegfried, 40n, 97n, 98n
Brezhnev, Leonid I., 5, 7, 13, 35n

Central Missile Design Office, 76–77
Chelomei design bureau, 54–55, 58, 77, 81, 83, 86, 87, 121, 124
Chelomei, V. N., 54, 76, 79–80, 83, 122n
Cherednichenko, M. I., 11n
Cohen, S. T., 30n
Colton, Timothy J., 9n
Command structure, 5; operational commands, 9–10; Supreme High Command, 5, 7, 9; theaters of military operations, 9–13
Committee of State Security. *See* KGB

Defense Council, 5, 7
Defense system. *See* Air defense system
Dementiev, P. V., 75
Deployment: air defense forces, 143–44; land-based missiles, 14, 90–93; sea-based missiles, 18, 95–96; strategic forces, 14–15, 18
Deriabin, Peter, 81n
Design bureaus: aircraft, 75; designer role, 78–80; development process, 76–77; establishment, 74; program life cycles, 81, 83–84; role, 3, 77–78
Dismukes, Bradford, 18n, 95n
Doctrine and strategy: background, 22–23; defined, 23–24; missile force role, 46–48, 63–64; nuclear, 24–27; principles, 24–37; sea-based forces, 58; trends, 71–72; U.S., 72–73; usefulness, 4; wartime objectives, 27–32
Donnelly, Christopher, 110n
Douglass, Joseph D., Jr., 19n, 26n, 27n, 28n, 29n, 34n, 41n, 118n
Dzhelaukhov, Kh., 30n

Erickson, John, 32n, 33n, 47n, 91n
Ermarth, Fritz W., 22n

167